Walking in EXTREMADURA

Discover Spain's Secret Paradise

Gisela Radant Wood

SANTANA BOOKS

WALKING IN EXTREMADURA

Published by Ediciones Santana, S.L.

Apartado 41
29650 Mijas-Pueblo (Málaga)
Spain

Tel: (0034) 952 48 58 38
E-Mail: info@santanabooks.com
www.santanabooks.com

Copyright © 2012 Gisela Radant Wood
Photos by Gisela Radant Wood

Cartography: The maps in this book are reproduced by kind permission from the Instituto Geográfico Nacional (IGN) 1:50,000 and 1:25.000 series.

Designed by: Cheryl Gatward

No part of this book may be reproduced or transmitted in any form or by any means without the prior written permission of the publishers.

Printed in Spain by Industrias Gráficas Solprint, S.L.

ISBN: 978-84-89954-95-3
Depósito Legal: MA 1813 - 2012

Acknowledgements

I would like to thank all those who have helped me in the preparation of this book. Alan and Gertrud at Santana Books for their enthusiasm for the project, Cheryl Gatward at New Image for inspired design, Guy Hunter-Watts for advice during the initial stages and my husband, Roger Wood, for turning my excited scribblings into coherent text and making endless pots of tea.

Thanks are due to Agustín Cabria Ramos at the Centro Nacional de Información Geográfica for permission to reproduce the maps and such a nice e-mail exchange. To Manuel Flores Mancebo at Cartex, Cáceres, who valiantly organised all the maps in all the sizes I wanted to purchase. Jakki Cosway for huge dinners after marathon walks in the Sierra de Gata and to the many friendly tourist officers whom I encountered along the way, especially in Losar de la Vera, Guadalupe and Mérida.

For test-walking routes, and checking that I know my left from my right, thanks go to Sally and Geoff Barnard from England, Marlene and Peter-Dirk Nachrodt from Germany and Paul Jenkins from Ecuador.

Special thanks must go to my many friends in the Almoharín Walking Group who guided my first steps in Extremadura.

However, this book is dedicated to Augusto Torres Palomino and Esteban Acedo Avila who waited for me the first time I walked in the Sierra de Gredos.

Photography
All photographic images are by the author.

cover photos:
above, View of Trevejo Castle, Sierra de Gata
below, Visigoth Church, Sierra de Montánchez

Contents

Foreword	8
Map of Extremadura showing 30 walks	9
Introduction	10

1 The Sierra de Montánchez — 28

The Walk of the Cork Oak Valley	36
The Walk of the Valley of the Mills	44
The Walk over the High Sierra	58
The Walk of the Medieval Sheep Track	70
The Walk of Country Lanes and Hidden Paths	80
The Wild Walk on Cancho Blanco	88
The Walk up to La Hoya	102
The Walk of the Oak Tree and the Pilgrim Hospital	108
The Walk of the Peonies	118

2 The Roman Waters — 128

The Walk around Proserpina	136
A Walk in Cornalvo Natural Park	142
The Walk of the White Cliffs of Zarza	148

3 The Sierra de Gata — 158

The Walk of the Natural Pool	164
A Walk to the Hermitage of the Holy Spirit	170
The Walk of the Pass of San Martín	178
The Walk by the Riverside	190
The Walk of the Bandit's Castle	196
The Walk of Pico Jálama	204

4 The Sierra de Gredos and La Vera — 218
The Walk of Yuste Monastery — 226
The Walk of the Mountain View — 238
The Walk of the Four Rivers — 244

5 Monfragüe National Park — 250
A Walk into Monfragüe — 256
The Walk of the Mediterranean Oasis — 262
The Route of the English — 268

6 Las Villuercas — 278
The Walk of the Hermitages — 286
The Pilgrimage Route of Isabel the Catholic — 294
The Hunting Route of Alfonso XI — 302

7 City Walks — 310
The Walk of the Roman Citizen — 316
A Walk in a Renaissance City — 326
A Walk with the Conquistadores — 336

Glossary — 350
Identifying flowers around Extremadura — 352

Foreword

I've been walking all my life. I grew up in the depths of the Devonshire countryside where public transport was something we knew about but didn't really believe existed. As a family we walked everywhere. Well, my parents walked. I would walk three steps and wail, "My legs are tired — carry me." It's still a family joke over fifty years later.

Visiting Extremadura for the first time was a revelation. The public transport was on a par with that of Devon in the 1950s but so was the way of life and I was enchanted. On moving here, six years ago, I started to explore by walking around. I joined the local walking group and made friends fast.

They taught me about their countryside and showed me how to find Extremadura's hidden paths. They gave me the confidence to be adventurous and strike out on my own. Just as well. Although the walks clearly exist there's almost no organised information available in English. Our many visitors wanted to go walking, not only where we live, but further afield in Extremadura. I found I was able to make plans and suggest routes for them based on their particular interests and level of walking fitness.

I began to record my favourite walks, the ones I've walked many times. I started a web site, walkingextremadura.com five years ago and, although the site is small, it has grown in popularity to become the foremost site about walking in Extremadura in English. That's not hard. It's the only one. The site's basic information has led to requests for 'the book' from walkers across the world.

Some of the walks in this book are old favourites but many are new. None is on the web site. However should something happen to change any of the walks in the book, I will post updates on the web site. Meanwhile we can all enjoy Extremadura, truly a paradise for walkers.

30 Walks in Spain's secret paradise

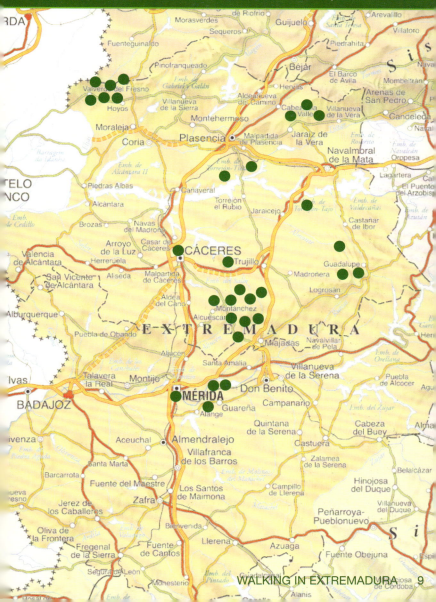

WALKING IN EXTREMADURA

Introduction

People who love walking will find the sheer space of Extremadura exhilarating, extraordinary and exquisite. It's exclusive, too. Extremadura remains Spain's least-known and least-visited region. The two provinces, Caceres and Badajoz, are tucked up against Portugal's border and hemmed by mountains. Extremadura has an impressive network of modern roads, largely funded by the European Union, making previously remote areas accessible. Once in these areas, people will find exploration on foot is the best way of uncovering the secrets of a land rich in History and blessed by Nature.

Geography

At over 41,600 square kilometres Extremadura is just larger than Switzerland. From the Sierra de Gredos in the north, still snow-covered in May, to the southern border with sunny Andalucia is 280 kilometres as the eagle flies.

Extremadura has some impressive forested mountain ranges. The Sierra de Gredos rises to a height of 2,592m and, still in the north but further west, the Sierra de Gata attains just over 1,500m. The Sierra de las Villuercas, in the east, rises to nearly 1,600m. In the centre are the lower Sierra de Montánchez and the Sierra de San Pedro. The Sierra Morena lies between Extremadura and Andalucia in the south.

Two of Spain's five biggest rivers, the Tajo and the Guadiana run right across Extremadura. A network of smaller rivers all contribute to important habitats for many species of wildlife and plant life. Extremadura is land-locked, but astonishingly, thanks to its innumerable lakes and reservoirs, it has more miles of 'coast' than any other Spanish region. It also has more water within its boundaries than any other comparable area in the whole of Europe.

Puente de Cuartos, Losar de la Vera, July

INTRODUCTION

History

Although many walkers may come here first and foremost for the glorious countryside and the diversity of the flora and fauna, Extremadura offers more. Many walks pass ruins from former times and they are scattered, without much warning, throughout the countryside. No one visiting the historic cities of Mérida, Cáceres and Trujillo in particular, and Guadalupe, Plasencia or Coria as additional attractions, could fail to be impressed at the richness of the evidence of a very long history. Monuments of occupation by the Romans, Visigoths, Moors, and Christians survive virtually undisturbed. There are dolmans, ancient tracks and roads, Roman theatres, amphitheatres, aqueducts, viaducts, reservoirs, bridges, Visigoth ruins, Moorish castles, forts, alcazabas, Christian castles, cathedrals, churches, monasteries, convents and small, preserved, granite-built cities, almost untouched by time. The best way to discover all these treasures is on foot, literally, walking in the footsteps of history. Therefore, at the back of the book are walking guides to the cities of Mérida, Cáceres and Trujillo. Take a camera and binoculars and prepare to be amazed.

Flora

In spring it is impossible to do some of the walks in this book without stepping on carpets of colour created by thousands of wild flowers. Extremadura's natural habitats support an enormous diversity of flowers, flowering bushes, trees and vegetation. The indigenous trees are the oaks — holm, cork and Pyrenean — the Spanish chestnut, the terebinth and alders. The eucalyptus trees were an imported idea during the last century but they are slowly being phased out in favour of replanting oaks. Trees such as the olive, cherry, orange, almond and fig have been cultivated for well over a millennium. Cistus, broom, retama, lavender, Mediterranean Daphne, curry plant, chrysanthemum and other flowering bushes

Yuste Monastery, June

form a backdrop to most of the walks in the spring. Flowers are everywhere. In the Sierra de Montánchez alone there are over a hundred varieties including the tall Spanish iris, foxglove, asphodel, snake's head fritillary, lupin, clover, yellow and white daisy and the purple viper's bugloss. Included at the back of the book is a guide to the most common flowers a walker may see during the spring.

Birds

Extremadura has long been known as a birdwatchers' paradise. It is on many migratory routes, with diverse species stopping off to summer or winter here. Each autumn the *grulla* (crane) announces its arrival from the north of Europe with its distinctive call. High in the sky they come in, wave after wave. There are many thousand — yes, thousand — of these birds wintering in the wetlands in central Extremadura. A remarkable sight. The mountains provide habitats for many species of vulture, eagle, harrier, buzzard, kite and hawk. The river valleys are home to the heron, stork, lapwing, grebe, ducks and any number of smaller birds. The countryside in general is home to the distinctive azure-winged magpie, colourful bee-eater, flashy hoopoe, crested lark, owls and song birds. However, the best place for a walk with bird-watching in mind is in Monfragüe National Park and there is a chapter on Monfragüe in the book.

Mammals

The wildlife in Extremadura is still genuinely wild. Depending on the habitat and the time of the year red deer, wild boar, rabbit, Iberian hare, fox, badger, wild cat, pine martin and genet, and the mongoose could, in theory, be seen. Even the lynx still prowls here — but there are no bears.

Villages

Extremadura is sparsely populated in modern terms. It has only

Snow-capped mountains above Tornavacas, November

25 residents per square kilometre. England has 395. Cáceres, the provincial capital, is a big city by local standards yet has less than 100,000 inhabitants. Extremeño towns and villages are well separated and this gives rise to the individual character of each settlement. The people of Extremadura are genuinely open and friendly. They are fiercely proud of their home villages but in recent centuries history had side-stepped the area. It has known periods of hunger and poverty, and many people left to find work in Northern Europe only returning to their village after a lifetime away. Even today, no matter how far they travel in search of work, every August will find them back for the holidays. While well aware of what is going on in the wider world, people prefer to live Life in a simpler way. Care of the family, the village, the countryside, the traditional way of life: this is what matters to the local people.

INTRODUCTION

A keen interest in conservation is growing. There is a realization that the region's centuries of isolation has handed down a precious heritage. Enormous tracts of Extremadura are in a pristine and untouched state. Many of the mountain areas are so unpolluted that their rivers run with the clearest drinking water. I know, I've drunk from many, many sources and no water could be sweeter. Unspoiled Extremadura also offers walkers a fabulous heritage of traditional food, crafts, music, dance and art.

When to walk in Extremadura

Everywhere in Extremadura can be walked during March, April, May and June. They are the best times to visit if you are a lover of wild flowers. The long lazy Extremeño spring sees the countryside covered with hundreds of wild flower varieties. March can start cool but by June it can be hot. There may be rain in early spring but, as in the autumn, it clears all too quickly for the farmer's liking. May and June are optimum times for many breeding birds.

July and August are hot. Rain is rare. The grass dries up to a scorched yellow, but the green of the forests and olive groves indicate that the countryside is just sleeping ... not dead. The best times to go out are early morning, late afternoon and evening. The middle part of the day can be very hot indeed but most villages, even the smallest, have a pool, open from mid-June to mid-September. Why not stop for a swim? Alternatively, choose a route with a lake, take a picnic. Spend the afternoon swimming and lying in the shade of a tree. During these months it's best to walk in the north, in the Sierra de Gata and the Sierra de Gredos.

All of Extremadura can be enjoyed in September, October and November. They are glorious months with the full range of autumn hues making the wooded slopes of the sierras a blaze of colour. September days can still be hot, but even the middle part of the day in November is warm by North European standards. Evenings are cool going into cold by the end of November. There is a chance of rain in October and November. This usually clears away quickly to reveal sunshine and blue sky but, occasionally, it can rain all day. Don't let that put you off. Some walks are wonderful in the wet.

The lower sierras are a good location for walking during the winter. December, January and February can be cold but if you enjoy walking with an extra jumper then this might be the time for you. Snow is not usual, but when it falls it is a pretty sprinkle on the mountain peaks rather than a major problem but in the north the sierras can have substantial falls of snow.

Always check the weather before setting out. A good, and in my experience, accurate, web site is:

http://www.eltiempo.es

You can search for villages individually to get local forecasts.

The routes

The majority of routes in this book lie in Cáceres Province. The reason for this is that Cáceres has more mountains, rivers, valleys and, to my mind, more interesting places to walk. I think it's both more spectacular and prettier than Extremadura's southern province, Badajoz. The areas featured have distinct characteristics and walking in them inevitably leads to a different experience. In the most accessible area, the Sierra de Montánchez, I have listed more walks than in other areas. This is not only because it lies at the centre of the Mérida, Cáceres, Trujillo triangle but also because of its wonderful natural diversity. In this area I have chosen a wide variety of routes from almost flat, requiring a low level of fitness, to some quite strenuous climbs, even for fit walkers. There are short routes, lasting only two hours, and some are much longer; all-day adventures. The purpose of including such a broad choice of routes is that I feel everyone will want to do some walking here.

INTRODUCTION

No holiday or visit to Extremadura can be considered complete without at least two or three rewarding and enjoyable walks. Conversely, in an area like the Sierra de Gata there are a few easy walks but a medium level of fitness is required to enjoy the area fully.

How to use the walking notes

Each chapter contains walks in a distinct area to make a walking holiday easier to plan. Chapters start with an overall introduction to the area.

Each route will have its own introduction with an outline of any historical background, natural information and what to look out for along the way. There is a map, detailed description of the all-important starting point plus the distance measured in kilometres and time to be allowed for the route. Some routes offer alternatives with short-cuts or longer additions.

The degree of difficulty for each walk is determined by average fitness and the terrain and elevation a route will cover. A short walk with steep climbs may be graded 'medium' while a longer, flat walk might be 'low'. Walks both long and upward would be graded 'hard'. It's fairly logical. However, routes are not listed with the easiest first and the hardest last but geographically from west to east within their chapter.

The time taken to complete a walk depends entirely on how fast you walk and how often you stop. The time, therefore, can only be a guide.

The maps in the book are reproduced with permission from the

INTRODUCTION

Instituto Geográfico Nacional and are 1:50.000 or 1:25.000. They show where the route lies. The green line is the recommended route. The purple line is an option; either a short cut or an extension. Very occasionally a path will not appear on the map. Don't worry. It exists because I've walked it and you are probably standing on it, looking at the map. Follow the directions.

The GPS points are an additional guide to double-check important locations but I have not included them for obvious places. They are listed in ° and ' and " because that is what is on the maps. However, you will be able to complete the walks without a GPS by following the route description and using a map.

Definitions of English words and often used phrases in the route descriptions are:

Lane — usually in a reasonable condition made either of concrete or compacted dirt. It is normally near a population centre and is for lots of users; vehicles, horses, bikes, people.

Track — made of almost anything and is definitely in the countryside. It is wide enough for transport suitable for the terrain, plus horses, bikes and people.

Path — anything from granite paved or very rocky to grassy or dirt. It is much narrower than either a lane or track and is for horses, donkeys and people.

Stream bed — might be dry or very wet depending on the rainfall during the previous winter.

Flowering bushes — generally lavender, cistus, broom and retama.

Wall — dry stone wall unless otherwise stated.

In season — exactly that. The promise of spring flowers is not possible in the autumn.

INTRODUCTION

Equipment

Walking in Extremadura takes in every environment from mountains and valleys to meadows and forests, from rivers and lakes to dry plains and rocky slopes. Walking here can be on any surface from granite paved footpaths dating back to Roman times to soft grass in a water-fed meadow.

• Appropriate footwear is essential. I discovered that boots with inflexible soles are not ideal here, because they cannot cope with small rocks. It's like walking with two planks of wood on the feet. They also slip on wet granite. Better, by far, are boots with some 'give' in the sole. Two pairs of thin socks are better than one thick pair and a spare pair in the (comfortable) rucksack is always a good idea.

• In summer, wear shorts if you want to, but in winter, with long trousers on, tuck them into your socks. You really do not want the sensation that something unusual has just started to climb up your leg.

• Water is absolutely essential year-round; at least 1 litre per person, per walk.

• A high energy snack like nuts, pure black chocolate or dried fruits for longer walks. Dried figs are a speciality of the Sierra de Montánchez area and very good for day-long walks.

• Map, compass, GPS.

• Mobile phone, torch, knife.

INTRODUCTION

- Camera, binoculars.
- Weather kit: a hat, sunscreen and sunglasses are useful all year round, waterproofs.
- Basic First Aid; plasters, antiseptic cream, bandage.
- Many routes pass rivers or lakes. Take swimming kit for a cool, refreshing dip — a wonderful experience.
- One thing that you must carry is a stick. They help going up and down mountains. They measure the depth of streams, fords, giant puddles and even rivers on occasion. They hold back brambles, branches and other vegetation. They are useful to hold out to, and pull up, fellow walkers who just can't get up one bit of the mountain. They are great for flicking the odd snake (not dangerous just alarming) out of the way and for threatening aggressive dogs (but I've never met any). Sticks are also pretty good for resting on and catching your breath while admiring the view.

The Via de la Plata

No book on walking in Extremadura could fail to mention the Via de la Plata. It is an ancient communication road laid down by the Romans over 2000 years ago. However, its name 'plata' does not mean 'silver' as many people believe but comes from the Moorish word for 'paved'. In the Middle Ages it became a popular pilgrimage route to the tomb of St. James in Santiago de Compostela, Galicia. It starts in Seville, Andalucia. There is also a route from Granada which joins the Via de la Plata in Mérida. It covers 1000 kilometres, 300 of which pass through the length of Extremadura, often shadowing the E-803 main road. While it attracts fewer pilgrims than the northern route, starting in France,

INTRODUCTION

it is gaining in popularity. 14,000 pilgrims walked the route during 2010. The route is also known as the Ruta de la Plata and the Camino de Santiago and is called the Way of St. James in English.

Organized walks

There is a huge tradition of walking in Extremadura and many towns and even small villages have a walking group. These meet normally every Sunday for local walks. Once a year, the larger groups organize a route for public participation. The walks are always well sign-posted and marshalled with stops for free drinks and sometimes a traditional free meal at the end of the route. The walk itself may not be everyone's idea of a peaceful experience. The short Charles V route in Jarandilla de la Vera has 2000 walkers on the day and is very busy and noisy. The Valley of Ambroz attracts over 10,000 people during the autumn weekends. However, the atmosphere is excellent and it's a good way to meet up with walking enthusiasts from all over Europe who come just for the walk.

Walking solo

Many people ask if it's safe to walk alone in Extremadura. The answer is always the same; anyone can have an accident and twist an ankle. Provided you tell someone where you are going and what time you expect to be back and have a mobile phone, know the emergency numbers, speak Spanish and can accurately describe where you are ... go for it.

Wild walking

For those of you who want the freedom to explore off what is already a pretty wild track, orient yourself carefully before you start. Check where the visible mountains are and the sun and the time. If you go up you can expect to come down and if you are doing a circular route you can expect to turn right more than

Woodland path, Sierra de Montánchez, April

INTRODUCTION

left in a clockwise route and vice versa. Wild walking in the Sierra de Montánchez is great fun and relatively easy. Remember that mist can come down quickly in the autumn months and take precautions accordingly. Wild walking in the Sierra de Gata or the Sierra de Guadalupe is more risky as the areas are remote. I wouldn't recommend wild walking at any time in the Gredos mountains unless you are a very experienced walker. Although I do a lot of solo wild walking, I have lived here for over six years and walk daily. I am able to get unlost when I get lost. Be on the safe side. Take a companion. Share the fun.

The working countryside

Extremadura is a natural paradise but even in paradise people work. The countryside around villages, on lower slopes and hills, is organized and worked. There are many productive fincas and they are tended by the owners and farmers. Olives are harvested in December. The olive trees are usually pruned immediately afterwards but certainly by February when new flowers form. Bonfires, with licences, dispose of unwanted agricultural debris. These can be busy months in the campo and not everything is hand done with pannier-laden donkeys taking the produce to the village — although some farmers still work that way. A degree of low-tech mechanization is used. It's normal. Figs are harvested in the summer months when the lanes seem more full of tractors than walkers. Apart from that the countryside can be remarkably quiet even just a few hundred metres from the village.

Something about hunters

Hunting with shotguns and dogs is extremely popular in Extremadura during the months from mid-October to mid-March. Local restaurants can testify to the success of this sport with venison, wild boar, rabbit, partridge and other game birds on their menus. Hunters go out on Sundays and Public Holidays and

INTRODUCTION

they can shatter the quiet of a walk. They make so much noise sometimes it's a wonder they shoot anything at all and it's easy to be irritated by them. However, these hunters care as much about the countryside as we do and they are largely responsible for keeping open the higher mountain paths that we enjoy walking the rest of the week.

Reminders

- Never, ever light a fire in the countryside. There are strict rules about this. Bonfires, even campfires and barbecues, need a permit from the local Town Hall.

- Take all your rubbish with you but fruit peels and biodegradable organic waste is fine to leave behind — buried.

- If you go through a gate, close it behind you carefully.

Although I have described each route as unambiguously and as accurately as possible, please remember that, very occasionally a route may change — a landslide in the mountains, a diverted stream, a fallen tree, etc. I've tried not to use descriptions like 'red metal gate' because that might so easily become a 'blue wooden gate' but some descriptions and some landmarks are necessary. With this book, a map and a good orienting before the start of any walk I feel confident that you, my fellow walker, will not get lost ... for long.

A headache of a different sort is definitively identifying larger roads. It depends on the map. Most roads have two identifiers with EX and CC as the prefix but some roads also have CCV and different numbers. Even the motorway from Madrid to Badajoz is the EX-90 and A5. Wherever possible I have used numbers from actual

INTRODUCTION

roadsigns and the latest maps but these may change.

Useful books

Books on Extremadura in English are rare. However, Crossbill Guides has published a very good guide to the natural environment, *Extremadura* by Dirk Hilbers. ISBN 978-9-05011-381-6

Collins Wild Guide *Wild Flowers* by John Akeroyd.
ISBN 13: 978007177936 ISBN 10: 0007177933

A good, but very heavy, book on birds: *Bird* by Peter Hayman & Rob Hume. ISBN 978-1-84533-338-6

A more manageable, but still large, bird book with great photography: *Birds of Iberia* by Clive Finlayson & David Tomlinson. ISBN 84-89954-28-3

Maps

The maps in this book are reproduced by kind permission from the Instituto Geográfico Nacional (IGN) 1:50,000 and 1:25.000 series. I strongly recommend that you use the IGN maps to plot any of the additional routes mentioned in the chapters. It is not enough to start a walk in the Sierra de Gredos, for example, with a line drawing from the tourist office.

IGN maps are available from:

Centro Nacional de Información Geográfica
General Ibánez de Ibero 3, 28010 Madrid
consulta@cnig.es • www.cnig.es

Cartex
Avda. de España, No11 2ºC (number 11 on the second floor), Cáceres 10004. (It's in a block of flats to the right of the Banco Santander as you look at the buildings.)

gisiberica@gisiberica.com • www.gisiberica.com

Maps can also be obtained in the U.K. from:

Stanfords
12-14 Long Acre, London WC1
sales@stanfords.co.uk • www.stanfords.co.uk

The maps in the book have numbers to locate the GPS points but they are a guide to how far you have walked even without the GPS information. The numbers are quite large and hide some of the map. I have tried to position them to be close to where they need to be but without obscuring important information.

Accommodation and Eating Out

This book is not intended to be a general purpose tourist guide but in some chapters I have included a few places to stay where walkers are especially welcome. Tourism is still in the early stages in Extremadura but that is part of its charm. Plane-loads of tourists do not arrive here hourly and thank goodness for that. However, Extremadura has exceptionally high-quality casa rurales tucked away in the countryside or in small villages. If you prefer luxury mixed with history, the chain of Paradors in larger towns is very impressive. Remember, recommendations listed are not a definitive guide and you will need to do your own research.

A Word about the Words

I have used lower-case letters, where literate, for names of animals, birds, trees and plants simply to aid the flow of the text.

View from Montánchez path in June

The Sierra de Montánchez

1	The Walk of the Cork Oak Valley	36
2	The Walk of the Valley of the Mills	44
3	The Walk over the High Sierra	58
4	The Walk of the Medieval Sheep Track	70
5	The Walk of Country Lanes and Hidden Paths	80
6	The Wild Walk on Cancho Blanco	88
7	The Walk up to La Hoya	102
8	The Walk of the Oak Tree and the Pilgrim Hospital	108
9	The Walk of the Peonies	118

INTRODUCTION

The Sierra de Montánchez

The Sierra de Montánchez is my home area and where I do most of my daily walking. It is a series of hills rising from 300m to a height of 994m behind the small town of Montánchez. The sierra is predominantly granite. Huge formations of boulders are a striking part of the landscape. The trees are mainly holm and cork oaks, and terebinth or turpentine (a member of the pistacia family) but once over 500m Pyrenean oaks and Spanish chestnut predominate. These deciduous trees make walking possible all year round with shade in the summer, colour in the autumn, filtered sunshine in the winter and pale budding leaves in the spring.

The first big attraction for any walker is the thousands of interconnecting tracks and pathways going back to Roman times. It is possible to walk for hours in deep countryside and not meet anyone. That is the second attraction; the feeling of peace within the huge space. The quiet and the natural environment provide a perfect habitat for wildlife especially rabbits, hares, foxes, wild boar, partridges, small song birds and birds of prey, especially vultures and hawks. Lavender, gum cistus, broom and retama grow abundantly. During the spring the wild flowers are everywhere making it impossible to avoid stepping on them. In autumn footsteps are muffled by fallen leaves. It's quiet.

Naturally, the north side of the sierra is more rugged as it is exposed to the colder wind. The south facing slopes are altogether softer and prettier with more meadows covered by flowers in the spring. It is very accessible for walkers. Throughout the sierra there are numerous streams and water courses. The springs, as far as I have experienced, are safe to drink; the water is cool and soft, but be warned, not every blue line on the map is a stream at the height of summer.

There are signs of man's involvement with the sierra going back over two millennia. Slopes are terraced in almost inaccessible

THE SIERRA DE MONTÁNCHEZ 1

The high sierra, December

INTRODUCTION

places. The lower hills are covered in fincas given over to olive, fig and vine production. Orange trees grow almost wild. In February whole mountainsides are dotted with the pale blossom of almond trees. Animals graze both lower and higher slopes. Ruins of the past agricultural life abound. Every water course seems to hide a disused mill. Many are in varying stages of rubble or restoration. Hidden hermitages, shrines and ruins of grander houses from past times all prove the long association between man and the land.

The sierra lies at the centre of the cultural triangle formed by the historic cities of Cáceres, Trujillo and Mérida. It is a perfect base from which to explore the fascinating history of these cities. However, the sierra itself is dotted with villages; some, like Almoharín, lie in valleys as low as 308m, while Montánchez is the highest at 707m. The villages are mainly dependent on agriculture and are solidly built. Rural time-keeping means that, especially in the summer, places appear deserted between 14.00 and 17.00. This is not modern Spain. However, all villages can offer a few shops and a bar or two and the bigger population centres run bus and taxi services and have banks and cash machines. Rural tourism is in its infancy but there are a few good places to stay.

Practical information

Almoharín is a village of 2,000 inhabitants. It is alleged that the village was founded over 1200 years ago by a Moorish leader who was visited by the Virgin of Sopetran on the eve of a battle with the Christians. Overcome by her beauty and goodness he converted to Christianity and founded the village — hence its Moorish name. The Virgin of Sopetran is the Patroness of Almoharín. The village boasts a sheep cheese centre — they export the famous Torta de Cásar world-wide — with an exhibition in six languages. There is also a yummy fig factory specialising in chocolate figs which has led Almoharín to be dubbed 'The Fig Capital of the World'. The village has shops, banks, cash machines, cafés, restaurants and

THE SIERRA DE MONTÁNCHEZ

Looking south-west from the Sierra de Montánchez, October

a garage. There are numerous places to stay, all known to me and recommended.

La Casa del Limonero is our own spacious, comfortable and fully-equipped house in the heart of Almoharín — we live in the countryside. I'm happy to give advice on walking, suggest routes, lend maps and do some guiding if needed. Roger looks after the practical side of life — like wood for the two wood-burning stoves during the winter. www.walkingextremadura.com

Las Gamitas is a welcoming and comfortable casa rural. It is surrounded by Nature at its best and is just 3km outside Almoharín. Carlos speaks good English and is very knowledgeable about wine. Irina cooks like an angel. Las Gamitas offers superb and inventive cuisine. We stayed here in our early days in

INTRODUCTION

Almoharín. Irina was particularly impressed by her first English guests — we took our muddy boots off at the front door! www.lasgamitas.com

La Atalaya is a spacious casa rural in a lovely part of the countryside just outside Almoharín. Enjoy superb rural views and delicious peace and quiet. www.almoharinrural.com

Casa Rural La Plaza is a newly refurbished, modern apartment right in the centre of Almoharín. www.casarural-laplaza.es

Montánchez is the capital of the area with a world-class reputation for *jamon* (ham). One of the pleasures of the town is a cool beer and a plate of jamon in the Plaza de España. Montánchez is an ancient town, originally founded by the Romans but it was the Moors who built the defensive castle in 713. Alfonso IX took Montánchez for the Christians in 1230 and strengthened the castle. Gradually it fell into disrepair but is now being restored. It is completely free and well worth a visit especially for the phenomenal views of the surrounding country. The ramparts of the castle are a favourite with bird-watchers who come in the spring to see the black wheatear among other important birds.

Montánchez boasts two hotels and numerous casa rurales but prices vary enormously.

The Casa Rural La Fontano is clean, comfortable and reasonably priced — perfect for walkers. It is in the heart of Montánchez and recommended by toprural.com as an excellent place to stay. I can agree with that. The web site is in English and Spanish and the welcome you get will be very friendly. www.casaruralfontano.com

In Salvatierra de Santiago try the **Casa Fiona**. This is a rural apartment in a tiny but historic village. www.toprural.com

THE SIERRA DE MONTÁNCHEZ

Other walks

There are hundreds of other walks in the Sierra de Montánchez and surrounding area but they are not available in any language anywhere. This book is a start. However, there are a few villages with mapped walks and information boards at the start of the routes. The maps are usually just lines and it is best to plot the route on an IGN map before you start.

In Alcuéscar there is the Route of the Cork Oaks which takes in the Visigoth Church and interpretation centre.

In Robledillo there is a good 11.5km walk along the Cerro Molliquero.

In Botija there is a 4km out-and-back walk along the River Tamuja to the excavations of Villasviejas, a Neolithic Village. The walk can be made longer by starting in Benquerencia.

Walkers with a grasp of Spanish can ask in village Town Halls for information on local walks but what you get back will be in Spanish.

Maps

Even the smallest scale maps, listed below, do not show all the paths in the area. The best advice is to use the descriptions to follow the walks. The GPS points are a back-up and so are the maps but the descriptions are the real guide.

Map: IGN 730-I Valdefuentes 1:25.000

Map: IGN 730-II Ibahernando 1:25.000

Map: IGN 730-III Montánchez 1:25.000

Map: IGN 730-IV Escurial 1:25.000

or

Map: IGN 730 Montánchez 1:50.000

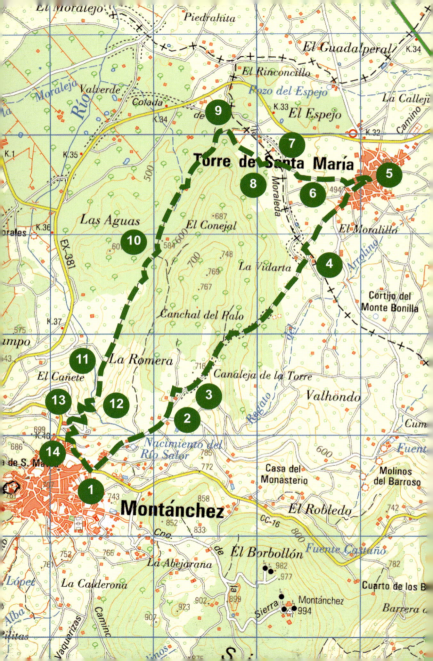

THE SIERRA DE MONTÁNCHEZ 1

1 The Walk of the Cork Oak Valley

Start: Montánchez

Finish: Montánchez

3 hours plus stops

10 km

**Low: 494m
High: 699m**

Easy

Montánchez → Torre de Santa María → Montánchez
Map: IGN 730 Montánchez 1:50.000

Cork oak wood in March

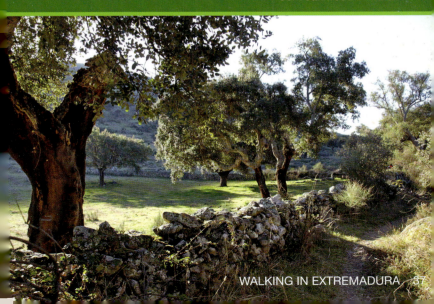

THE WALK OF THE CORK OAK VALLEY

Introduction

This walk starts in Montánchez although it could start from Torre de Santa María. However, the former town has greater scope for refreshments and more interesting things to explore — like the castle. The walk links the town and village and is surprisingly easy other than the very beginning and the very end. There is a descent, steep in places, on the outward stretch but the return goes upward very gradually until the final kilometre which is steep. Its charm is the path itself. It starts on the road but very quickly finds an old granite-paved path that runs all the way to Torre. On the return path runs alongside an extensive cork oak wood with bird-spotting and flower identification opportunities. Towards the end of the walk the views of Montánchez and the open vistas across the plains of Cáceres, dotted with villages, are the highlight.

This walk is perfect all year. In summer, if the walk is done early or late it is mainly shaded on the return but take the usual precautions of extra water, a hat and sunscreen.

Directions

Start from the roundabout — essentially a crossroads — on the main road in to Montánchez from everywhere. ❶ With your back to the town take the small road on the other side of the roundabout. Ignore all turnings but walk ahead for 800m to come to a large building on the left. The building has no name but it is huge, with a lot of windows on two floors, has buff coloured walls and a burgundy roof. Just before this building is a path, left. ❷ Take this path and walk to the end of the building where there is a Y junction. Go right.

Pass a pretty house on the left. This is an area of vines, olives and small fincas with little gates. There is a good view of Montánchez Castle behind. Ignore a turning, left, and walk on to a Y junction.

THE SIERRA DE MONTÁNCHEZ

Montánchez Castle

Go right. The path goes up and down and twists and turns. The verges are full of flowers, in season, and deciduous oaks start to dominate the view on the left. As the path crests a small rise, ahead is a wonderful view of ranges of mountains stretching all the way to the Sierra de Gredos in the north. Torre de Santa María is visible ahead.

The path descends steeply. On the right the path seems to bend back in a U turn but ignore this. ❸ Our path goes ahead. Pass a granite water trough on the left. It has a pipe and drinkable running water. The path narrows considerably and is paved, roughly, with granite. It runs, downhill, all the way to Torre but, take care, as it is extremely steep in places. On the right are the views and on the left is a slope of a spur of the Sierra de Montánchez, covered in granite boulders, oak trees and flowering bushes. After 1.25km,

WALKING IN EXTREMADURA

THE WALK OF THE CORK OAK VALLEY

and ignoring all junctions, the path comes out at a T junction with a lane. ❹ Turn left to follow the lane as it bends to the right and heads for the village. A lane from the right joins the one we are on and the two become Calle Asunción. Walk ahead into the Plaza Generalisimo and explore Torre.

To return to Montánchez from the square, ❺ with the church in front of you, take the road on the right called Calle del Campo. At the end of the road there is a 5-lane junction. Go straight ahead to the lane with the electricity tower, passing two lanes on the left and one on the right. At the Y junction ❻ take the left turning and put the Sierra de Montánchez on the left and ahead. The lane narrows and becomes a track. At the next Y junction go right. Pass into an area of olive groves with a few holm oak trees. At a third Y junction, take the left path. At the T junction, go right on to a bigger track going slightly uphill. Within a few metres, by a metal gate on the left, the track makes a decisive turn to the right. Ignore this. On the left is a tiny grassy path with a dry stone wall on the left and a holm oak tree on the right. ❼ Take this tiny path. It runs almost parallel to the low mountains on the left. The agricultural landscape drops behind and the path takes on a much prettier aspect.

The path is very narrow with many flowering bushes on either side; broom, lavender and cistus. There are boulders to negotiate but it is very tranquil with the feeling of deep, deep countryside even though the village is only fifteen minutes away. Pass through an area of old holm oaks forming a shady tunnel that ends in a good view of the countryside ahead. After 250m there is a wide junction. Bear right. ❽ After another 500m the path swings around to the right but do not go that way. Take the tiny path to the left. ❾ It goes in the direction of the mountains. It narrows considerably, gets rocky and goes up. As it levels off for a while there are open views to the right across to the village of Albala with its fortress-like church tower. The path is flat along this stretch and then rises

View of Torre de Santa María from Montánchez, January

slightly. The cork oak woods start on the right, obscuring the views.

The path is long. It winds a little but continues without junctions through a deep countryside area. As it gradually climbs the views behind become extensive. This is an area of many flowering bushes and a jumble of small holm oak saplings. The cork oaks continue on the right. On the left are huge pastures with isolated cork oaks; typical dehesa. As the path comes out from the trees momentarily and bends around to the right there, in front, is Montánchez with the castle on the hill. ⓵⓪

The path meanders past a large boulder strewn expanse on the left. The cork oak wood thins on the right. As Montánchez gets closer the path becomes a well-used track. On the right the view

THE WALK OF THE CORK OAK VALLEY

becomes pastoral with huge meadows, hills and mountains in the distance. As the track approaches Montánchez there is a jamon factory on the horizon in which thousands of pigs' legs are hanging in air-dried conditions for up to four years. It's what Montánchez is famous for.

On the outskirts of Montánchez there are a few junctions but ignore these. The path comes to a stream bed on the right. ⑪ This is the birth of the Rio Salor. Do not cross the stream bed but keep it on the right. The path rises very sharply. There is a gate on the left up a rocky, grassy ramp. ⑫ Leave the path which continues right, to the stream. Walk up the rocky ramp on the left to the gate. There is a tiny granite paved pathway that zig-zags up steeply, crossing the stream further up. Follow the path up ignoring other turnings. Look behind for spectacular views. The path comes out on a small road. ⑬ Go straight across to pick up another little path that bears right. This goes up to join the main road into Montánchez with the jamon factory on the left. ⑭ Walk left along the road to arrive back at the roundabout.

THE SIERRA DE MONTÁNCHEZ 1

GPS Points
The Walk of the Cork Oak Valley

1. N39° 13' 36.67" W06° 08' 48.23"
2. N39° 13' 53.86" W06° 08' 17.41"
3. N39° 14' 14.20" W06° 07' 58.91"
4. N39° 14' 47.04" W06° 07' 22.74"
5. N39° 15' 10.40" W06° 07' 02.14"
6. N39° 15' 12.33" W06° 07' 10.17"
7. N39° 15' 16.76" W06° 07' 34.06"
8. N39° 15' 15.89" W06° 07" 44.45"
9. N39° 15' 27.60" W06° 07' 55.83"
10. N39° 14' 44.64" W06° 08' 24.81"
11. N39° 14' 06.74" W06° 08' 45.70"
12. N39° 14' 01.72" W06° 08' 45.49"
13. N39° 13' 53.53" W06° 08' 54.55"
14. N39° 13' 50.19" W06° 08' 59.88"

WALKING IN EXTREMADURA

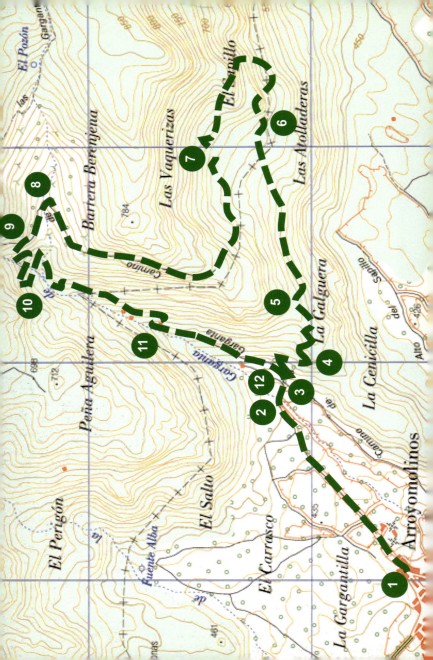

THE SIERRA DE MONTÁNCHEZ 1

2 The Walk of the Valley of the Mills

Start: Arroyomolinos

Finish: Arroyomolinos

3-4 hours plus stops

7.5 km

Low: 425m
High: 712m

Medium

Arroyomolinos → Barrera Berenjena → Arroyomolinos
Map: IGN 730-III Montánchez 1:25.000

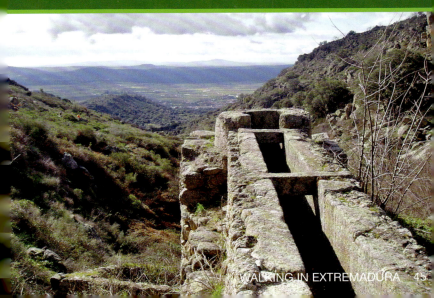

Mill race above Arroyomolinos, November

THE WALK OF THE VALLEY OF THE MILLS

Introduction

This is a variation of a popular visitor walk, The Route of the Mills. My version is better, I feel, because fewer people know about it, it is less disturbed and it offers a greater contrast of scenery. The main attraction of this walk is the valley of the mills which stretches up from the village of Arroyomolinos, to just a few kilometres from Montánchez. The word 'arroyomolinos' translates as 'millstream' and there is, indeed, a stream running the entire length of the valley. The Romans first started using the power of water to turn mill stones. The Moors perfected the system. Water coming down from the Sierra de Montánchez was harnessed through a series of channels. The water fell down to turn the mill stones in the mills below to make flour for the people of the village and to grind up animal foods. Sadly the mills and the water channels gradually fell into disrepair. However, there are ruins left to convey what a mighty undertaking this once was. Some of the mills have been restored — not all sympathetically.

The first part of the walk is the most demanding. The climb zig-zags up and crosses over a spur of the Sierra de Montánchez revealing views to the south. It is a good bird-spotting zone and includes the chance to see hawks and eagles. The middle part enters a deep, quiet cork oak wood, then crosses back over the sierra to follow a high mountain path. The last part of the walk winds down the impressive valley of the mills. The return offers fewer chances to spot birds as this is a popular route — especially at weekends. Apart from the cork oaks the trees are mainly deciduous oaks. There is abundant yellow and white broom with some lavender and cistus bushes adding splashes of additional colour in the spring with a profusion of wild flowers on the return through the valley.

This walk is lower and shorter than the Walk of the High Sierra. However, for walkers of medium fitness, who want the experience

THE SIERRA DE MONTÁNCHEZ

of crossing the sierra and doing a walk with views, it is an excellent option. For walkers with a higher level of fitness an extension can be done to walk into Montánchez and return. Additionally, the whole of the Ruta de Donde Nace can be added making a walk of 18kms. Details of the Donde Nace are in the information section and map of the Walk of the High Sierra.

The walk can be done year-round but take extra care if it has been raining as the granite-paved paths can be slippery and that is not to be recommended on the highest path as there is nothing to stop you falling off the edge of the mountain. In autumn it can occasionally be foggy restricting the view. Start early if you are walking in the summer and take extra water. Take binoculars.

Arroyomolinos was, of course, the site of a terrible beating during the Peninsular Wars for French troops at the hands of the British, Spanish and Portuguese force 200 years ago. The French, taken by surprise at dawn, threw down their weapons and fled up the sheer slopes of the sierra. Walkers today can take a much more leisurely approach.

Directions

From the CC-60/CC-117 Montánchez-Almoharín road, turn at the Arroyomolinos sign which has the crest of the village displayed on a roofed pillar. This will be the first turning left into the village, coming from Montánchez, or the last turning right, coming from Almoharín. Drive straight down the road. At the first Y junction go left into Calle Bolos. At the second Y junction turn right into Calle Membrillos. Take the first junction on the left into Calle España. Drive all the way up Calle España ignoring any other junctions until there is a Y junction. Turn left into a small lane which widens out into a large area with grass, boulders and agricultural buildings. ❶ Park. Walk directly towards the radio mast. By the mast is a map and information board of the Route of the Mills but, as already

THE WALK OF THE VALLEY OF THE MILLS

indicated, we are going to do a different walk.

Turn left and walk straight up the concrete track towards the mountains ahead. Ignore turnings left and right and pass Finca Alameda on the right. There are pastures on the left where a few cattle usually graze. Pass a *chozo* (a round shepherd's hut, typical of the trashumancia era) on the right. Also right a few metres later is a picnic area. The concrete track goes uphill and, at the first of the ruined mills ahead, there is a T junction. Turn right, then left. On the left and right are spurs of the Sierra de Montánchez and ahead is the valley of the mills.

The track bears right ❷ and crosses a ford. In the rainy season the stepping stones on the left ensure a dry-footed crossing. To the right is a good view of the church in Arroyomolinos. The track goes up sharply and finishes at a Y junction. Turn right. Within 10m there is a wide boulder-strewn area on the left with three possible paths over the boulders. Look at this area — the easiest path is on the extreme right. Walk along the very rough little path. It is strewn with a lot of rocks but the path is clear and follows a wall on the right. It veers to the right and climbs up.

After about 50m there is a junction with a small granite-paved path rising up on the right. ❸ There is an indistinct red arrow pointing up the path on a boulder to the left of the path. (Confusingly there is a white arrow pointing left but ignore it.) Take this paved path that goes up. It very quickly narrows and the paving almost acts as a staircase as it goes up very steeply. The direction is back towards Arroyomolinos but the path zig-zags. Keep to the granite path and avoid any dead-end junctions. Occasionally there are granite boulders with a helpful red blob. The path narrows again and flowering bushes encroach on the path. Sometimes there are smaller paths that go up even more steeply cutting off the zig or zag but keep to the zig-zag path to avoid getting confused. After initially pointing back to the village, the zig-zag path strikes

THE SIERRA DE MONTÁNCHEZ 1

Mill ruins, May

THE WALK OF THE VALLEY OF THE MILLS

decisively in the direction of the valley head and shadows the valley of the mills, below, before turning away once more. ❹ Look back for the view. The near village is Arroyomolinos and the far one is Alcuéscar with its white hermitage on the hill to the left of the village.

The bushes encroach on the path even more during the spring. With the zig-zags this can be confusing but if you cannot find the granite path you have gone wrong. Do not rush but look around. It is certainly there. Below an imposing granite outcrop there is the suggestion of a Y junction but the granite path is on the right — the other path is not granite paved so do not take it. Pass the granite outcrop with it on your right and continue upwards through the broom bushes, flowering white in the spring. Continue the path as it shadows the valley once more with the rocky outcrop now behind and the valley head in front. As the path approaches the sierra top it becomes flatter, wider and easier to follow with a low granite wall on the left. The path bends decisively to the right and continues up. ❺ To the left, on a big rock, is a reassuring faded red arrow. To the right is a very good view of Arroyomolinos.

The final climb on this part of the walk comes up over the top of the sierra. The views of the plains to the south stretch away in the distance. To the left are higher outcrops of granite with old deciduous oak trees on the lower slopes. Ahead are further peaks of the sierra. The path is wide but narrows and widens as it follows in a more-or-less straight line along this side of the sierra. It is still granite-paved in places. Occasionally the path is impeded by enormous granite slabs and flat boulders but they are easily negotiated. There are many oaks, wild olives and flowering bushes but nothing here is cultivated. In spite of the faded red arrows and blobs on granite rocks this is a hidden path and a perfectly unspoiled stretch of the Sierra de Montánchez. It is an excellent place for spotting birds and even hawks. In spring the bird song is deafening.

THE SIERRA DE MONTÁNCHEZ 1

The path is lined by walls in places and continues fairly level but as it descends for a few metres there are wild chrysanthemum bushes on the left. The path goes up again, enters a copse of oaks and winds around left and right. Here there are enormous boulders to negotiate but they are not high — this is not mountaineering. The path narrows to a tiny earth track where there is usually a 20m stretch of water underfoot. There are handy stepping stones to help negotiate this section. They were placed, one year, by members of the Almoharín Walking Group — me included. Enormous boulders impede the path once more but beyond them is an open grassy area. Bear left where there are even more enormous boulders of granite to negotiate. ❻ Whether you go to the left or right of the biggest boulders makes no difference — both paths go around. Once past the boulders the path narrows and strikes into the mountains. For the eagle-eyed, with your back to the plains, look left, there is a white farmhouse with two small granite buildings to its right. As a point of orientation the path is headed in that direction, seemingly back towards Arroyomolinos — check the map.

Continue on the path with walls on either side. Almost immediately the path enters a cork oak wood. There are still glimpses of the plains on the left but the attraction now is the silence and beauty of the wood. The path bears left and at a Y junction bears left again. Ignore the small path to the right. The path goes up sharply, heads directly towards the mountains in front and is granite-paved once more. On the right is an abandoned farm building. We now enter into the deepest part of the wood. The cork is harvested every nine years and there is evidence of successive years harvesting — not all of the trees are harvested in any one year. Access is by donkey so it is just as well the crop is light-weight. As the path continues the view on the right is of barren and rocky tops of a spur of the mountains which makes the vegetation around the path that much more enjoyable. As you might expect,

THE WALK OF THE VALLEY OF THE MILLS

the deep woods are home to many song birds.

The path rises slightly and passes an old building tucked away in the trees before going downhill again and veering left. It comes to an open grassy area with the white farmhouse, seen earlier, on the left. There is no junction at this point and the path, granite-paved and going up, leaves the open area on the right. It veers to the left. The wood is left behind although small copses of trees continue to line the path, especially on the left. Pass the granite houses on the right. ❼ The path is quite high now and as it climbs higher it narrows and zig-zags through denser cork oaks and flowering bushes with an abundance of lavender. At the top of the climb the path drops down over the sierra once more. First Alcuéscar, then Arroyomolinos, become visible on the left.

The granite-paved path winds around the side of the valley of the mills. On the right are higher parts of the sierra but the stunning view on the left is of the valley. Way below, on the left, the concrete path from the start of the walk can be seen and some of the mills can be picked out. The return to Arroyomolinos is along the valley bottom. Continue with care on the high path — there are no barriers to the drop on the left — but it is not dangerous; with just under a metre wide there is plenty of room for single file. Pass a huge boulder on the left and then two others opposite each other. Don't rush this part of the walk as there is a lot to see with occasional wide areas for a more leisurely look. The path gets narrower with cistus and broom bushes and oak saplings on the left and oak copses on the right. It climbs up to the highest part of the walk and then drops down. From here on the walk is downhill. As it descends the path becomes less paved and less rough.

After about two hours of walking — and very little sign of man's hand on the countryside — the path passes a metal gate on the right and drops down more steeply into an area of terraced olive farming. It widens into a track and the granite paving gives way

THE SIERRA DE MONTÁNCHEZ 1

Sierra path in fog, November

to earth. Pass little agricultural buildings, gates and various small turnings. Ahead on the sierra slopes there is a concrete track that is part of a tourist track into Montánchez and this walk will join that track at a junction. Continue on the downward track as it passes the first of the mill races on the left. At the bottom of the descent there is a stream bed that can be anything from a raging torrent to a trickle. 8 Cross the water by using the stepping stones if necessary. Bear left up a track to a T junction. Turn left. As you walk along the broad flattish track look left to see the terraced slopes planted with olives but higher up there are the deciduous oak woods we came through earlier.

Within 100m the dirt track becomes granite-paved, then concrete, and it goes on up into Montánchez. If you want to do that option

THE WALK OF THE VALLEY OF THE MILLS

keep to the track all the way to Montánchez and then return to this point ❾ to continue the walk.

On the left is a small rough granite-paved path that goes back on itself with a small gate and gatepost left. Take this path to zig-zag the start of the descent into the valley of the mills. On the left is another mill race, but the views down into the valley are quite stunning from this spot. At a clearing on the left there are two finca gates but the path zig-zags right. On the left is another finca gate and below it is a beautifully restored mill, Villa Granado. Continue on the path as it zigs, then zags to come out below the mill. Here there is a chance to walk ahead to see a small waterfall and a pool of water in which lies an abandoned millstone. ❿ After exploring retrace the 10m back to continue left on the zig-zag path.

The path winds around and crosses the stream once more. Use the stepping stones. The water continues down the valley and it can be heard from the path but the stream bed is so overgrown with vegetation it can only be seen occasionally. The next part of the walk needs little explanation. The path gets wider, narrower, rougher, flatter, goes downwards and passes mills on the left and one on the right. There are no junctions. The valley is filled with vegetation especially flowering bushes and deciduous oak trees and, lower down there are holm oaks. The middle part of the valley is not cultivated at all. Cattle occasionally graze on the opposite slope but the higher slopes of the valley are rugged granite with huge boulders only softened by hardy broom bushes.

The path decisively zigs to the right, ⓫ then zags to the left at a recently restored mill. Continue in the direction of Arroyomolinos and as the path drops lower towards the village the valley sides appear to get higher. Keep a look out for hawks and the occasional eagle circling above the high sierra. The path comes to a boggy part but there are stones to help negotiate this stretch. Be careful, if the stones are wet they can be slippery. At a T junction

THE SIERRA DE MONTÁNCHEZ 1

Above Arroyomolinos, May

go left towards the village. The path comes out at the rough boulder area ⓬ where there were three options for crossing the boulders. Negotiate them and turn right on the concrete track to retrace the track back to the parking area.

THE WALK OF THE VALLEY OF THE MILLS

Footpath going up, May

THE SIERRA DE MONTÁNCHEZ

GPS Points
The Walk of the Valley of the Mills

1. N 39° 11' 19.03" W 06° 9' 35.72"
2. N 39° 11' 35.43" W 06° 9' 10.31"
3. N 39° 11' 35.19" W 06° 9' 03.37"
4. N 39° 11' 33.08" W 06° 9' 01.68"
5. N 39° 11' 34.12" W 06° 8' 54.31"
6. N 39° 11' 37.91" W 06° 8' 24.65"
7. N 39° 11' 43.47" W 06° 8' 35.18"
8. N 39° 12' 10.26" W 06° 8' 32.70"
9. N 39° 12' 11.43" W 06° 8' 39.67"
10. N 39° 12' 09.40" W 06° 8' 42.69"
11. N 39° 11' 50.46" W 06° 8' 55.96"
12. N 39° 11' 34.75" W 06° 9' 06.14"

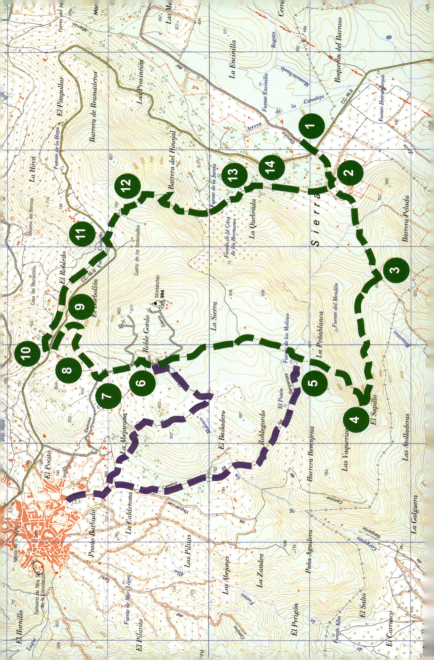

THE SIERRA DE MONTÁNCHEZ 1

3 The Walk over the High Sierra

Start: The Quebrada Valley

Finish: The Quebrada Valley

4.5 hours plus stops

11.75 km

Low: 462m
High: 900m

High / Medium

Quebrada Valley → Montánchez → Quebrada Valley
Map: IGN 730-III Montánchez 1:25.000

The south of the sierra, December

WALKING IN EXTREMADURA 59

THE WALK OVER THE HIGH SIERRA

Two of the paths on this walk do not appear on the map. However, the directions are very precise. The paths exist because I've walked them many times. Keep to the directions.

If starting and finishing in Montánchez, and/or including La Ruta de Donde Nace **Time: 7-8 hours Distance: 18.25 kilometres**

Introduction

Although the Sierra de Montánchez is not very high compared with some mountains it still gives plenty of opportunities for fit walkers to stretch themselves. This walk has a climb of 438m — most of it in the first hour. It is one of my favourite walks, contrasting the south and north faces of the sierra, with amazing views on both sides. It is hard going for at least the first hour and in places it is steep enough to zig-zag the zig-zags but the immediate scenery, plus the views, make it worth the effort. The middle part of the walk, along the sierra top is almost flat with a chance to relax. The final part of the circuit is downhill and passes through an area that should be declared one of 'Outstanding Natural Beauty'. You'll see what I mean. In spring there are flowers and blossoms everywhere and even the holm oaks have catkins. In summer there is shade on all but the top of the sierra. In autumn the reds of the deciduous oaks and chestnuts are vivid and in winter it is the unclothed landscape itself that is the attraction. Take binoculars.

The walk starts in the countryside but if transport is problematic, and you are a fit walker, it is possible to start and finish in Montánchez. Start the longer walk at the roundabout by the swimming pool and the Avenida de los Toreros. There is a sign and information board about the Ruta de Donde Nace, a popular easy route. Walk the Donde Nace clockwise — the recommended route is anti-clockwise. Join the Walk over the High Sierra at point 6 on the map. Follow all the directions until point 2 where you will start the long climb back over the sierra to rejoin the Donde Nace

THE SIERRA DE MONTÁNCHEZ 1

Walking up the south side of the sierra, April

THE WALK OVER THE HIGH SIERRA

at point 5. Complete the Donde Nace by walking clockwise back to Montánchez. The Donde Nace is fully waymarked with blue boards. Take something to eat and extra water but there is a water source between GPS points 7 and 8 on the map.

Walkers coming from the Quebrada can, just as easily, add the Donde Nace and stop in Montánchez for lunch. The Donde Nace is a good walk with excellent views over Arroyomolinos to the west and some deep chestnut woods to the east.

Directions

On the CC-117, between Arroyomolinos and Almoharín, turn on to the CC-160 and follow the sign for Montánchez and La Quebrada. As the road bears around to the left and dips down into the lowest part of the valley there is a small crossroads and a weekend house on the right with a sign for Finca El Hinojal. Park in the right turning where the road is widest. Cross the CC-160 to walk up the small concrete track directly opposite. ❶ There is a sign on the left advising that no motorbikes or quads are allowed on the sierra and that's very nice for us walkers who like the quiet. The Sierra de Montánchez is on the right and all around are pastures, holm oaks and flowering bushes including retama. There is a low range of hills to the left as the track goes into a spur of the sierra.

At the T junction with two metal gates ahead turn right. The concrete track goes up very sharply and comes to a second T junction with a small dirt track going to the right. ❷ Ignore this — it is where the return route joins the circuit in several hours time. Turn left and pass fig plantations and olive groves. The track winds past three successive metal gates on the right and continues up. As it winds left it goes downhill slightly and then bears right decisively. It comes to lovely countryside with a deciduous oak wood on the left and views of the higher sierra on the right. Behind is Cancho Blanco. On the right are two restored agricultural

THE SIERRA DE MONTÁNCHEZ **1**

buildings set against the mountains. The ascent becomes steeper on the final push up this part of the walk.

At the top of the track there is a T junction, at which we turn right. However, to the left is a wide turning with a small path which leads more-or-less in a straight direction to Arroyomolinos. This is a nice walk for another day. For now, look immediately right. There is a small earth path that is flat. **3** Take this path. It follows a ridge that has views down to Arroyomolinos on the left and back to the Quebrada valley and Cancho Blanco beyond on the right. Ahead is the Sierra de Montánchez and this walk goes over what you can see in front of you. The flat path is very pretty and it winds its way up and down bearing gradually left. In addition to lavender, cistus, white and yellow broom and retama there are many tall spikes of dark mullein, foxgloves and smaller wild flowers — all in season. The earth path comes to a wider track and goes sharply up. Keep on the wide track which, thankfully, zig-zags. Don't hurry this part of the walk. The views to the left are stunning and on a clear day you can see ... forever. Don't forget to look back as well.

At a crossroads both right and left turnings are closed off by wire fencing. Take the small granite-paved path ahead. The path zig-zags and goes up past a tiny building. Pass a second crossroads with both right and left turnings fenced off. Continue up the granite-paved path and ignore the next junction left. The path bears very sharp right and enters an old oak wood carpeted with tassel-headed hyacinths, bluebells and white campion in spring. **4** It's hard to know where to look as each time the path zigs the views are different from the zags. The wood shelters many birds and it is a peaceful place. Not many people come here. There are a few small olive groves and these are harvested in December in the traditional way — with donkeys and panniers.

As the path levels off nears the top of the sierra it becomes extremely narrow with high walls on either side. For 100m, as the

THE WALK OVER THE HIGH SIERRA

path crosses over from the southern slopes to the northern side, the views are restricted by the walls and trees. On the right there are glimpses of higher outcrops of granite but this walk does not include them. Behind there is still a phenomenal view to the south but ahead there is nothing to see for a few minutes until the path widens, the walls lower, and the top of the sierra is reached.

The area is surprisingly large and flat with many vineyards and a few fig plantations and olive groves. However, much of the area is walled rough pasture where hardy cattle graze. There are fewer trees and the vegetation is sparse. There are granite outcrops that give the scenery a bleak and dramatic look after the pretty climb up from the southern side. In spring the trees on the northern side are several weeks behind those already in leaf on the south side. In autumn the oaks and chestnuts are red long before the change occurs to trees on the southern slopes.

To the right, on the very top of the sierra is the almost inevitable collection of radio masts, however, there are plenty of other places to look. As the path winds around there are views to the north. The lakes at the Casas de Don Antonio can be seen on the left ahead. At a T junction on the right is a blue waymark of the Ruta de Donde Nace, a circular route around the top of the sierra starting from Montánchez. **5** Our route turns right on to a flattish track and follows the waymark signs for 1.5kms. The track passes two turnings on the right which both wind down to the Quebrada valley but ignore these. The track passes the entrance to the radio masts with a sign 'Roble Gordo' and the highest part of the walk. At a T junction the track joins a concrete lane. On the left the Ruta de Donde Nace drops back into Montánchez but we take the concrete lane, right. **6**

The concrete lane goes downhill towards the east. On the left are a few weekend houses — one extremely modern and somewhat incongruous. Ahead are views out over the plains of Cáceres

Pigs in the chestnut woods, December

THE WALK OVER THE HIGH SIERRA

and extensive vineyards. As the lane descends there is a deep gully to the left which runs to a small but solid building. It is an old reservoir, now disused, but you can hear the water within. Just before you get to this building, ahead and to the left, is a good view of Montánchez Castle and the hermitage next to it. A few metres after the reservoir building there is a crossroads with a tiny earth path both left and right. Turn right. ❼ Ahead is a conical hill and to the left are vineyards and views of Torre de Santa María and further in the distance, Valdefuentes. On the left is a junction with huge granite water troughs. The water coming from the pipe is drinkable.

Continue on the path, which becomes a wider track, towards the conical hill and circles the hill in a clockwise direction. Just ahead is a gateway into a finca. To the right by the gatepost is a tiny path with granite boulders. ❽ Take this path. It climbs up the side of the conical hill. On the left is a low wall which disappears within a few metres. The path goes up sharply but then levels off and widens out slightly. By a metal gate it bends around to the left and descends steeply. Stay on the path but take care as last year's oak leaves hide boulders underfoot. Pick the way carefully but at the same time watch that none of the low hanging twigs from the oak trees poke your eyes out. There are also the incredible views to look to — take your time. There is a wall on the right as a guide. Continue down. Ahead there is another wall and when you can see this other wall cut across diagonally to the left to continue with the new wall on the right. ❾ The path is quite rough but drops down to the CC-160 which is visible below.

Once on the CC-160, turn left. After 150m take the first turning on the right by a small metal gate with gateposts. ❿ The turning is an earth track that briefly shadows the road. It quickly becomes a concrete track. Pass agricultural buildings, left and right. Go down the track while ignoring all turnings. Ahead is a gateway with a metal gate leading to a house. On the left of the gateway are two

THE SIERRA DE MONTÁNCHEZ **1**

earth paths; one left, one ahead. Take the path ahead — the one closest to the house. The CC-160 is high above to the right. To the left are olive fincas and tremendous views out over the plains to the north. The path descends. It is paved with granite, lined with flowering bushes and accompanied by bird song. Ahead is one side of the Sierra de Montánchez terraced with olive trees. As the path descends ignore the two next turnings left. The path enters an oak wood and becomes wider, less rough and levels. At a broad Y junction keep right and follow the path, now a track, until it comes out at the CC-160 once more, by a small house on the left.

Turn left on to the CC-160, cross over, take the first turning right on to a rough path lined with walls. **11** On either side there are terraces of fruit trees, including cherry trees. The path is partly granite-paved and it zig-zags up to panoramic views out over the south once more. The many flowering bushes are dotted between the granite boulders and the oaks are growing wild. It is a very pretty part of the walk — especially in spring. At a Y junction turn right. **12** Stay on the granite-paved path as it descends. On the right the slopes of the sierra are covered in oaks and chestnuts — colourful in the autumn. As the path goes down more sharply it zig-zags and comes out at a T junction. Turn right on to a concrete track. **13** On the right is a newly built house. Follow the concrete track down until there is another T junction. Leave the concrete track and turn right on to the granite path once more. (The concrete track is a new one put in to access the house by vehicles and it criss-crosses the granite path.) Pass a finca entrance on the right and a junction on the left. **14** Ignore this. Go straight on, down the granite path. At a T junction turn right, then left at another new house on the right. Follow the path downwards through a small copse of trees.

The path comes to a low area that always seems to have a small stream of water running alongside. This is never a problem as

Quebrada lane, December

there are stepping stones and higher parts of the path to walk on if needed. To the left are pastures and cork oaks and to the right are olive groves and the slopes of the sierra. At a Y junction, go left. There is a huge granite boulder in the path but it is easily negotiated; just take care in the wet. The stream continues and the wild flowers are diverse and profuse. At a multiple junction keep left. The path becomes less rough but continues to descend. At a T junction turn left to complete the circuit. (❷, again) By two metal gates on the right is a Y junction. Turn left to descend back to the Quebrada road and the parked car.

THE SIERRA DE MONTÁNCHEZ 1

GPS Points
The Walk over the High Sierra

1. N39° 12' 06.12" W06° 06' 17.65"
2. N39° 12' 01.67" W06° 06' 34.00"
3. N39° 11' 44.52" W06° 07' 11.01"
4. N39° 11' 51.45" W06° 07' 57.00"
5. N39° 12' 09.32" W06° 07' 48.14"
6. N39° 12' 58.35" W06° 07' 50.41"
7. N39° 13' 13.04" W06° 07' 58.57"
8. N39° 13' 18.72" W06° 07' 49.38"
9. N39° 13' 22.24" W06° 07' 36.60"
10. N39° 13' 28.85" W06° 07' 45.54"
11. N39° 13' 11.17" W06° 06' 57.80"
12. N39° 13' 07.73" W06° 06' 45.88"
13. N39° 12' 43.36" W06° 06' 45.08"
14. N39° 12' 36.68" W06° 06' 44.40"

THE SIERRA DE MONTÁNCHEZ

4 The Walk of the Medieval Sheep Track

Start: swimming pool, Almoharín

Finish: swimming pool, Almoharín

4 hours plus stops

13.75 km

Low: 298m
High: 465m

Easy

Almoharín → Valdemorales → Almoharín
Map: IGN 730 Montánchez 1:50.000

White broom on the cordel, March

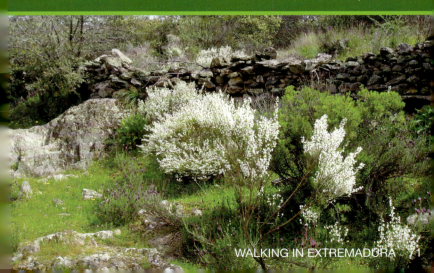

THE SIERRA DE MONTÁNCHEZ 1

View of Almoharín, March

Introduction

This easy walk is a perfect introduction to both the countryside and the agricultural history of Extremadura as it takes in part of the Cordel from Mérida to Trujillo. A cordel is a line along which sheep were moved in the trasumancia era. The walk has long stretches of pretty paths with good views of the Sierra de Montánchez and the surrounding countryside. There are streams in the wet season; a profusion of flowers from February to June and good bird-spotting opportunities in the small rocky valley of the Hornillo. The walk also links the small town of Almoharín with the even smaller village of Valdemorales. Time could be spent in either location relaxing or exploring. As the route enjoys some shade for different parts of the way it can be walked in summer either very early or late. A late walk through the open stretches where the fragrant

THE WALK OF THE MEDIEVAL SHEEP TRACK

retama grows is intoxicating. Wear boots if it has rained recently as three small parts of the route can be damp but if the rainy season has been prolonged it will be more wet.

Directions

Start at the Almoharín swimming pool on the west of the village on the EX-206 Cáceres-Miajadas road. ❶ There are plenty of places to park by the pool. With your back to the EX-206 and the pool on your left, head off down the lane going directly ahead. Pass a metal electricity tower on the left. Almost at once you come to a small ford with a concrete bridge on the right. Cross over. The lane goes uphill very slightly. As you go over the brow of the hill look right. There is a rocky elevated slope with a narrow path. Take this path and follow it as it winds along. After only a few minutes it turns to the right but a small, steep, rocky path goes down, left. Take this left path. Cross over a stream bed by way of stepping stones. The path climbs up ahead. To the right is a splendid example of an old mill. Its setting is pretty; in winter there are oranges on the trees and in early spring the almond trees are in blossom. The path continues up and turns sharply left, still going uphill gently. Just after the top of the climb look right for a magnificent view of the Sierra de Montánchez. The path descends to meet the earlier lane. Turn right. ❷ This stretch is home to both hoopoes and azure-winged magpies. Ignore a turning left to stay on the lane. At a Y junction with the house 'La Redonda' stay on the lane as it bears left. Pass the occasional finca on the left with a house and past an impressive entrance over the stream bed of the Hornillo to a big cattle finca, 'La Mariposa'. Ahead is a wide junction ❸ with options; left, across the stream bed, straight, on a narrowed rocky path or right, uphill. Take the path straight ahead.

In spring this path is beautiful with an abundance of flowering bushes and wild flowers. The high hills of the finca on the right are often a good place to spot birds; including small birds of prey.

THE SIERRA DE MONTÁNCHEZ

The path is lined with walls and is a mixture of grass, earth and granite slabs and small rocks underfoot. It meanders slightly and dips down where stepping stones cross the stream bed of the Hornillo. A little further on is an area of reeds and tall grass but the path is well defined. This bit can be boggy in the rainy season but it is possible to pick the way forward by using the strong tufts of grass and reeds as stepping stones. Continue ahead until the path widens out and meets the old Cordel de Mérida a Trujillo at a wide T junction.

Look around. To the right is a stone-walled finca with a terrific view of Cerro San Cristobal and Cancho Blanco in the distance. Behind is Almoharín. To the left is the way to Mérida (and it is possible to walk there on this cordel). Look ahead across the cordel and to the left. There is a wide finca gate but it will not be locked; this is a public right of way. Pass through closing the gate behind you. The path is ahead.

This part of the walk is along the left bank of a small but steep-sided valley where the Hornillo flows when there is enough rain. It is an area of game birds and small wild mammals. There are, sometimes, lazy sheep grazing who run away at the sight of walkers. Follow the path along the valley taking care to negotiate the rocks in the path carefully. As the climb goes up the valley, look back occasionally for the views down towards Almoharín. The path meanders with a few tricky bits where the rocks are 'in the way'. Take your time. After ten minutes or so, the valley ends in a wide open space dotted with retama bushes — very pretty in spring and deliciously fragrant on summer evenings. Keep on the path ahead. It bends to the left slightly. There are several paths now but it matters not which you pick as long as you are going forward and to the left a bit. Look ahead. To the right is a series of wooded hills. After a few minutes, to the left, is a long, low farmhouse and outbuildings which are a point of orientation. After about ten minutes the path joins a track from the right. Go right.

THE WALK OF THE MEDIEVAL SHEEP TRACK

It will come out from the retama dotted area to a T junction with a wide track with a fence on the opposite side. (You should be by the farmhouse gate but don't worry if you are not. The path from the valley must bring you to the track. Look at the map to check.) Turn right. ❹

Walk straight up this wide track with the retama dotted area on the right and the wire fence on the left. The track crosses a cattle grid and narrows considerably to become a path. Keep straight ahead (all the way to Valdemorales). The path goes through a narrow section where your stick will come in handy to peg back the branches or bushes. Once through this slightly overgrown stretch the path becomes a glorious progression of Extremeño countryside at its best. Enjoy the trees, bushes, flowers, animals, birds, silence and views. The path is narrow and occasionally has granite slabs or bigger rocks to negotiate but nothing serious. To the left is rising ground and there are small fincas. To the right are some spectacular views of Almoharín and the countryside beyond. Pass a rock-strewn path going sharply downward on the right but continue on the path straight ahead. The views on the right disappear and give way to lush meadows, hills and holm oaks. Walk ahead to Valdemorales. At the junction with the EX-206 look left. There is a pedestrian crossing. Use it to cross the road then walk ahead into the village past the little park and benches on your right. Valdemorales is tiny but has two bars and a shop. Explore, then make your way to the church to continue the walk.

With the church on the left and the Plaza de España on the other side of the church, walk ahead. Once past the church, take the right hand road going straight on past a stone building with a big arched entrance. Almost at once you are in countryside again. Follow the road over a concrete bridge that spans a small stream bed and bear right but do not turn sharply right over a second bridge. The road comes to a wide junction with a small track off to the left. Do not take that. Keep on the wider road to the

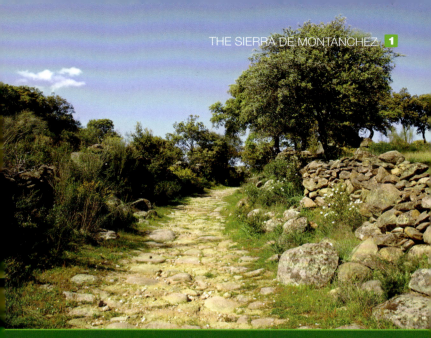

THE SIERRA DE MONTÁNCHEZ 1

Between fincas, March

right. There is a electricity mast with an open grassy area. Follow the road as it bears right then left to another junction with an information board, on the left, about local wild flower and plant identification. Take the road to the right. ❺ Pass an agricultural building on the right. Turn right at the next junction. Cross the EX-206 once more. Carefully. Go straight ahead down a grassy path that bears left. Cross the small stream bed using the stepping stones if necessary. To the right is a huge walnut tree laden with nuts in November and December. Once over the stream bed, turn left, and pass a strange walled construction on the right. Continue to a little lane and what looks like a junk-yard ahead. Turn right with an agricultural building on your left. Immediately after the building turn sharp left to pick up a grassy path. ❻ The path is the cordel again. It very quickly leaves the road behind and enters into glorious countryside again.

THE WALK OF THE MEDIEVAL SHEEP TRACK

Keep on the path. It meanders a bit at the start then enters a narrow stretch with flowering bushes on both sides. Views of the steeply wooded slopes are on the right. Look out for birds of prey as they circle above the granite outcrops. The path widens and the walking is very easy. Eventually you arrive back at the point where you went through the finca gate on the cordel.

Turn left to retrace the walk back to the junction with the house 'La Redonda'. Turn left. After a few metres, at a Y junction, turn left again. The lane goes up slightly with olive and fig fincas all around. The lane bends to the left then right. The view behind, in the distance, is of typical dehesa slopes. Ahead, to the right, Cerro San Cristobal is visible. The lane narrows and becomes a grass and reed path. It can be a bit boggy in the rainy season. Continue around a few boulders in the path and come out into a wide area with a utilitarian concrete bridge over a stream. ⑦ To the left, tucked away in the reeds, is the ruin of a mill. To the right is a view down the valley to Almoharín. Cross the bridge and continue on the path, more rocky now, as it runs parallel, but higher, to the stream bed on the right. The path becomes more grassy and meets a junction on the right. Turn right. Straight ahead is the stream and another ruined mill on the right. Growing in the mill is a magnificent almond tree bursting with blossoms every February. Turn and retrace a few steps from the stream and the mill. On the right is an tiny earth path. Take that path to meet a T junction with a slightly wider path. Turn left. Pass a finca house on the left. Walk straight ahead to cross a ford and reach the EX-206. ⑧ Turn right and walk 100m back to the swimming pool and the start.

GPS Points
The Walk of the Medieval Sheep Track

1. N39° 10' 32.40" W06° 03' 04.54"
2. N39° 10' 24.87" W06° 03' 37.94"
3. N39° 10' 47.98" W06° 03' 59.50"
4. N39° 11' 04.06" W06° 05' 16.69"
5. N39° 12' 09.93" W06° 03' 40.95"
6. N39° 11' 54.71" W06° 03' 59.85"
7. N39° 10' 38.27" W06° 03' 32.15"
8. N39° 10' 37.53" W06° 03' 11.04"

THE SIERRA DE MONTÁNCHEZ

5 The Walk of Country Lanes and Hidden Paths

Start: Plaza de España, Almoharín

Finish: Plaza de España, Almoharín

2-2.5 hours plus stops

6.5 km

Low: 308m
High: 456m

Easy

Almoharín → Almoharín
Map: IGN 730 Montánchez 1:50.000

Spanish Festoon (*Zerynthia rumina*), July

WALKING IN EXTREMADURA 81

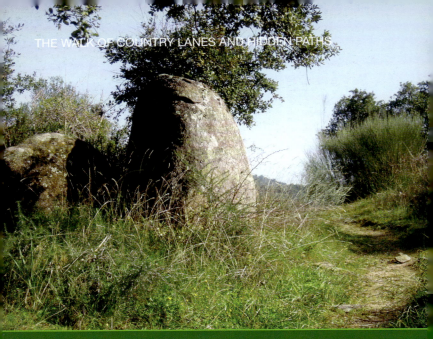

THE WALK OF COUNTRY LANES AND HIDDEN PATHS

At the top of the first hidden path, February

Introduction

This walk lies to the north of the village of Almoharín. The constant views of the surrounding mountains and hills form a lovely backdrop to the more domesticated working countryside through which this walk passes. It is a circuit that takes in well-tended fincas of olive, fig, orange and almond. There are many livestock fincas: cattle, sheep, pigs, horses and donkeys. It is a good walk on which to see how the village people express their love of, and care for, the countryside. The circuit consists of three wide lanes connected by two hidden paths. It starts with a gentle rise and fall along the first lane and joins with a small path, glorious in spring with flowers and blossoms. A short walk on the next lane joins the other hidden path. This one is more shaded and narrow and, in spring, full of bird song. The final lane of the circuit, the

Almond blossom with the Cerro San Cristobal behind, February

descent back to the village, starts with tremendous views down to Almohrín and beyond. It is undemanding, except in one short stretch on the first path and then a longer stretch, on the next one. However, the degree of difficulty is low. The walk is best in February for the spectacular almond blossoms but there is something of interest all year around. In high summer the trees give shade early and late but the lane back to the village has no shade.

Directions

Facing the church in the Plaza de España in Almohrín ❶ walk around to the north side of the church. Opposite is the Centro del Mayor, to the right of which is Calle Hernán Cortés. Take this road all the way, gently uphill, to the Hermitage of Santa Filomena ignoring all junctions. At the hermitage take the road on the right. It

THE WALK OF COUNTRY LANES AND HIDDEN PATHS

narrows and curves around left, then right, and divides at a wide junction. Ignore the lane to the right. Our lane goes left, uphill, with a clear view of Cerro San Cristobal to the right. On the left are glimpses of the Sierra de Montánchez. The lane quickly comes to a junction by a finca called 'Mil Colinas' on the right. Ignore the main lane straight ahead and take the lane on the left. ❷

At the top of the gentle hill the view, all the way around, of hills and mountains is one of the highlights of this section of the circuit. As the lane drops down on the other side of the hill it is possible to feel enveloped by the whole of the Sierra de Montánchez. Pass a concrete bridge over a stream bed near a house on the left. The lane winds to the left and then goes right. It passes tempting little paths, different gates, mature oaks and olives. On the right are meadows and pastures carpeted with white and yellow daises from January to June and the purple of viper's bugloss from March to July. Cattle very often graze here. The lane comes to a wide junction where the left fork almost doubles back on itself. ❸ This left fork, if followed, returns to the village near the swimming pool. Continue on the lane to the right. On the right is a lovely meadow with granite boulders and a big *charca* (pond) that never goes dry — even in the summer.

On the right, by a metal gate there is a blue and orange waymark on a stone in the wall. Ignore it. (These are waymarks for the Almoharín walking group's invitation route held every April but not included in this book. If you want to do that walk another day, it is easy but 18km. Just follow the waymarks.) Next to the waymark is a small earth path. ❹ Take this path. It is strewn with small loose rocks and larger, partly buried, granite boulders. There's a good view of wooded hills on the left. The path continues in a straight direction with various stretches of earth, grass or rocks underfoot. It goes up slightly, then becomes level and then there is a much more rocky, steeper part with a short climb. At the top are shady trees and a very large boulder on the left. This is a good

THE SIERRA DE MONTÁNCHEZ

360 degree viewing point out over the surrounding countryside and hills. Follow the path down; it is not as rocky as the upward stretch. To the left, almond trees are dotted amongst the olives and figs.

At the bottom of the descent is a very large boulder right in the middle of the path — a distinctive landmark. The path widens out and comes to a broad junction. Turn right on to a lane. Follow the lane past a small agricultural compound on the right where there is usually a friendly dog, and a few piglets. The lane passes a path on the left, again with a blue and orange waymark on the stones. Ignore it. Keep straight on in the direction of the village. Pass two fincas with imposing gateposts on the left and one with equally imposing gateposts on the right. The lane continues almost flat and straight. As the lane begins to bend slightly to the right there is a junction to the left. The path is grassy with a few rocks. Turn left on to this path. ❺ Straight ahead is a gate with Cerro San Cristobal directly above. Immediately left is a turning on to a very narrow path. Take this path.

After a few metres the views of cultivated fincas are left behind. The path is seldom used and is rocky, narrow and twisty in places but it has no junctions. It is pretty when the bushes are in flower. It goes up slightly and is shaded by trees. Enjoy the glimpses of views and the music of seasonal song birds. As the path evens out into a soft earth footpath the views are all to the left with Cerro San Cristobal looming larger with each step towards it. The path narrows and enters a deeply shaded section. It becomes more rocky and goes upward. The high points on the route, when the trees thin, afford lovely views behind and to the left. The path opens out and goes to the right. Here there is a small grassy area perfect for a picnic. Follow the path as it bends right and continues up then bends left around a large boulder, and starts to descend, past big, old cork oaks on the right. The path widens with walls on either side and views of small fincas to the right. Working a finca

THE WALK OF COUNTRY LANES AND HIDDEN PATHS

up here can only be done by access on foot or donkey but that is what makes this path so enjoyable — the quiet.

As the path comes out from the trees, on the left are very good examples of huge meadows with holm oaks; the dehesa of Extremadura. It is a little more rocky underfoot again but the descent is gentle. The earth path finishes abruptly and become one of concrete. To the right is a small weekend house and the path joins a larger rough lane. ❻ Follow the rough lane to the right. Directly ahead is a view of Almoharín. The lane descends past a small house on the left where there is a stream bed, very pretty when full of water. The lane becomes flatter and joins another one at a T junction. Turn right to follow this lane towards the village ignoring other junctions until the wide junction at the start of the circular walk. Retrace the route into the village.

GPS Points
The Walk of Country Lanes and Hidden Paths

1. N39° 10' 35.49" W06° 02' 38.49"
2. N39° 10' 56.27" W06° 02' 39.93"
3. N39° 11' 16.13" W06° 03' 18.15"
4. N39° 11' 23.87" W06° 03' 27.75"
5. N39° 11' 23.56" W06° 02' 47.15"
6. N39° 11' 18.96" W06° 02' 21.23"

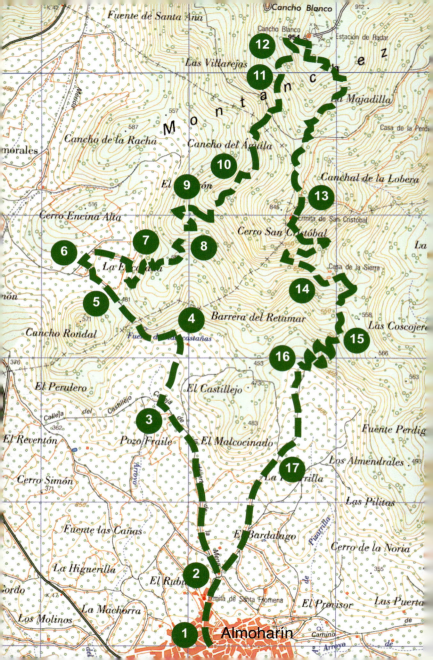

THE SIERRA DE MONTÁNCHEZ 1

6 The Wild Walk on Cancho Blanco

Start: Plaza de España, Almoharín

Finish: Plaza de España, Almoharín

6 hours plus stops

13.75 km

Low: 308m
High: 940m

Medium-High

Almoharín → Almoharín
Map: IGN 730 Montánchez 1:50.000

Cancho Blanco, January

THE WILD WALK ON CANCHO BLANCO

Introduction

This walk takes in the two highest peaks behind Almoharín: first, Cancho Blanco, with its distinctive white radar station, and second, Cerro San Cristobal. The degree of difficulty for the walk is medium-high as the climbs zig-zag rather than go straight up. However, the walk does need a good level of fitness because it involves long stretches of unrelieved ascent plus two peaks. The level of climb is 632m from lowest to highest point — more than, for example, the two linear walks in Las Villuercas, so don't be lulled into thinking it's going to be that easy. There are also a few low stone walls to clamber over and other rocky bits to negotiate, but there is no actual mountaineering. However, walkers choosing to tackle this route need to be experienced because the path is vague in places. Finding the way relies on good orienting skills if landmarks are missed. A regular walker will not get lost in any event; this is the Sierra de Montánchez and not the Hindu Kush. Its very charm is the wild walking. However, if you do not feel confident enough to wild walk, but want a good, long climb, do the Walk over the High Sierra instead as it follows clear paths.

The foothills of the peaks are made up of hundreds of small fincas, enclosed in the typical dry stone walls of granite. As the climb gets higher the fincas disappear and the terrain becomes open. The dominant bushes are broom and retama. The three types of oak tree; holm, cork and deciduous (above 500m) all grow on the slopes and there are small copses of these oaks right at the tops of both peaks. In spring there are hundreds of wild flowers, including peonies, and almond blossoms are dotted everywhere. Song birds nest in the thicker cover of the lower slopes. In autumn the deciduous oaks make the sierra very colourful with their falling leaves. On cold winter days, with the sun shining, walking here is perfect.

There are also a few historical surprises along the way. There are

THE SIERRA DE MONTÁNCHEZ

The Village of Valdemorales, February

landmarks everywhere quite apart from the radar station; ruined houses, imposing gateways, granite watering troughs, drinkable springs, the ruined Hermitage of San Cristobal, a 500 year old boundary marker between Almoharín, Valdemorales and Zarza de Montánchez and, of course, the tremendous view. One of the best known landmarks is the house of a local rich family. In the early days of Alfonso XIII, over a century ago, when the summer got too hot down in the village, the redoubtable grandmother would pack up her entire household and transport everything, by donkey, to the house in the mountains where the cooler breeze blew. Every day someone would go to the village for bread but everything else, water, milk, vegetables and meat was provided by the grand finca that went with the 'summer house'. In autumn, everything was packed up again for the descent back to the village. Nowadays,

THE WILD WALK ON CANCHO BLANCO

we have air-conditioning and few donkeys. The once magnificent house and outbuildings are falling into further disrepair with each passing year but it is still breezy with extensive views. It makes an excellent picnic spot.

The directions for this walk are rather precise but the number of rocky outcrops, holm oaks, dry stone walls and granite boulders can all add up to confusion unless you are a very methodical walker. I've walked up here many times — but never the exact same route twice. Better by far is to follow the points of orientation and pick out the best paths yourself. Use the map and your eyes and enjoy the walk. Take binoculars.

Directions

Park in the Plaza de España, Almoharín. Walk to the other side of the church. Next to the Centro del Mayor is Calle Hernán Cortés. ❶ Take this road. It goes all the way, gently uphill, to the Hermitage of Santa Filomena. Here the road divides in two. Take the road on the right. It narrows and curves to divide at a wide junction. Take the lane on the left. ❷ It quickly comes to junction by a finca called 'Mil Colinas' on the right. Take the main lane that goes straight ahead and ignore the left turn.

The lane goes gently up. Ignore all left junctions and two on the right. At the third junction on the right turn up a narrow concreted path. ❸ There is a blue and orange waymark on a large stone to the left. (These are waymarks for the Almoharín walking group's invitation route held every April but not included in this book. If you want to do that walk another day, it is easy but 18km. Just follow the waymarks.) We follow these waymarks for a time. Look up the path; a hill lies dead ahead. The concrete quickly becomes earth and grass and the hill ahead looms large. By a big metal gate, on the right, the path becomes even more narrow with many flowering bushes close up on either side.

THE SIERRA DE MONTÁNCHEZ **1**

The path widens out, starts to climb gently and becomes rocky. At one point it splits in two but rejoins after it passes a clump of trees. The path makes a 90 degree turn to the left ❹ and becomes an enchanting, partly-paved, stretch with views down towards Almoharín on the left and a wooded area on the right. This wood is a great place for nesting song birds. As the climb becomes more pronounced the path zig-zags with a helpful waymark on a rock every now and then. The views to the left disappear as the hills close in. Keep straight. As the path widens out it becomes a small grassy lane. Ignore tiny paths left and right. At a big junction follow around to the left as the lane becomes a flat, concrete path. ❺ There is a view of the radar station in the distance. Enjoy this flat part of the walk as the going will be upward soon.

At the next junction take the small earth path to the right with the waymark. It quickly joins an earth track. Path and track become a single wide lane. Turn right at the next junction. ❻ The lane becomes concrete. This is an area of working fincas, although some do seem a little wild. Look out for flowers in the meadows. The next junction is within 100m. Follow the concrete lane to the right and start climbing up. There are various tempting tracks going off but keep on the concrete path as it winds up very steeply. Look back for good views of Valdemorales and the surrounding landscape.

At a ruined house, above head height on the right, the concrete lane comes to an end in a turning circle. ❼ There are various finca gates and a path, right. Ignore it. Ahead is a tiny grassy path. It may look a bit overgrown but take this path. It is flat with broom and retama bushes on either side. It is narrow, but clear. Push back bushes with your stick if necessary. To the left is a super view of the Sierra de Montánchez. The going, inevitably, starts to be upwards. Keep the wall on the left as a guide when the path opens out. The views, right, are towards Almoharín. Come to an enormous granite boulder that lies across the path. Go around

THE WILD WALK ON CANCHO BLANCO

it and immediately climb over the dry stone wall on the left. It is not hard. Use the stones as steps but take care. ❽ As an extra landmark, as if the boulder is not enough, there is a big almond tree to the left where you climb over the wall.

Once over the wall, a steep side of a hill, horizontally terraced and with low walls, is ahead. Climb up. Carefully negotiate the low walls interspaced with flat grassy stretches. It doesn't matter if you go a few metres left or right in picking out the best way to go up as long as the view of Almoharín is behind and you keep going up. Eventually you will arrive at a broad track that runs across the way up. ❾ To the left is a low ruined house. To the right is a drinkable spring with water running into granite troughs. If you are not exactly at this point, don't worry as long as you have found the track — which you must find if you have gone straight up. Turn right on to this track and follow it up.

The track is wide. As it winds its way up, the side with the view changes, depending on the direction of the zig and zag. As the climb ascends the radar station is in full view and directly ahead. As the radar station disappears from view behind a line of holm oaks the track curves, decisively, to the right. It becomes rougher but the outlook is even more spectacular with both Valdemorales and Almoharín in view. There are no real junctions on the track but if in doubt, go up. At a wide open grassy expanse the radar station comes into view once more and the track goes to the right. As it goes up it is, surprisingly, flat in stretches.

Out over the left is a lovely view of the wooded side of Cancho Blanco. In the middle is a huge granite outcrop surrounded by almond trees. It has splashes of lime green on it. It looks like paint but is a lichen indigenous to the area. The radar station has disappeared behind the ridge once more but the way ahead is now very clear, defined by a series of walls. The track widens but goes up more steeply. On the left are granite boulders and

THE SIERRA DE MONTÁNCHEZ

Cerro San Cristobal from the Jagged Dog's Teeth, February

THE WILD WALK ON CANCHO BLANCO

outcrops with wonderful views behind them. Many different, colourful mosses and lichen grow on the granite. The track makes a 90 degree turn to the right and after 500m it peters out to become vague. **10**

Now is the time for some wild walking and zig-zagging in the direction of the top. Most of the low walls that get in the way should have gaps for passing through but, if you are not in that position, just climb over them. Cross over the first wall. You will be in a lane. Cross it and the next wall. Continue up. As the climb comes over the horizon a long wall is in front. Turn left to walk towards the (hidden) radar station. Keep the wall on the right as a guide, 20-30m away, and pass various granite outcrops on the left. The wall starts to come across the line of vision as you go higher. As you walk towards the wall you have to climb over it. There is a place where there is a large rock close to the wall with a tiny path between it and the wall. It is not so high here. Use the protruding stones to climb over the wall.

You are now in an area of rocky outcrops and small deciduous oak saplings. Pick the way to the left, the wall you climbed over is soon 10m to the left and will fall away sharply the higher you climb. Ahead is a big outcrop with a large single holm oak growing from the centre. **11** Once past the outcrop and holm oak on your left continue upwards. You can see the radar station. Pass through a gap in yet another low wall. Straight ahead is a wider grassy path with a line of rocks on the left and stunted trees on the right. This part of the walk, through a delightful small copse, is flat and easy.

Go right along the wall on the left until you find a gap with an old metal gate abandoned to one side. Walk through the gateway into a meadow dotted with oak trees, possibly with grazing cattle. Go through a second gap in a second wall. This is the top of Cancho Blanco with the fenced radar station directly ahead. For an even higher point, turn left and climb the giant granite boulders, settle

THE SIERRA DE MONTÁNCHEZ 1

down and rest, picnic and look at the view. ⑫ As a guide, this part of the walk, from Almoharín to radar station, usually takes 2.5 hours but if you are looking at views, plants, flowers, trees, bushes and birds and pacing yourself it will take longer.

For the way back, retrace through the meadow and walls but stay left. There is a little path that goes down with a wall on the left. Go through the gap on the left and there is a sharp downward path with another wall ahead and Cerro San Cristobal directly ahead and sometimes slightly to the right. The view of Valdemorales is on the right. Follow the path as it zig-zags through bushes and rocks but always going down in the direction of Cerro San Cristobal, on which, quite clearly, is a wall running from the bottom to halfway up the slope. Keep that in mind as a point of orientation. With an outcrop like jagged dog's teeth on your left continue down and go slightly left. Pick your way. Below Cerro San Cristobal are some distinct open meadows. Make for those. You come to a wall that limits the deciduous oaks. Climb over into the meadows. The path, now clear, goes to Cerro San Cristobal. Pick up a wall coming from the left as a guide and follow it. The path comes to a large outcrop on the right that makes the path narrow against the wall. It needs careful negotiating but continue downward and slightly left to cross over the wall that has been the guide on the left.

Walk through a grassy space. Look ahead and left. There is a good view of the reservoir on the River Burdalo, scheduled to open for swimming and non-motorised sport in 2013. Keep the rocky outcrops right, with another wall, left, as a guide until you pass through a gap in the wall to a lane. Cross this and the next wall. You are in a wide open area. To the right is Valdemorales. To the left is a deep valley with the reservoir in front in the distance. Walk straight over the space and straight up the soft hill in front. The path goes ahead with a wall to the right — the wall we saw from a distance. Pass through a small gap to put the wall on the left. Choose a path but go up. The wall drops away very quickly.

THE WILD WALK ON CANCHO BLANCO

Go up. At the top, go left by the rocky outcrop with trees and pick up a wall on the right. Go around the rocky outcrop. Keep on the path to the next outcrop also with trees on top.

Once at the top of Cerro San Cristobal there is a small flattish area ringed by trees. Pick up the clear path that goes around to the right. The boulders here are more rounded and softer. There are many peony plants. Turn leftish to go around the rocks. Turn slightly right to walk the ridge. Here are the ruins of the Hermitage of San Cristobal. **13** It must have been quite a building at one point as, around the left corner, through a gap in ruined walls, are the ruins of the original gateposts. Look to the right of the gateposts for the granite boundary marker mentioned in the introduction. Impressive — just like the view from here.

Go past the main hermitage entrance on the right and pick up a small path that goes down, to the right and then turns sharp left to go downward keeping the hermitage on the left and all the view on the right. After a few metres a clear path is visible. Follow the path as it goes down gently towards a wall and a large almond tree ahead. The path goes right and zig-zags very gently downwards. You can see Almoharín ahead and can orient yourself. The path goes right for a long way. Do not try to go down too quickly; the descent is much more gentle than you might expect at this stage. After about 15 minutes Almoharín is directly ahead in the distance and the reservoir is on the left. The path descends more sharply with zig-zags that begin at a rocky outcrop. Ahead, and to the right, below is a large ruined property; the one in the introduction. That's the point of orientation.

The path enters a more shaded area with rocks and trees. The going down is quite steep. Leave the wood and enter an area of bushes and wild olives. Pick the way down. The walk comes out into a copse of holm oaks. Straight ahead is the reservoir. Keep on zig-zagging down. To the right, ahead, are glimpses of Almoharín.

THE SIERRA DE MONTÁNCHEZ **1**

Suddenly, the ruins of the wealthy local family's house, the Casa de la Sierra, are before you. **14** This is a good place to rest. The house on the left was the family house, the one on the right the servants quarters. Look back to see how far down you have come from the hermitage.

The onward path goes through the middle of the two ruined houses. To the right is a wall and a path. Put the wall on your left. The path has granite steps for the first 20m and bears left, then right as it goes down. Go right over a low wall, right on a grassy path that zig-zags towards an open area with a huge cork oak on your right and, for about 100m, bear left, away from the village, through a deep cork oak grove. The path then turns back towards the village and continues gently downwards. From here always choose the best path for going down, through gaps in any walls to save clambering over them and bear right in the general direction of the village.

There is the old lane that connected Casa de la Sierra with the village, but it has long been abandoned. However, you should be able to find it and keep it on your right as a guide. Come to a pleasant flat grassy expanse that is dotted with retama bushes and, occasionally quiet grazing animals. Make your way ahead on a distinct path. The path comes to a wall that cuts across it. Turn right at the wall to have it on the left and walk to a huge holm oak, about 20m away, and climb over the wall. Do not worry if you are not at this exact point. Look for the wall, the tree and the path beyond the wall. Once over the wall you are back on the blue and orange waymarked route partly followed at the start of this walk. Turn right. **15**

The next part of the walk has tremendous views ahead and to the right, but the path is very rocky and twisty and goes downwards for quite some way. It needs concentration. Remember to look at the view occasionally. At the bottom of the last zig-zag follow

Valdemorales from the oak woods, February

the path to the left. ⓰ It is still a bit rocky but more level and is bordered with broom and retama. On the left is a magnificent example of a big meadow with holm oaks; the dehesa of Extremadura. The hillsides are covered in granite boulders and holm oaks. In spring the meadow is yellow with daisies.

The path comes to a junction with a small lane to the left and a broader concreted lane on the right that goes to the village. ⓱ Go right. This lane comes out to a junction with a wider earth lane by a small house on the right. Take the main lane going down to the village. Follow this lane all the way down, quite steeply to start with, back to the village and the square.

THE SIERRA DE MONTÁNCHEZ 1

GPS Points
The Wild Walk on Cancho Blanco

1. N39° 10' 35.49" W06° 02' 38.49"
2. N39° 10' 51.12" W06° 02' 37.46"
3. N39° 11' 30.00" W06° 02' 54.60"
4. N39° 11' 47.72" W06° 02' 49.14"
5. N39° 11' 54.71" W06° 03' 09.81"
6. N39° 12' 01.36" W06° 03' 18.60"
7. N39° 12' 00.61" W06° 03' 00.31"
8. N39° 12' 05.50" W06° 02' 48.34"
9. N39° 12' 12.69" W06° 02' 47.48"
10. N39° 12' 17.37" W06° 02' 38.71"
11. N39° 12' 47.76" W06° 02' 19.96"
12. N39° 12' 53.53" W06° 02' 17.98"
13. N39° 12' 09.36" W06° 02' 28.39"
14. N39° 12' 01.02" W06° 02' 09.10"
15. N39° 11' 49.49" W06° 02' 02.26"
16. N39° 11' 41.91" W06° 02" 13.69"
17. N39° 11' 22.85" W06° 02' 16.31"

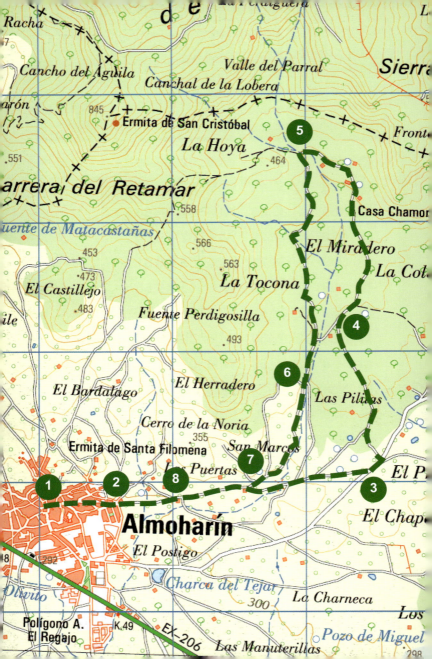

THE SIERRA DE MONTÁNCHEZ 1

7 The Walk up to La Hoya

Start: Plaza de España, Almoharín

Finish: Plaza de España, Almoharín

3 hours plus stops

10.25 km

Low: 292m
High: 434m

Easy

Almoharín → Almoharín
Map: IGN 730-III Montánchez 1:25.000

La Hoya in spate, December

THE WALK UP TO LA HOYA

Introduction

This walk explores the countryside on the south facing slopes of the low hills of the Sierra de Montánchez. It starts on a wide back lane from Almoharín that goes into the area known as Las Gamitas. The beginning of the circular part of the walk goes up the small valley created by the Hoya, a stream, delightful in winter but dry in the summer months. Holm oak trees are the main feature of the area and that means the opportunity to spot plenty of birds. Small birds of prey circle the mountain peaks as the walk goes deeper into the countryside. The return to the village is along a track that goes gently downhill. Apart from the sound of bird song in season the area is remarkably quiet given that you are never more than a few kilometres from the village.

This walk can be experienced year-round but I feel it is best in the autumn or winter after the rains because then the Hoya flows delightfully in the valley and the surrounding vegetation is lush. In spring there are flowers and birds. An early or late start is recommended in summer as there is no shade on the lane.

Directions

Facing the church in the Plaza de España in Almoharín ❶ walk around to the north side of the church and straight down Calle Real. At the bottom of the hill come to a T junction with a shop on the left. Turn right. Take the third turning on the left into Calle Gran Capitán. Do not take any junctions. After 300m come to a wide multiple junction. Ignore the two left turns. Ignore the turn into Calle V Centenario and a line of modern terraced houses on the right. Walk directly ahead ❷ on to a wide lane which passes olive and fig fincas. The low hills of the Sierra de Montánchez are on the left and the village is behind. The lane is going due east. Do not take any turnings or junctions but keep on the main lane. There will be three distinctive turnings left — keep more to the right and ahead if in doubt.

THE SIERRA DE MONTÁNCHEZ **1**

After 2.5km the wide lane joins a minor road at a T junction **3** where there is a small house on the left. Turn left. Pass a second, neighbouring, small house and on the left is a wide grassy track. Turn left on to the track. Cerro San Cristobal and the Sierra de Montánchez are directly ahead. Stay on the track. At a Y junction ignore a turning left. Enter an area of flowering bushes, trees, birds, views and deep, deep quiet.

The track narrows and goes up very gently. There are a lot of flowering bushes on either side. The countryside is very wooded and is almost undisturbed. After passing a stone-built house on the right the oak trees thin slightly and the views become more open with a few farmed fincas in sight. There is a junction with a little path joining the track from the left — ignore this, it runs back to the road from the village. **4** Follow the track as it bends decisively to the right. After a left bend the track becomes narrower, rougher and goes up slightly. It levels out and the figs and olives fall back. The oaks increase. Continue gently uphill. The low hills in front loom larger as the track goes deeper into the countryside. It bends to the left slightly, narrows and goes up steeply. An abandoned farmhouse is on the left, surrounded by almond blossoms in early spring.

The track becomes even narrower and is effectively a path. The pointed peak, ahead, with the very top cut off, is a place to spot lesser hawks. On the right is a low white farmhouse. There are lavender and broom bushes and low oak trees. The mountains are encircling. As the path passes a stone built house on the left look back for extensive views. The path bends left, then right and enters a shady stretch with the flowering bushes continuing all around. It becomes very rocky. On the left are large boulders over which the Hoya cascades when in spate. Even in dry times there should be pools of water amongst the boulders. The path is clear and paved. This is a good place to stop and explore, picnic or sit

THE WALK UP TO LA HOYA

quietly. The tops of the mountains are good for spotting birds and, in spite of the oak trees, there are good views back along the path.

Cross the stream bed by using the stepping stones. The path goes straight over the stream bed and comes to a T junction with another path. Turn left. ❺ The path, which winds back down to the village is narrow, wide, flat and rough by turns. There are a few junctions but ignore all turnings. It is lovely in a quiet and wild way with copses of oaks and a few grazing cattle here and there. In the summer, in the evening, rabbits play in the grassy expanses. Look to the mountains, right, for birds.

The path bends left by metal gates opposite each other. It comes out to two concrete bridges on the left that cross a wide stream bed with a track that continues left. ❻ Do not cross the stream bed or go left. Continue right as the path becomes a track. After about 50m is an old well on the left. The water is drinkable and there is a tin attached to a long string for drinking purposes. Yes! I know — but everyone, including me, does it.

Continue straight on the track ignoring turnings to left and right. By a small shed and gate on the left the track narrows considerably to become a path once more. It bends to the right. In the rainy season the stream bed on the left is full of water. Continue ahead and pass some agricultural buildings on the left. Ahead is a wall with a huge metal door and a T junction. Turn left. ❼ At the next T junction turn right to return to the village which is in sight. At the Y junction ❽ with the circular concrete dais and the covered well, it is possible to take either lane as they both go back to the village. The left lane returns to the starting point.

THE SIERRA DE MONTÁNCHEZ 1

GPS Points
The Walk up to La Hoya

1. N39° 10' 35.49" W06° 02' 38.49"
2. N39° 10' 37.57" W06° 02' 15.67"
3. N39° 10' 47.77" W06° 00' 58.02"
4. N39° 11' 25.33" W06° 01' 09.61"
5. N39° 12' 06.57" W06° 01' 22.75"
6. N39° 11' 09.86" W06° 01' 18.56"
7. N39° 10' 42.93" W06° 01' 35.24"
8. N39° 10' 39.62" W06° 01' 59.53"

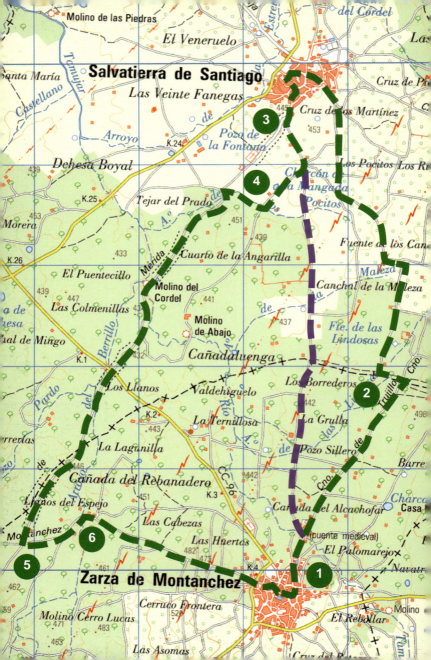

THE SIERRA DE MONTÁNCHEZ 1

8 The Walk of the Oak Tree and the Pilgrim Hospital

Start: Zarza de Montánchez

Finish: Zarza de Montánchez

4.5 hours plus stops

15 km

Low: 425m
High: 476m

Easy

Zarza → Salvatierra de Santiago → Zarza
Map: IGN 730 Montánchez 1:50.000

Holm oaks near Zarza, March

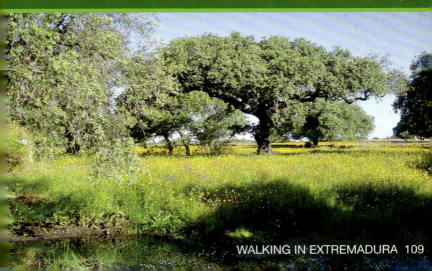

THE WALK OF THE OAK TREE AND THE PILGRIM HOSPITAL

Short option: start and finish in Zarza de Montánchez
Time: 2.5 hours plus stops **Distance:** 10 kilometres

Introduction

This walk is almost completely flat. The delight of this walk is the linking of two rural villages: Zarza de Montánchez and Salvatierra de Santiago. The route passes a medieval bridge, an 800-year-old oak tree, a pilgrim hospital in which Carlos V passed a night in 1526, an old church, a hermitage, an ancient waymark cross and a clapper bridge of untold age. The pilgrim hospital is now simply a large empty house but the crests under the top windows bear testimony to a much earlier history. It was reputedly build, and run, by the Knights of Alcántara to look after pilgrims who had fallen sick on the nearby Via de la Plata, also known as the Camino de Santiago or Way of St. James, on route to the shrine of St. James at Santiago de Compostela in Galicia. There is, of course, lovely countryside all around; flowers in spring, vultures in summer, colourful trees on the sierra slopes in autumn and streams in winter. Ask locals about the previous few week's rainfall before you walk as, to be honest, although this walk is lovely most of the year I think it's best after a few inches of rain.

There are two return options from Salvatierra. The shorter route returns via a straight flat lane with open countryside all around. Everyone can do this little walk. The only fitness level needed is to be able to walk for 2.5 hours. It's ideal as a walk before breakfast on a sight-seeing day, or a post-dinner walk.

The second option is longer and follows a wide, medieval sheep track used during the trasumancia era. The going underfoot is softer than the lane and the route passes along wide verges lined with lavender and broom. At a crossing of the River Tamuja there is a old clapper bridge reminiscent of those found on Dartmoor, England. It is a good place to pause and spot birds coming to

THE SIERRA DE MONTÁNCHEZ

enjoy the water. If you have time, do the longer walk.

Neither route is suitable for high summer as there is little shade on more than half the route.

Directions

Head towards Zarza de Montánchez on the CC-146, from a signposted junction on the EX-206 Cáceres-Miajadas road. As you approach the village take the first left junction to by-pass the village. At the end of the by-pass, stop at the junction and turn right in the direction of the village. On the left is the café bar Encina la Terrona with a small wooden sign of the same name on the wall. Turn left at this café to have it on the right as you go down the lane. Pass the Infant School and playing field on the left. Park at the big space outside the Piscina Municipal. ❶ Walk around the swimming pool, using either side, to get to a wide, straight lane leading away from the village. Take this lane. In a few moments there is a well-preserved medieval bridge over the River Tamuja. There is a lane to the left which is the return via the short cut. Cross over the bridge and walk ahead on the wide flat lane.

The area is one of small fincas but the olives and figs, habitual to the area, soon fall behind in favour of the dehesa of Extremadura. On the right is the Sierra de Zarza and behind is the Sierra de Montánchez. The holm oak and pastures support cows, horses, donkeys, goats, hens, sheep and a great many black pigs running free in the meadows. The pigs live on the acorns and make the most prized, and expensive, jamon (ham).

After only 20 minutes of walking the lane passes a conservation area on the left. Enter by the small gate that crosses over a cattle grid. This is the park with the Encina la Terrona, an oak tree reputed to be 800 years old. The actual oldest tree in Extremadura is a chestnut in the north near the village of Segura de Toro, but this tree is the oldest oak. The branches of the tree

THE WALK OF THE OAK TREE AND THE PILGRIM HOSPITAL

are propped up by huge black cylindrical poles but they are not intrusive. It's 16.4m high and the trunk is 7.7m in circumference. There are benches to rest and admire the tree from all angles and there are information boards but only in Spanish. The tree supports many small birds and nearby it is possible to spot larger birds, even the Booted Eagle.

Come out from the park and turn left to continue on the lane. After only five minutes, on the right, is a wide space with a sign for the Charca de las Lindosas, a small pond. It's normally full of water and is an important spot for nature but it can be dry in the height of a long summer. Just after the pond there is a crossroads with a track going left and another going right. Take the left track.
❷ The Sierra de Montánchez is visible on the left. At two metal gates opposite each other there is a small path that goes ahead but keep on the track as it bends sharply to the right. Ignore all junctions ahead. The track has many low-growing trees and flowering bushes to the left. They make this part of the walk very pretty — even when the bushes are not in flower. At two gates on the right and one straight ahead the track turns to the left. It winds to the right at two more gates opposite each other. To the left the views become very open with villages in the distance. The oaks thin and fincas with olives appear. Look ahead to the left; the village of Salvatierra de Santiago is visible. The track comes to a small turning right but do not take that. Go around to the left to cross a stream-bed with stepping stones. The stream is called the Arroyo de los Pocitos and there is a large well with smaller granite drinking troughs around. It is clearly an important source of agricultural water. The track winds its way through the countryside as it continues towards the village.

At a multiple junction ignore two left turnings and take the path to the right. Pass agricultural buildings and untidy evidence of human habitation on the right to make for the village centre on the left. Look left. The roof of the hermitage and the ancient stone cross

THE SIERRA DE MONTÁNCHEZ 1

Salvatierra de Santiago from the Hermitage, February

can be seen. As a point of orientation the route leaves the village from there. Salvatierra de Santiago is small with a population of around 355 people. Explore the village at leisure but stop off at Bar Fé just before the Town Hall for refreshments. Worth seeing are the Pilgrim Hospital across from the Town Hall and to the left, the Church of Salvatierra de los Barros, the Hermitage called the Capilla y Panteón Santa Catalina, and the stone cross. Ask for any keys at the Town Hall. Written directions are not needed as the village is tiny.

To continue the walk leave the hermitage behind to the left, with the view of the church to the right, and the radar station on Cancho Blanco dead ahead, take the lane to the left. Do not take the road. Pass a building signed the 'CRA Orden de Santiago' on the right and take the wide lane ahead. ❸ Pass a copse of

THE WALK OF THE OAK TREE AND THE PILGRIM HOSPITAL

eucalyptus on the right with a picnic area and what looks like a lot of rubble. There is a track going to the right there. This leads to part of the Cordel de Mérida a Trujillo, an ancient sheep track (a different stretch but the same cordel as in The Walk of the Medieval Sheep Track) and the longer route back to Zarza.

For the short route, stay on the main lane. The lane goes straight to Zarza so do not be tempted by any paths at junctions. There are many opportunities for bird watching in the skies above the dehesa. Vultures are fond of this area because of the chances to feed off a variety of dead animals, especially the birth casualties during the spring. After only 45 minutes Zarza appears and the lane comes back into the village via the medieval bridge. Retrace your steps to the other side of the swimming pool and the car.

For the longer route, take the track to the right at the picnic area with the rubble on the right. This is a small diversion to pass a big pool on the right and an opportunity to see birds — depending on the time of day and the season. The track narrows and becomes a path. Pass a metal gate and small agricultural building on the right. The path comes to a crossroads at a very wide, boulder-strewn grassy area. Take the small track to the right. ❹ It's soft, narrow and winds gently up and down. After about 100m there's another wide area with an enormous flat boulder in the middle but there are no junctions and our track continues straight ahead. There are pastures on either side with many oak trees that are shady. After another 100m the track joins another one in a T junction. Take the left turning. This is now the medieval sheep track and we follow it for a good hour.

The Sierra de Montánchez is straight ahead. The track is clear and winds its way through an area of flowering bushes. There is little shade but there are oak trees on either side of the wide verges. In the rainy season water flows in the channels on either side of the track and, where there is water, there are birds and a profusion

THE SIERRA DE MONTÁNCHEZ

of flowers. The track comes to the River Tamuja, which can be anything from a stream to a serious body of water depending on the rainfall. There is a sign indicating the name of the river and the Molino de la Angarilla. There are stepping stones on the right to cross the river. Cross over and continue to follow the course of the river keeping it on the left for a few hundred metres before the river bends away. The track becomes narrower and rougher and goes up and down slightly and meanders. The bushes, especially lavender, grow more profusely in this area — typical Extremeño countryside: wild, remote, beautiful, silent. At a wide Y junction the track seems to split but just goes around some flowering bushes. Suddenly the track comes to a small back road, the CC-96 linking the tiny village of Benquerencia to Zarza. Cross straight over and pick up the track directly on the other side of the road.

The track is much narrower once over the road and the trees and bushes encroach. Cross a wide steam bed with pools of water year-round. The many clumps of reeds indicate that a wide area becomes wet during some winters. However the track is easy to follow as it bends left. Tucked in between the banks of the stream bed is an old clapper bridge made of granite. It is worth investigating. Continue with the stream bed on the left. The track comes to a wide expanse with a gateway to a huge finca on the left but our track goes ahead. It comes out at another extremely wide junction. The track itself goes around to the right, and on the right is a gateway to a finca. Our direction is left and we leave the sheep track here on a lane that doubles back to the left. **5**

The lane is lined with walls and there are fincas with oak trees and pasture. On the right is a dense copse of oaks. The lane joins another one cutting across it in a Y junction. Take the left turning. It is wide and passes a small stone shed on the right before coming to a concrete bridge that goes over a stream bed. On the left is a small pool. The lane goes ahead and passes a couple of ramshackle agricultural buildings to the left, then winds around

THE WALK OF THE OAK TREE AND THE PILGRIM HOSPITAL

the last building — a small house — to come to a junction. ❻ One lane goes completely left, one goes left then right, one goes straight on. Take the lane going straight on; it leads directly to Zarza.

The lane is wide with fencing on either side and passes open pasture and dehesa on either side. In spring these meadows are purple with viper's bugloss. As the lane continues it is joined by another one coming from the right to form a Y junction. Both lanes merge to the left. Go left. The lane becomes narrower and rougher and goes uphill. Suddenly the oaks thin and olive fincas take over. At the top of the small hill there is a crossroads of paths. Continue straight on. Zarza is visible ahead. The lane widens to come out at the village on the by-pass that you came in on at the start. Cross the by-pass, enter the village and explore, or return to the swimming pool car park for the car.

THE SIERRA DE MONTÁNCHEZ 1

GPS Points
The Walk of the Oak Tree and the Pilgrim Hospital

1. N 39° 15' 36.47" W 06° 01' 52.59"
2. N 39° 16' 37.86" W 06° 01' 10.28"
3. N 39° 17' 57.53" W 06° 02' 00.48"
4. N 39° 17' 31.57" W 06° 02' 08.42"
5. N 39° 15' 40.82" W 06° 03' 39.94"
6. N 39° 15' 50.10" W 06° 03' 11.18"

WALKING IN EXTREMADURA 117

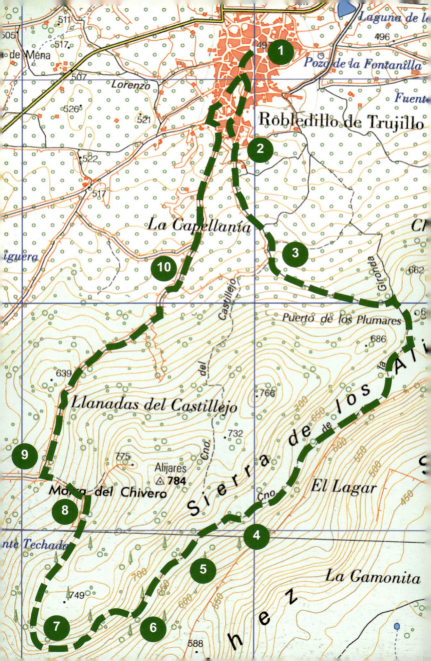

THE SIERRA DE MONTÁNCHEZ 1

9 The Walk of the Peonies

Start: Pl. de España, Robledillo de Trujillo

Finish: Pl. de España, Robledillo de Trujillo

3 hours plus stops

7.5 km

Low: 480m
High: 750m

Mostly Easy

Robledillo de Trujillo → Robledillo de Trujillo
Map: IGN 730 Montánchez 1:50.000

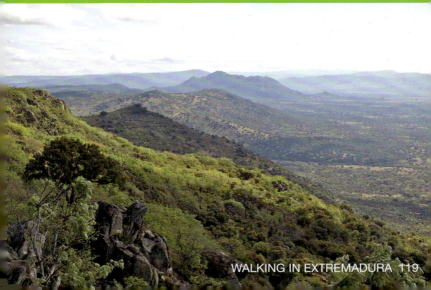
View towards the Sierra de Santa Cruz, April

THE WALK OF THE PEONIES

Introduction

This is simply the prettiest route to walk during the spring. It explodes with colour on every step; yellow and white broom, purple lavender, white and pink gum cistus, bluebells, deep pink peonies, yellow daisies, new pale green leaves on Pyrenean deciduous oaks, dark green holm oaks, yellow catkins, red leaves on terebinth trees and blue skies.

The first part of the walk leads out from the village of Robledillo in a very gentle climb. There are wonderful views towards the left while on the right are tree-covered sierra slopes. The middle part of the walk has a short, sharp climb giving extensive views behind towards the Sierra de Santa Cruz. This is followed by a gentle descent through expanses of wild peonies in April and May. The final part of the walk is a steeper descent back to the village flanked by a profusion of flowering bushes. Throughout the walk, with the flowers, come the birds, bees and butterflies.

Everyone with a basic level of fitness can do this walk but take the short, sharp climb slowly. There's no need to rush. The route can be walked throughout the year. However, the best time to walk for flowers is from late February to early June — depending on rainfall and temperatures. Late October to early December is when the deciduous oaks and terebinth trees make a glorious display as their leaves turn golden then red. The route is circular and can be walked in either direction but the following directions describe the clockwise option.

Directions

To get to the village of Robledillo de Trujillo turn off the Cáceres-Miajadas EX-206 at the sign for Zarza de Montánchez. Pass that village and keep going on the Carretera de Zarza-Montánchez until you get to Robledillo. Robledillo can also be approached via Trujillo and the village of Ibahernando. Start the walk from

THE SIERRA DE MONTÁNCHEZ

the pretty Plaza de España where there is parking. ❶ With the church, and the fountain, on the left, walk ahead up Calle Gabriel y Galán. At the wide junction keep right to walk straight ahead up Calle Extremadura. At the Y junction with the telephone box, Calle Extremadura bears right. Keep going, ignoring any small junctions left or right. Once past Calle Manuel Montero on the right there is a Y junction. Take the left turning – the return is via the right turning. The road becomes much narrower. Bear left and continue past a row of picturesque old houses. At the end of the road, in front of a house numbered 74 and at a Y junction, turn left. This is now open countryside. ❷

Climb up the concrete lane. Ignore a turning left and, bear right, to start up a rough dirt track. Just after a wide rough space pass an agricultural building on the left of the track which now gets narrower and very rocky. There is an olive finca on the right but deciduous oak trees start to appear on either side of the track. At a Y junction bear right over some large granite boulders on to a small rough path climbing upwards. Ahead is a pretty view of a rounded hill covered in oak trees. Keep on the rough path as it climbs up. Come to a wide, open space on the left and the path bears slightly right and continues up. ❸ The oaks and flowering bushes become thicker and encroach a little on the path which settles down and becomes almost level and less rough. Ignore a tiny path, right. Continue ahead. A lot of big flat boulders pave the path — parts are ancient and were first paved hundreds of years ago. There are a few tiny paths to the left and more to the right but ignore all of these. The path goes up steadily through an area still dotted with small olive fincas and gates. The oak trees grow thinly but there are many flowers underfoot between the granite slabs and rocks because the path is used very infrequently. In season, look out for low growing red spurrey, paronychia capitata and stonecrop. At the sides of the path there may be white, pink and red vetch, bright blue periwinkle, bluebell, short barbary nut and

THE WALK OF THE PEONIES

tall Spanish iris, white campion and foxglove. If you look harder in amongst the broom and retama there may be the slender Spanish fritillary.

The views between the trees to the left are of Robledillo. To the right are the slopes of the rounded hill seen earlier, covered with trees and glorious in autumn. Pass a well, also on the right — but take care, there is nothing to stop you falling in. As the path climbs higher the views become more extensive. Over the wall on the left are distant views to the north — Trujillo is easily spotted and beyond, the Sierra de Gredos. The ascent continues and enters the start of a deciduous oak wood, past clumps of lavender and broom where granite paving acts as steps. The trees on either side shade the path which then levels a bit and becomes softer underfoot. At the top of the climb the path becomes almost completely flat, narrows and goes through tall swathes of cistus and lavender. This part of the walk is like strolling through a wild and natural garden. The view passes from the Robledillo side of the sierra to a different aspect altogether, towards the south, over huge flat plains down towards Mérida. The path goes through towering bushes of cistus with their sweet sticky resinous smell in the air. The variety of cistus with the brown-red fleck on each white petal, is known as Jara in Spanish. It is the flower of Extremadura. There are many trees including the terebinth. The path runs in a reasonably straight line for a long way. Walking is easy. It is flat. On our left is a considerable drop to the plain below. On the right is a small range of hills topped by rocky outcrops. This is a fabulous viewing point. ❹ The path, paved once more, zig-zags slightly. The path continues with a wall on the left and tall cistus bushes on the right. It enters a copse of oak trees before going up slightly then dropping down to a large open meadow with multiple granite water troughs. These catch flowing water for animals. ❺ This is a good place to stop, rest, explore and look at the views.

Continue on the path, which leaves the meadow on the opposite

THE SIERRA DE MONTÁNCHEZ 1

Lavender, cistus and broom, April

THE WALK OF THE PEONIES

side of the point of entry — it is the same path. It is narrow, sometimes paved or rocky, but mostly dirt. There are lavender and broom bushes and the deciduous oaks continue but there are now a few holm oaks as well. Ahead is a huge and dramatic rocky outcrop that we will pass later. At a small clearing there is a tiny path, left, but ignore this. The path bends 90 degrees to the right ❻ and becomes a very steep, rocky but wide track for about 100m during which the climb is 86m. At the top of this energetic climb veer left. The path narrows and within 20m there is a deciduous oak copse. Continue down, then steadily up the path all the way through lush vegetation underfoot to the dramatic rocky outcrop seen earlier. Look behind for the view of the Sierra de Santa Cruz but, more importantly, look out for peonies, asphodels and orchids all along this path. Once at the top of the climb, by the rocky outcrop, stop to look all around at the views. Look for orchids near the base of the outcrop. Over the peak of the climb the descent reveals yet another view. Use the walls on either side of the path as a guide. Where the path dips, hug first the left wall, then, as the path makes a diagonal move, then rises, hug the right wall. Within 50m, hugging the right wall, the path turns 90 degrees to the right and becomes a wide track. ❼

After a few uphill steps there are carpets of peonies and bluebells and tall deciduous oaks. The track is very soft underfoot and the walls, either side, are far apart. The view ahead is of the plains to the north-west and the village of Salvatierra de Santiago. As the track descends there are still a lot of peonies but gradually these give way to other flowers: campion, foxglove and vetch. The broom, lavender and cistus bushes continue to line the track. The path narrows but continues downhill through the oaks. On the left the village of Zarza de Montánchez comes into view. On the right is the other side of the sierra we saw during the first part of the walk. After a good 15 minutes, the path comes to a terraced picnic area with wooden tables, benches and a barbecue. ❽ It is

THE SIERRA DE MONTÁNCHEZ

a high area overlooking Zarza below. The path makes a decisive left turn to go downwards. The descent is sharp with zig-zags and boulders but it is not difficult. Within about 100m the path narrows and is lined with white broom. It comes out at a large open expanse of grass by a metal gate in a wall on the left. There is a Y junction. Ignore the left turn and go right. **9** The path is narrow. On the left, over a low wall, there are views of small fincas laid to pasture. On the right are tree-covered hills. Look behind for a good view of Cancho Blanco. Ahead and to the left is a rugged hillside covered in boulders and bushes. It is a good bird-spotting area. The path enters a stretch where the trees and bushes encroach and give shade. It narrows and continues downward. Robledillo comes into sight and beyond is a view of the Sierra de Santa Cruz. In the distance is the Sierra de Gredos.

At a Y junction, keep left – the right turning only goes into a finca. The path comes out to a large rocky area but continue straight down along a clear, rocky path. At the next Y junction, keep left. The path becomes closed in by trees and, apart from the village ahead the views are restricted. As the path approaches the village it passes gates and fincas and a few signs of human activity. Ignore a junction right and keep left. At the following junction ignore the left path and bear right passing more gates. **10** The path passes a huge granite-paved area — take care when it is wet — with a lovely view of the church ahead. It narrows once more, flanked with high hedges as it comes to the first outbuildings of the village. Go left at the first Y junction on to a lane. At the next Y junction keep right past 'Villa Juan Ruiz 2011'. The lane bears right. At a T junction with one of the main roads in the village, turn right and walk all the way down the road without taking any junctions. At a Y junction, where we went left at the start, join Calle Extremadura to retrace our steps to the starting point. Back at the Plaza de España visit the church, if it is open, or go around the back of the church, turn left, and go into Bar Seville for refreshments.

THE WALK OF THE PEONIES

Robledillo de Trujillo, April

GPS Points
The Walk of the Peonies

1. N39° 16' 10.74" W05° 58' 49.51"
2. N39° 15' 57.32" W05° 58' 52.40"
3. N39° 15' 51.89" W05° 58' 51.29"
4. N39° 15' 05.75" W05° 58' 43.11"
5. N39° 15' 04.86" W05° 58' 45.23"
6. N39° 14' 56.60" W05° 58' 59.97"
7. N39° 14' 49.49" W05° 59' 17.88"
8. N39° 15' 05.76" W05° 59' 17.27"
9. N39° 15' 07.87" W05° 59' 24.58"
10. N39° 15' 50.05" W05° 58' 57.33"

Quiet reflection, Proserpina, March

The Roman Waters

1	The Walk around Proserpina	136
2	A Walk in Cornalvo Natural Park	142
3	The Walk of the White Cliffs of Zarza	148

INTRODUCTION

The Roman Waters

When, in 25BC, the Romans chose Emerita Augusta (modern day Mérida) as the site for the capital of Lusitania, the most westerly province of their empire, they settled down believing they would be there forever. One of the most important needs of any centre of population is water and the Romans constructed reservoirs to serve their city.

The first water supply system, 16km to the north-east of the city, was called Agua Augusta — presumably in honour of the Emperor Augustus. The actual date water started to come to the city from this source is uncertain but it was brought all the way via an aqueduct. There's still some confusion as to how the water was channelled into the aqueduct because there is evidence that the actual dam, and the creation of the reservoir, came later. This complex was called Caput Aquae, or more likely, Cornus Albus, which has been corrupted over the years to become Cornalvo.

The city's second water supply was from underground springs some 5km north of Emerita Augusta and brought to the city via the Rabo de Buey-San Lázaro aqueduct. The remains of this aqueduct can be seen on the Mérida city walk.

The third water supply, however, was another reservoir. This reservoir, known as Albuera de Carija, collected rainwater and water from the River Adelfas and River Pardillas. In the 18th century a Roman plaque invoking the Goddess of Spring was found near the reservoir and the site was renamed 'Proserpina' in her honour. The reservoir was much closer to the city than the first — only 5km away. It was easily reached by the Via de la Plata, the main arterial road of the province. Water was brought via a pipe and an aqueduct, Los Milagros, the impressive ruins of which can be seen in modern day Mérida. The dams at both Cornalvo and Proserpina were constructed around the same time, during the first century A.D. and the rule of Trajan. It's interesting to suppose

THE ROMAN WATERS 2

that the chief architect for dams was constantly busy across the Empire and designed the dams as a joint project on a rare visit to the remote province.

Eighteen kilometres to the south of Mérida lies Alange. In Roman times it was called Aquae. It was an extremely popular spa with naturally occurring thermal waters at a temperature of 28°C with a flow of 216 litres per minute. By the 1st century A.D. it was a flourishing centre, complete with Roman Baths built during the time of Flavius. These fell into disuse during the medieval period but gained a new popularity during the 18th century when the ruins were reconstructed and new buildings erected. Although further reconstruction work was carried out in 1820 and 1860, and in more recent years, parts of the present buildings still date to Roman times. The Alange reservoir, however, is 'modern 'and is fed by three rivers, the Matachel, Palomilas and Valdemedel. Archeologists are certain that many important Roman sites lie under the water.

Cornalvo and Proserpina reservoirs are surrounded by huge expanses of typical Extremeño dehesa, but they give a very differing walking experience. Cornalvo is further away from any large town and much of the land is divided into privately owned fincas and estates — *cortijos*. This has helped to keep the area unspoiled and tranquil. It is home to such a wide range of bird, animal and plant life it has been declared a Natural Park. Walking in Cornalvo has almost no man-made distractions from the views and enjoyment of the surrounding deep countryside.

Proserpina, on the other hand, has developed over the last few years to become a popular leisure area for people escaping from Mérida, especially at weekends and during the summer heat. This does not detract from the bird life which uses the reservoir, especially in the winter, but the summer months are given over to swimming, picnics, café-life and ice creams.

INTRODUCTION

The walk overlooking Alange is different again — it's longer and higher. Walking along the ridge of the Sierra de Peñas Blancas, among the granite rocks and flowering bushes while looking at the water below, is a very satisfying experience. The ridge is wild and totally unspoiled while the views are breath-taking.

Practical Information

The walks in this chapter are all in Badajoz Province, the southern half of Extremadura.

Mérida is the best place to seek accommodation and facilities in the area. The Tourist Office is in the new building next to the car park, Calle Cabo Verde, 06800, Mérida. They speak English, are helpful and friendly.

Proserpina is a summer holiday resort with accommodation and camping. Out-of-season the campsite is closed but on many winter walks here I have encountered hardy nature-lovers who simply camp under the trees and the stars. There are a good range of cafés and restaurants providing everything from hot coffee and cold beer to a full 3-course meal but only Lago Pinar stays open all day, every day.

Cornalvo is severely restricted with both accommodation and eating places — there aren't any. There is a bar just outside the park next to the Interpretation Centre and it is welcoming but limited. The hunting trophies mounted on the wall are a bit incongruous.

In **Alange**, the Gran Hotel Aqualange is modern, yet built in the style of Art Deco. Walk into the foyer and admire the architecture.

Gran Hotel Aqualange - Balneario de Alange
Paseo de las Huertas 3, 06840 Alange, Spain

There is a good open-air café just behind the hotel overlooking the gardens. It is an informal place to eat but I can recommend it for

THE ROMAN WATERS 2

Cornalvo after the winter rains, January

the setting alone especially when the flowers are in bloom.

In Calle Baños there's an excellent hotel and restaurant called Varinia Serena. The food is very good — especially in the colder months as they do a fine hunting menu.

Other Walks

Both the Via de la Plata, also known as the Camino de Santiago or Way of St. James, and the Cañada Real de Santa María Araya can be walked from Mérida to Proserpina. They are well-established walks and are clearly marked on the map — the Camino de Santiago with a pink scallop shell. However, here are the necessary directions starting and finishing in the Plaza de España, Mérida.

INTRODUCTION

To walk along the Camino de Santiago, choose the nicer EP (Embalse de Proserpina) route, as the CR (Calzada Romana), follows the N630 for most of the way. Both routes are waymarked. For the EP route leave the Plaza de España by the northern corner (to the left of the Town Hall) and walk down Calle de Santa Julia bearing right. Turn left into Calle Trajana and walk under Trajan's Arch. Turn right, then left into the Plaza de la Constitución. Walk ahead into Travesia de Almendralejo and left into Calle Almendralejo, then right into Calle Calvario. Walk under the railway line via the underpass and turn left then right to cross the River Albarregas by a small Roman bridge. The impressive Aqueduct de los Milagros, which brought water from Proserpina, is on the right. Walk down the Via de la Plata for 100m and pick up the Avenida del Lago to keep on that road, following the signs and waymarks, until you get to Proserpina.

After walking around the water return to Mérida on the Cañada Real de Santa María Araya (marked on the map IGN 777 Mérida 1:50.000). This medieval sheep track comes out at the River Guadiana to the west of Mérida. Turn left to walk along the river to return to the Roman bridge, turn left again into Calle del Puente and the Plaza.

These routes are historic and ancient however they offer little in the way of shade — take extra water. If walking up from, and returning to, Mérida, add 14kms to the route and start the walk around the reservoir at the Roman dam.

Cornalvo Natural Park has an Interpretation Centre located just outside Trujillanos. Although information in English is limited, the exhibitions and displays are easy to understand. Maps of five additional walking routes — ranging from 1km to 15km — can be picked up here. This is important as walking off-route is discouraged. Most of Cornalvo is still private land but the main reason for controlling where people walk is to leave the wildlife

THE ROMAN WATERS 2

undisturbed. Unfortunately many of these additional routes are linear but it is possible to piece together sensible circuits. Be aware that shade is limited in Cornalvo because, despite the thousands of trees, they are well spaced.

Nature Park Interpretation Centre,
Ctra. Trujillanos-Embalse Cornalvo, s/n
Phone: 0034 630 125172

Los Canchales Reservoir to the west of Proserpina is also a good area for walks near water. It is an area designated 'Special Protection for Birds' and several hides have been built for the patient bird-spotting enthusiast. To access the walk it is best to start at the village of Garrovilla just off the EX-209 west of Mérida. From here the walk is signposted. It's 7.5km to the water and a further 23km around the reservoir. However, it's not essential to do the entire 30.5km — pace yourself for an out-and-back walk.

Maps

Map: IGN 752 Mirandilla 1:50.000

Map: IGN 753 Miajadas 1:50.000

Map: IGN 777 Mérida 1:50.000

Map: IGN 778 Don Benito 1:50.000

Map: IGN 803 Almendralejo 1:50.000

Map: IGN 804 Oliva de Mérida 1:50.000

Cornalvo is divided by four maps: IGN 752, IGN 753, IGN 777 and IGN 778.

THE ROMAN WATERS **2**

1 The Walk around Proserpina

Start: Lago Pinar Rest., Proserpina

Finish: Lago Pinar Rest., Proserpina

1.5 hours

5.5 km

Low: 240m
High: 240m

Very Easy

Proserpina → Proserpina
Map: IGN 777 Mérida 1:50.000

Looking south-west across the water, May

WALKING IN EXTREMADURA 137

THE WALK AROUND PROSERPINA

Introduction

Proserpina can be walked by everyone. It is a totally flat route around the edges of the reservoir. There are many inlets and small creeks which, combined with the surrounding dehesa landscape make the place a haven for birds. During the course of walking here I have seen white storks, grey herons, cattle egrets, cormorants, mallard ducks, tufted ducks and shovelers on the water — all in their season, of course. In addition, birds of prey including sparrowhawks and red kites circle the sky, drawn from the dehesa to the water. Song birds, including the crested lark, keep busy near the water. Around the reservoir are Mediterranean pines and stands of eucalyptus. There are many types of grasses and reeds, retama and lavender bushes and low growing flowers including paronychia, candytuft and campanula.

The walk can be done all the year around. For maximum opportunities to spot birds, including migratory species, walk early on a winter's morning — you'll get the reservoir to yourself. Take binoculars. In the summer months, after walking very early, spend the rest of the day swimming. The water is soft and refreshing.

Directions

'Embalse de Proserpina' is sign-posted from the N630 approximately 5km north of Mérida. Follow the signs and drive about 3km along a narrow road, in a very bad state of repair, to arrive at the reservoir. Park among the trees at the Lago Pinar restaurant. This is a *chiringuito* (open-air snack bar) that stays open all year around, all day, every day, serves good food and has some handy toilets.

Directions for this simple walk are a bit unnecessary — just walk around the water. Our route takes us clockwise. There is a footpath that goes all the way around and is illuminated at night. However, there are some features of the walk worth describing.

The Roman dam, March

Look out for birds all the way around, not only on the water but also overhead. Walk as close to the water's edge as you like but at times it is necessary to get back on the footpath to cross over small bridges where streams feed the reservoir.

Directly in front of Lago Pinar is an open shoreline dotted with trees, mainly Mediterranean pines. ❶ This area is very popular for swimming and, consequentially there is less bird activity on this side of the water. Over to the left, is a very strange modern-looking white building with a spiral tower ending in a cross. ❷ According to the map this is the Hermitage of San Isidro but judging by the abandoned look of the place he is not very popular. The building is usually locked.

Across the water is Proserpina village, a cluster of expensive houses with gardens, very unlike the typical Spanish village. Many

THE WALK AROUND PROSERPINA

of the houses are empty except for the summer — and the village is quiet even then. The village side of the water has many inlets, some choked with reeds. These are frequented by waterfowl especially during the breeding season and when chicks are young. As you walk you may encounter fishermen in the stretch of the walk before the village as the reservoir has many fish which attract herons, storks and cormorants.

A feature of Proserpina are the huge granite promontories which are popular with birds. There are also a few viewing areas and, with patience, some rewarding bird spotting opportunities.
❸ Each bend around the reservoir brings new birds, reeds, vegetation and a new view out over the water.

Historically, the Roman dam is the highlight of the walk. ❹ It is protected under Mérida's UNESCO World Heritage status. In recent years a new bypass for vehicles means walkers have the dam completely to themselves. Spend some time looking at the information boards. They are remarkably good with clear diagrams and an explanation of the history, construction and function of the dam in Spanish, Portuguese and ... English. The feat of engineering to build the dam 2000 years ago was amazing — especially as Proserpina is alleged to have been the largest reservoir in the Roman Empire at that time.

Proserpina is not a difficult walk yet it is not to be missed, not least for the chance to see so much bird activity.

THE ROMAN WATERS 2

GPS Points
The Walk around Proserpina

1. N38° 58' 36.51" W06° 21' 39.54"
2. N38° 58' 36.47" W06° 21 27.33"
3. N38° 58' 09.55" W06° 21' 44.69"
4. N38° 58' 11.55" W06° 21' 58.94

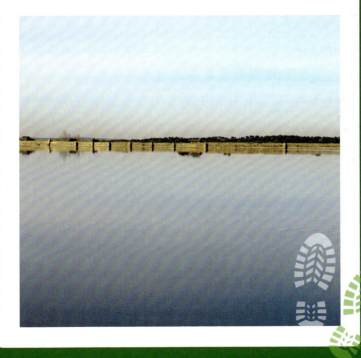

THE ROMAN WATERS **2**

2 A Walk in Cornalvo Natural Park

Start: Info. board at the Roman Dam

Finish: Info. board at the Roman Dam

4 hours

11.5 km

Low: 299m
High: 330m

Easy

Cornalvo → Cornalvo

Maps: IGN 752 Mirandilla 1:50.000
IGN 753 Miajadas 1:50.000
IGN 777 Mérida 1:50.000
IGN 778 Don Benito 1:50.000

Still waters, May

A WALK IN CORNALVO NATURAL PARK

Short option: start and finish as above
Time: 2 hours   Distance: 7 kilometres

Introduction

Cornalvo, which covers nearly 11,000 hectares, is a protected Natural Park with a Roman reservoir and dam as one of the man-made features of interest. The name Cornalvo probably comes from the Latin 'Cornus Albus' meaning White Horn after the white water of the River Albarregas which springs from below the horn shaped dam. The dam has been protected since 1912 but Cornalvo did not become a Natural Park until 1998.

Most of Cornalvo is dominated by pastures with holm and cork oaks — the Extremeño dehesa. For centuries this land was owned by a few very wealthy families, some of whom built huge *cortijos* (farmhouse estates). The landowners, who were mainly absent, did not change the land use over centuries. This has kept Cornalvo almost untouched. However, it was probably to the detriment of the poverty-stricken land workers. Today it is still used mainly for grazing livestock; sheep, cattle, horses, pigs and goats. Cornalvo also features two low mountain ranges, the Sierra del Moro and the Sierra Bermeja. Numerous rivers feed the park but the main one is the Aljucén which rises in the foothills of the Sierra de Montánchez.

Cornalvo boasts outstanding animal, bird and plant life. Depending on the time of year and day it is possible to see rabbits, badgers, genets, Iberian hares, wild boar, otters, species of toads and, of course, fish. Black and white storks, Booted Eagles, Bonelli's Eagle, vultures and lesser hawks hunt the dehesa. In addition to the oaks the park supports smaller trees including the strawberry tree and any number of flowering bushes such as retama, broom, lavender and cistus. Wild flowers bloom freely in spring.

THE ROMAN WATERS 2

No camping or swimming are allowed.

The short walk goes around the reservoir and the directions are straightforward but the longer walk includes a stretch along a stream, the Arroyo de las Muelas which feeds the reservoir. Be aware that in times of flooding it may be necessary to take a much wider line around the water and stream. It may even be necessary to resort to the lanes and this will mean an increased distance. I've walked this route in both dry and wet conditions and the wet is definitely more fun. Everyone can do the walk as it's almost flat. It is recommended in spring especially, but can be walked most of the year. Keep to the short route in summer where there is some shade and take the usual precautions of hat, sunscreen and extra water.

Directions

Cornalvo is sign-posted from the E-90 (A5 Badajoz-Madrid) motorway at Trujillanos. As you approach the park there is an Interpretation Centre on the left. It's worth visiting. Continue on the small road from the Interpretation Centre as far as the reservoir. Park just after the restored wall of the dam. There's an information and map board on the right. It shows the birds and flowers of the Natural Park and outlines suggested routes.

Start by walking across the Roman dam on the broad road. ❶ On the left is the restored wall of the dam and the water but on the right is a view out over a wooded valley. At the end of the dam, turn left ❷ to pick up the clearly defined path to walk with the water on the left. This part of the route is flat and runs close by the water's edge. The path goes through a dense area of cistus bushes — some taller than head-height. Follow to the left to follow the edge of the reservoir as it curves around. ❸ In times of flooding make a wider sweep but keep the water in view. The path separates from the water edge slightly and goes through open sweeping meadows of oak trees before returning to the water's edge.

A WALK IN CORNALVO NATURAL PARK

The path turns right ❹ to follow part of the Arroyo de las Muelas. How much water is in the stream bed will depend on the rainfall of the winter before the route is walked. The stream bed is a wonderful place for wild flowers and water-loving creatures. Continue ahead keeping the stream bed on the left. The path becomes more rocky and goes very slightly uphill. After 1.6km it comes to a small tarmac road. Turn right on to the road. ❺ After only 200m turn right off the road on to a path which bears right to a bridge over a small stream and pools of water. ❻ In the area around the bridge are granite boulders, tall reeds and flowering bushes. This is an excellent area to stop and do some serious exploring of plants and wild life, including butterflies and dragonflies, and to spot birds.

Keep the stream bed on the left as you retrace the steps back to the reservoir. ❼ Walk through deep areas of cistus bushes, many waist-high. Look out for wild flowers in spring. The path comes to an area with open meadows dotted with oak trees where, very often, horses graze freely. ❽ The route is clear through this open expanse. The views of the water, on the left, are lovely. In summer it is tempting to swim but resist the urge as it is not allowed. However, I have known people (mentioning no names) to take off boots and socks and walk in the water. Bliss!

The path continues anticlockwise around the water to arrive back to the starting point.

THE ROMAN WATERS 2

GPS Points
A Walk in Cornalvo Natural Park

1. N38º 59' 21.00" W06º 11' 31.30"
2. N38º 59' 15.56" W06º 11' 26.66"
3. N38º 59' 10.20" W06º 10' 52.40"
4. N39º 00' 09.29" W06º 10' 43.47"
5. N39º 01' 08.50" W06º 10' 40.91"
6. N39º 01' 09.82" W06º 10' 47.63"
7. N39º 00' 09.23" W06º 10' 48.19"
8. N38º 59' 26.50" W06º 10' 59.35"

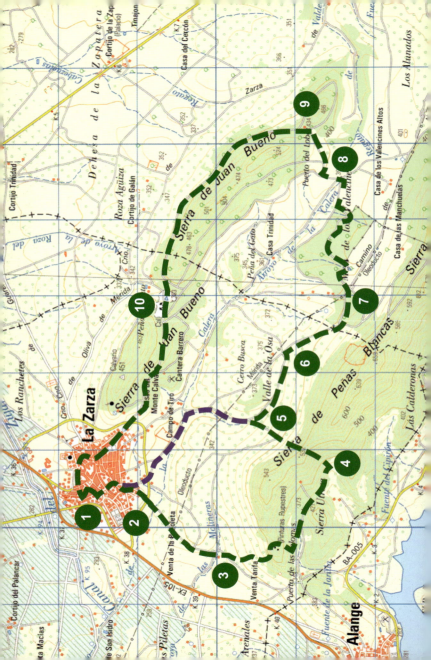

THE ROMAN WATERS **2**

3 The Walk of the White Cliffs of Zarza

Start: La Zarza, near Alange

Finish: La Zarza, near Alange

6 hours plus stops

18 km

Low: 227m
High: 514m

Medium

La Zarza → La Zarza
Maps: IGN 803 Almendralejo 1:50.000
IGN 804 Oliva de Mérida 1:50.000

View of Alange Castle, April

THE WALK OF THE WHITE CLIFFS OF ZARZA

Short option: start and finish as above
Time: 3 hours plus stops   Distance: 8 kilometres

Introduction

This route starts in the village of La Zarza, just off the EX-105, north of Alange. The first hour of the walk goes uphill with the last 100m, before the summit of the Sierra de Peñas Blancas, (roughly translated as white cliffs or rocks) especially steep. In spite of that, the walk only needs a reasonable level of fitness because the height of the climb is only 287m and it is not long. Just before the top of the climb is the Cueva de la Calderita which contains pinturas rupestres (cave or rock paintings), made between 2000 and 5000 B.C. Although the location is called a cave it's really only an overhanging rock so claustrophobes need not fear. There are information panels in the cave to explain the paintings. The walk along the top of the sierra gives fantastic views over Alange, the Roman Spa town, and the lakes in the distance. Take binoculars.

The short option only covers this first half of the route, returning to La Zarza after the descent from the sierra.

The longer route continues almost flat and passes through a typical agricultural landscape, pine woods, eucalyptus forests and meadows. Towards the end of the route is a huge mine that gives La Zarza its title of *La Tierrablanca* (Land of the White Earth). Cal is mined here. It is the mineral used in the traditional white paint for the outside of Spanish houses to keep them cool in the summer. The mine was started over 100 years ago and cal was sold throughout southern Spain by salesmen carrying it in panniers on donkeys. The mine is still worked today but only employs a handful of men — yet cal is still extremely popular, especially as it allows damp walls to 'breathe'.

The 'official' route is waymarked with white and yellow horizontal

THE ROMAN WATERS 2

bands on wooden posts, tree trunks and rocks but our route is slightly different.

The walk is best in late January and February for the hundreds of almond trees in blossom. From March to April the lavender, cistus and broom are in flower on the top of the sierra. In May the flowers are at their best and the sun is not too fierce.

Directions

Start in La Zarza at the junction of Calle de Juan Andrés Valor, Calle del Pilar and the Plaza de España. ❶ Walk straight up Calle del Pilar. At the roundabout, turn left, pass Calle de la Carrera and Calle de la Virgin and go up the hill of Calle del Pozo. At the top of Calle del Pozo where it meets Calle Valdelirios, turn right. Turn left to go straight down Calle de la Calderita. Straight ahead is the Sierra de Peñas Blancas. Walk straight ahead past turnings and a small shop on the left. The path climbing into the sierra can already be seen ahead. Follow the Calle de la Calderita as it leaves the village and becomes a small road. Ahead and to the right can be seen Culebra Hill with the remains of the Moorish fortress. It was constructed in the 9th century on earlier Roman ruins, captured by the Christians in the 13th century, and finally abandoned 300 years later. In the immediate vicinity there are many almond trees and olive groves. The small road comes to a main road. ❷ Cross straight over and continue on what is now a rough compacted earth track. Follow this track, without taking any side paths, as it winds its way upwards.

The track is lined with almond trees and is very pretty in spring. Behind there are views of the village of La Zarza and on the left the sierra looms closer and higher. On the right are views of the organized agricultural landscape. The track comes to a crossroads ❸ with an information board indicating that the Shelter of Calderita with the paintings is 65 minutes away — but that's a huge over-

THE WALK OF THE WHITE CLIFFS OF ZARZA

estimation. There's also an information board about local wild life. Continue ahead. The track narrows, becomes a small path, gets rougher and goes up. It turns naturally to the left with a small flat grassy area on the right. This is a good place to stop, turn, and look at La Zarza and the views below.

The path gets even narrower. The almond trees have thinned and there are more cistus, lavender and broom bushes with oak trees giving a shady aspect. The going up becomes very steep indeed. The cave can be seen ahead. The path zig-zags a little as it's simply too steep to go straight up. To visit the cave paintings turn right at the sign. The entrance is narrow but the paintings, although slight, are worth seeing. They depict figures but also trees and plants. On leaving the cave, go right to rejoin the path going up to the summit. It's very steep but quite short as the top is, literally, the top of the cave. The walk up from La Zarza usually takes me an hour but this excludes time looking at the cave paintings and the views.

The summit is wide open and remarkably flat. There are a lot of granite rocks and outcrops. The view on one side is towards La Zarza but the view from the other side is over the town of Alange and the huge reservoir. This is a very good place to spend some time; relax, explore, enjoy the views, spot the birds, examine the flowers and bushes and, in season, look out for butterflies.

To continue the walk the direction, with La Zarza behind and Alange reservoir ahead, is left, because the route now follows the top of the ridge. There's a waymark post that indicates the path. Meander along the ridge but keep unfailingly ahead. Keep the view of Alange behind and on the right, and watch out for the white and yellow bands painted on rocks. The area is wild and windswept but not barren. There are many flowering bushes and the heady smell of lavender in March and April is everywhere.

Pass an area where rocks have been dislodged, possibly during

THE ROMAN WATERS 2

Alange from the sierra ridge, April

THE WALK OF THE WHITE CLIFFS OF ZARZA

a wet winter, but they seem well embedded and do not move. On the left there is no longer a view, only the higher outcrops of granite but the view to the right is still superb. The path continues up and down slightly but then goes up more steeply to come out at another open space with a signpost indicating 'La Puerta de las Hoyas'. This is the highest part of the walk. On the right the view of Alange is lost to be replaced by a huge and dramatic wall of granite mountain. Ahead is a dense wood. To the left is a broad view of agricultural flatlands with La Zarza.

At the end of the open space turn left by the dry stone wall and waymark ❹ to start the descent. Keep to the path without any deviations but take care, it's extremely steep in places. Don't rush. The path runs through a small cork oak wood on the left. There is a Y junction but the right path only enters a finca and is not our path. On descending further the oak trees start to give way to almonds and olives. Lavender gives way to cistus. As the path comes nearly to the bottom it widens out to form a track. Ahead is a belt of eucalyptus trees on the Sierra de Juan Bueno. Behind is the Sierra de Peñas Blancas.

The track joins another one in a T junction. ❺ For the short route, turn left and follow the track ahead all the way back to La Zarza. There is a Y junction halfway along the track but both tracks lead to the village, however the left track follows a stream bed and is prettier. For the longer walk, turn right at the T junction and continue along the rough track.

After about one kilometre on the track there is a crossroads near a small house. ❻ The 'official' route goes straight on and is waymarked but this part of the route is along a very stony track that's hard to walk on and not very interesting. Our route, the one I prefer to walk, goes right at the crossroads. At a Y junction keep left. The track is easy to walk along and has lovely views all around. It dips down and then rises up and bears left to follow the

THE ROMAN WATERS 2

edge of a dense pine wood on the right. It comes out at a house with a distinctive small round house with cupola in the garden, and rejoins the 'official' route. ❼

There is a signpost indicating 'Pinar Los Valencines'. Turn right to go through some large metal gates. These gates should not be locked. Enter into the pine wood and follow the broad track through the trees. There are hundreds of cistus bushes covering the floor of the wood with large rosemary bushes dotted around. The rosemary looks very impressive in flower in March but by May the cistus will be the attraction with their white flowers. Between the trees on the right are glimpses of the Sierra de Peñas Blancas. This wood is home to many birds and flowers and its very denseness is an enjoyable walking experience.

About 200m into the wood there is a Y junction and our path is to the left. This is a glorious stretch with deep shade and the resinous smell of pines. Eventually the track comes out from the woods through a gate and, suddenly, to the left there is the Sierra de Juan Bueno with the eucalyptus trees. The track joins another one at a T junction. ❽ Go left. On the left, in the distance, is La Zarza. Continue ahead. Just before the electricity wire carrier, turn right as the track bears right. Ignore the next turning, left, but follow the track uphill through almonds and olives.

Just before a large ruined building on the right, the Casas de Don Andrés, turn left to enter the eucalyptus wood. There is a signpost indicating the way. ❾ Stay on the path all the way through the wood. There are many flowering bushes but the cistus dominate. On the right, in between the almond trees are extensive views of the plains. Cortijo de la Zapatera, marked as 'Palacio' on the map, is visible in the middle distance. In the far distance the Sierra de Montánchez can be seen. Along the route are very distinctive clumps of Lusitanian milk vetch and other flowers. At a Y junction the right track goes down but our track, the left one, goes uphill.

THE WALK OF THE WHITE CLIFFS OF ZARZA

After a short distance the track drops down and the Tierrablanca Mines ⑩ come into view. The track widens considerably to become a lane. To the left is an information board but, frustratingly, only in Spanish. On either side of the lane are open cast mines. The one on the left has a turquoise pool of water at the bottom.

As the lane winds its way from the mine the whole of the Sierra de Peñas Blancas stretches out on the left. On the right the tops of the Sierra de Juan Bueno are quite dramatic. The rocky outcrops are splashed with the distinctive lime green lichen so common here. The lane continues, crosses a road, and drops down into the village along Calle la Mina, then Calle la Independencia. Turn left for Calle la Cuesta, 2nd left for Calle los Pintores and right into the Plaza del Ayuntamiento. Turn left for Calle de Juan Andrés Valor and the Plaza de España for refreshments in one of the many bars and cafés.

THE ROMAN WATERS 2

GPS Points
The Walk of the White Cliffs of Zarza

1. N38° 49' 11.30" W06° 13' 15.85"
2. N38° 48' 44.20" W06° 13' 14.40"
3. N38° 48' 13.93" W06° 13' 38.88"
4. N38° 47' 43.89" W06° 12' 46.16"
5. N38° 48' 03.98" W06° 12' 29.44"
6. N38° 47' 51.34" W06° 11' 53.13"
7. N38° 47' 30.76" W06° 11' 22.51"
8. N38° 47' 29.54" W06° 10' 17.58"
9. N38° 47' 42.31" W06° 09' 51.00"
10. N38° 48' 41.60" W06° 11' 28.08"

Don't look down! Camino del Payo, June

The Sierra de Gata

1	The Walk of the Natural Pool	164
2	A Walk to the Hermitage of the Holy Spirit	170
3	The Walk of the Pass of San Martín	178
4	The Walk by the Riverside	190
5	The Walk of the Bandit's Castle	196
6	The Walk of Pico Jálama	204

INTRODUCTION

The Sierra de Gata

The Sierra de Gata is idyllic for walkers who enjoy open spaces, deep quiet, rugged sierras, fast flowing rivers, extensive woodlands and small cosy villages. It lies in the extreme north west of Extremadura and covers 1,211sq km. With peaks of over 1,500m, the sierra borders Portugal in the west and the autonomous region of Castile and León to the north. Ancient castles, fortified towns and villages dot both sides of the international border — relics of less friendly times when Portugal and Spain fought hard to claim the area.

Flowers come later here but last much longer. In June, when spring is over in the south, the Sierra de Gata are still covered with thousands of flowering bushes and gentle shades of green. Similarly, while the plains further south bake in summer temperatures of up to 40 degrees, the breezes are cooler in the Sierra de Gata. This makes the location ideal for walkers tied to holidays in July or August. More rain in the winter months makes the area greener and softer, with waterfalls, rivers and streams flowing throughout the year and creating natural swimming pools.

Geographically isolated, the Sierra de Gata is, today, a perfect destination for those who love the natural and rural way of life. The heavily forested area of deciduous Pyrenean oaks, ancient Spanish chestnuts and pine, is home to a small remaining population of Iberian lynx. There are birds of prey including eagles, hawks, buzzards and kites. It may be mostly forest, but villages are hedged about with flower strewn meadows in the spring where contented animals graze. Many woodland paths are shaded in the summer but dazzle with colour during the autumn as the deciduous trees shed their leaves. In the winter a dusting of snow on the higher mountain slopes adds a picture-postcard look. Throughout the calendar, this area is delightful.

Hundreds of paths and tracks link the villages dotted around

THE SIERRA DE GATA

the Sierra de Gata. There are several ancient pathways of communication that climb over the sierra to cross a *puerto* (mountain pass) and drop into Salamanca province.

Practical information

There are five featured villages in this chapter, three of them, Valverde del Fresno, at 490m, Eljas, at 610m, and San Martín de Trevejo, at 612m, lie in their own valley and are closest to Portugal. They retain an ancient language known as 'Falla' — a Romance language. It dates back to the 13th century, and the reconquest, when knights from Galicia, León and Portugal settled here bringing their own languages. These were mixed and kept alive by virtue of the isolation of the area. Although the language has no official status, knowledge of it in these villages remains extremely high. Street signs are often shown with the Falla above and the Castilian (Spanish) below. In Eljas there is an either/or mix for street names so the use of both in this book is not a misprint. San Martín has both languages on all street signs. Just south of San Martín lie the other two featured villages, Villamiel, at 738m, and tiny Trevejo, at 736m, with its distinctive ruined castle.

All these villages, excepting Trevejo (not to be confused with bigger San Martín de Trevejo), have a cash machine, grocery shops, butcher, health centre, pharmacy, café bars and a garage. San Martín has a tourist office where they are helpful but they do not speak English nor have literature in English.

Cars are the best form of transport for getting around as the area is sparsely populated. However, the villages can all be linked by walking and more on that to follow.

There are many places to stay and it is best to do your own research but **A Velha Fábrica** is a casa rural just on the edge of Valverde with a good restaurant and lovely gardens with a swimming pool:

INTRODUCTION

D. Miguel Robledo Carrasco 24.
10890 Valverde del Fresno, Cáceres, Extremadura
avelhafabrica.com

In Eljas there is a small modern house tucked into the old part of the village. It is self-catering and ideal for independent walkers:

La Casa de los Higos
Castelu Baixu, 47
10891 Eljas
www.walkingextremadura.com

In the tiny granite village of Trevejo there is a newly refurbished casa rural with two self-contained apartments. Full details here:

Calle Pizarro, 24 Trevejo, Sierra de Gata, Cáceres, Extremadura
www.apartamentos-afala.es

There are other places, of course, no less comfortable, scattered throughout the region.

Other walks

For those of you who want to walk really long routes all the walks described in this chapter are plotted so you can link them and create your own length of walk. Choose a starting point like Valverde and walk to Eljas via the Hermitage of the Holy Spirit, up to the Pass of San Martín down to San Martín and back to Valverde via Eljas (28.00km), or, starting from San Martín walk to Villamiel, detour to Trevejo and back to Villamiel, on to the Pass of San Martín via Pico Jálama and back to San Martín (30.55km), or, link smaller walks; the Holy Spirit route fits seamlessly with that of the Natural Pool (13.25km) or choose your own itinerary.

There are plenty of other walks throughout the whole of the Sierra de Gata. Ask in the tourist office in San Martín. Unfortunately, the routes are described rather basically in Spanish with sketchy line drawings for maps. It is best to plot the route on an IGN map

THE SIERRA DE GATA

before you start. Many routes are waymarked but, frustratingly, not necessarily from the start. One route in particular is still on my 'to walk' list — the PR-CC 188, Route of the Smugglers. It starts from the Plaza del Santo Cristo in Valverde where there is a map and information board for the 20km walk. Plot it on the IGN 572-IV Valverde map, listed below, and follow the waymarks and you should get a great walk to Portugal and back.

Maps

A mixture of small and large maps might be needed depending on the walk.

Map: IGN 572-IV Valverde 1:25.000

Map: IGN 573-I Navasfrías 1:25.000
(for the tip of the Walk of Pico Jálama)

Map: IGN 573-III Eljas 1:25.000

or

Map: IGN 573 Gata 1:50.000

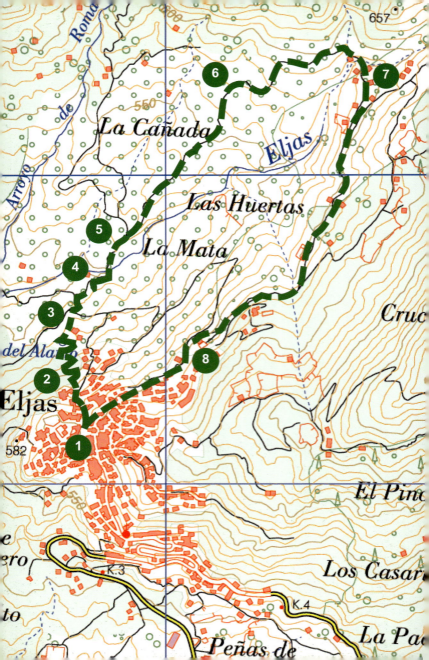

THE SIERRA DE GATA 3

1. The Walk of the Natural Pool

 Start: Plaza de la Constitución, Eljas

 Finish: Plaza de la Constitución, Eljas

 1.5 hours plus swimming time

 3.75 km

 Low: 505m High: 622m

 Easy

Eljas → Eljas
Map: IGN 573-III Eljas 1:25.000 or IGN 573 Gata 1:50.000

View of Eljas and Valverde

THE WALK OF THE NATURAL POOL

Introduction

The Sierra de Gata has many small rivers that never quite run dry. In the largest of these swimming pools have been formed. The pools are in varying degrees of 'naturalness' — some have steps going into them with shallow and deep ends, while some are substantial hollows in enormous granite boulders, sculpted smooth over millennia. However, all are open-air, in the countryside and with water that is flowing and 'refreshing'.

This short walk, centered on the village of Eljas, can be enjoyed for the natural countryside and the views all year round. However, it is one of the few walks in Extremadura that is also perfect for the long summer evenings, with a stop for a swim in a delightful setting, before returning to the village for a good local dinner.

Directions

Start in the Plaza de la Constitución, Eljas. ❶ Facing away from the square and with your back to the side door of the church (not the door opposite the Town Hall), look ahead. There is a building with a bar on the left. The name of the bar changes too often to be of use as a landmark but to the left of the bar is Calli Valvardi. As an extra point of orientation there is an information board on the left of the lane showing the PR-CC 184 walking route — but that is not this walk. Go down this lane. Ignore Calli Cunina within 50m on the left and walk to the next turning left, Calli San Bras. Turn left here and follow Calli San Bras as it bends right and goes down steeply. At a Y junction with the Medical Centre on the right do not go right. Go left down a steep lane and within 50m the name plate is on the left, Calli d'A Costa. ❷ On the left are agricultural buildings, ahead is a lane going down and right is another lane going down. Take the lane on the right. Ahead is an impressive view of the Sierra de Eljas.

Pass three granite water troughs on the right fed by a pipe with

THE SIERRA DE GATA **3**

running water. The lane narrows to a roughly concreted track which becomes paved with granite. Keep to the paved track as it zig-zags steeply down and away from the village. Pass an outbuilding, left, with a white and yellow waymark. A concrete road can be seen below and the track zig-zags to meet it. Turn left on to the concrete road and after 10m turn right, on to a stony path. There is a waymark on a stone. Take this path as it bends left and goes downwards. Pass an enormous boulder to the right with a waymark. At a Y junction **3** do not go left (this is the way to the Walk to the Hermitage of the Holy Spirit) but go right and follow the path to arrive at the River Eljas with two bridges over it. This is a pretty spot and a good place for looking at flowers and water-loving plants. Cross the river by either bridge. **4** On the right are the ruins of a once impressive house.

The path becomes wide and goes up towards the sierra, its rocky outcrops softened by many trees. Just after passing a modern finca gate on the right there is a Y junction. **5** Take the right turning going sharply uphill. The sierra is ahead and Eljas is to the right and behind. Pass through an area of olive fincas, deciduous trees and oaks. Follow the path. In season there are many flowers and plenty of birds, including hawks. Ignore a tiny path, left, just before a modern fenced building, also on the left. Follow the path with the fence on the left. Opposite is a small gate into a lovely wood of deep shade and bird song.

Pass a small reservoir on the left. **6** At a Y junction the path splits but rejoins within 30m. At the next Y junction the left path goes level around the head of the reservoir but we turn right to continue upwards. Eljas is on the right, Valverde is behind as the path bears left then turns sharply right. Ignore the tiny path on the left. Walk ahead. Pass very tall pine trees on the right as the path drops down into a wooded area of a few weekend houses; ruined, old and new. Ahead is a pine and deciduous oak wood. The path bends to the right and comes to a concrete bridge over the River

THE WALK OF THE NATURAL POOL

Eljas, a picnic area on the left and the natural pool on the right.

After that refreshing dip or just a rest, continue by walking ahead on the path. Come to an open space within 100m. Turn right. At a Y junction ❼ there is a track going through a gate on the right and a path going parallel, but higher, on the left. Choose either path as they join within 200m. The lower path does have an information board explaining how natural pools are formed and there are spaces for cars under trees. The higher path is prettier with the best views. Eljas is visible ahead. Walk on the joined paths towards the village. There are good views of the valley to the right with Valverde in the distance. Enormous granite boulders are to the left interspersed with foxgloves, flowering bushes and low growing scrub.

The path continues slightly uphill. A footpath joins the one we are on from the left at a small stream, also left. There are other small paths but keep to the main one and walk in the direction of Eljas. Look into the garden of the first house on the right — cherry trees. Pass the City of the Dead on the right. As the path now approaches the village it is illuminated at night. Pass a children's playground on the right with great views over the valley below. At the end of the playground is a Y junction ❽ with a right turning going sharply down. Stay left on the concrete path to arrive back in Eljas via Calle Currieira. Walk straight down this street all the way back to the square ignoring all turnings. At the Y junction keep going downwards. As the street drops lower it comes into the older part of Eljas with ancient and historical houses well worth studying. Pass the pharmacy on the right to arrive at the back of the church. Either way around the church will bring us back into the square and that tempting dinner.

GPS Points
The Walk of the Natural Pool

1. N40° 13' 01.73" W06° 50' 49.16"
2. N40° 13' 05.38" W06° 50' 50.99"
3. N40° 13' 15.00" W06° 50' 51.43"
4. N40° 13' 19.37" W06° 50' 47.25"
5. N40° 13' 23.79" W06° 50' 44.82"
6. N40° 13' 39.44" W06° 50' 27.26"
7. N40° 13' 40.17" W06° 50' 13.79"
8. N40° 13' 16.88" W06° 50' 28.19"

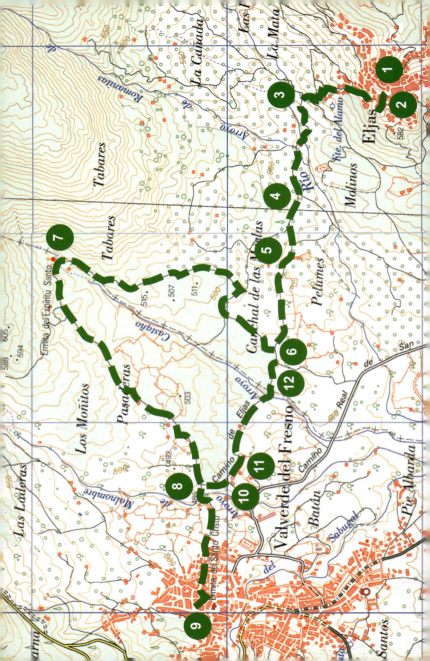

THE SIERRA DE GATA

2. A Walk to the Hermitage of the Holy Spirit

Start: Plaza de la Constitución, Eljas

Finish: Plaza de la Constitución, Eljas

3 hours

9.5 km

Low: 485m
High: 596m

Easy

Eljas → Valverde del Fresno → Eljas
Maps: IGN 572-IV Valverde del Fresno 1:25.000
IGN 573-III Eljas 1:25.000

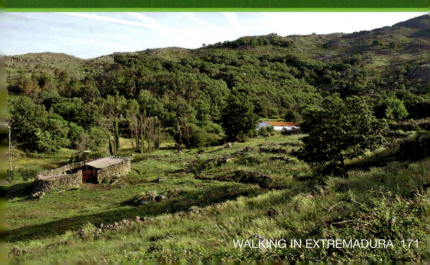

The Hermitage of the Holy Spirit, June

A WALK TO THE HERMITAGE OF THE HOLY SPIRIT

Introduction

This satisfying walk links the two villages of Eljas and Valverde del Fresno via a visit to the *Ermita del Espiritu Santo* (Hermitage of the Holy Spirit) set deep in a pretty valley. The walk is relatively flat and can be enjoyed throughout the year — even in the summer provided the start is very early or late. The lanes are mainly shaded by trees but there is one stretch without any shade. In winter, the sun will filter on to the paths as many of the trees are deciduous. There are two rivers to cross and both areas are full of water-loving plants and, with patience, are good bird spotting locations. Near the hermitage there is the possibility of seeing eagles. I saw two booted eagles last spring and smaller birds of prey are common. There are thousands of flowers in spring and the sweeping meadows below the sierras are carpeted in white, yellow, pink and purple.

Directions

Start in the Plaza de la Constitución, Eljas. ❶ Facing away from the square and with your back to the side door of the church (not the door opposite the Town Hall), look ahead. There is a building with a bar on the left. The name of the bar changes too often to be of use as a landmark but to the left of the bar is Calli Valvardi. As an extra point of orientation there is an information board on the left of the lane showing the PR-CC 184 walking route — but that is not this walk. Go down this lane. Ignore Calli Cunina within 50m on the left and walk to the next turning left, Calli San Bras. Turn left here and follow Calli San Bras as it bends right and goes down steeply. At a Y junction the Medical Centre is on the right but do not go right. Go left down a steep lane and within 50m the name plate is on the left, Calli d'A Costa. ❷ On the left are agricultural buildings, ahead is a lane going down and right is another lane going down. Take the lane on the right. Ahead is an impressive view of the Sierra de Eljas.

THE SIERRA DE GATA 3

Pass three granite water troughs on the right fed by a pipe with running water. The lane narrows to a roughly concreted track which becomes paved with granite. Keep to the paved track as it zig-zags steeply down and away from the village. Pass an outbuilding, left, with a white and yellow waymark. A concrete road can be seen below and the track zig-zags to meet it. Turn left on to the concrete road and after 10m turn right, on to a stony path. There is a waymark on a stone. Take this path as it bends left and goes downwards. Pass an enormous boulder to the right with a waymark. At a Y junction not go right (this is the way to the Walk of the Natural Pool) but keep on the path as it becomes a lane and bears left. ❸ Valverde is ahead in the distance.

Walk ahead keeping to the lane. Within about 150m, pass the ruin of a large wall on the right. It has a waymark. The wall is part of what was once a mill. A few metres further on, as the lane bends around the wall, come to the River Eljas and a bridge. This is an area for flowers and plants and deserves thorough exploration but take care — there are mill races and water channels everywhere, some hidden by vegetation. In season, dragonflies and butterflies dance to the music of croaking frogs. Cross the bridge. On the left, is a wall topped with vines and a waymark lower down. Come to a small stream bed with stepping stones for use in times of flood. Pass groves of oranges on the left and olives on the right. Hidden away there are productive vegetable gardens. The area is fertile and there are many deciduous trees. Look back for a view of Eljas.

The lane comes to a Y junction ❹ where a track goes left. Ignore it and continue on the lane. With vineyards, left, and a copse of deciduous oaks, right, come to a Y junction. Stay on the lane and ignore the path, left. As the lane bends to the right there are good views of the sierra ahead. The strange looking 'roads' high in the sierra are man-made fire-breaks. At another Y junction ❺ ignore the path to the right. Our lane goes straight ahead and climbs

A WALK TO THE HERMITAGE OF THE HOLY SPIRIT

up slightly to arrive at a large Y junction. ⑥ There is a multiple signpost: Eljas, Valverde, Ermita del Espiritu Santo. Turn right to follow the lane to the hermitage.

On the left, all the way, is a wild expanse of granite boulders, low flowering bushes, scrub, wild flowers and hawks circling above. There is no shade for the first 300m but after that there is a deciduous oak wood on the right. If walking early in the morning this wood gives shade in the summer. There are several entry points to the wood and it is possible to go in and explore but come back to the lane to continue the walk. Directly left is a view of Valverde but ahead and right is the sierra. As the lane crests a low hill the hermitage can be seen ahead, nestling at the head of a valley. The lane drops down to the hermitage. ⑦ This is a good place to rest or explore the building with its decorated doorway. There are foxgloves and peonies in May and over everything rests a deep quiet.

To continue the walk, with the hermitage behind, follow the path, right, towards Valverde. It goes up at the start with a copse of tall pines on the right. At the crest of the hill, look back for a view of mixed trees contrasted with the barren, boulder-strewn side of the hills opposite. Ignore the path to the right and keep ahead on the wide path. On the left is the other side of the wild expanse of granite boulders and low flowering bushes and as the walk continues Eljas comes into view beyond this expanse. The path drops down to copses and stands of deciduous trees and tall, impressive pines. The colours are superb in autumn. On the left is a white and green waymark but this is hardly necessary. Ignore the two little paths, left, as the main path becomes flanked by walls with verges of pink cistus. There are views of meadows, right, with the high sierra behind as the path enters a deeper pine wood.

Coming out from the pine trees, Valverde is close with a good view of the back of the 14th century church in the centre of the village.

Returning to Eljas, June

Pass a white building on the right where there is a Y junction. ❽ Go right to cross a small river over a bridge with green railings on either side. (The return to Eljas will be by the left fork.) The area is known as Fuente Petril and is a great place for flowers as there are multiple water channels. Once over the bridge, follow the path left, then right, where a track from the right joins our path. The outskirts of Valverde are near. Simply keep to the path to come to the road called the Avenida de Espiritu Santo. Ignore all turnings but walk ahead. The road comes to a small square, the Plaza del Santo Cristo with an ancient cross at the centre and, on the left is the Ermita de Santo Cristo. To the right is the start and information board for the 20km Route of the Smugglers, the PR-CC 188.

To explore Valverde, visit the church and take refreshment, walk ahead. At the T junction turn left, then right, into Calle Salvaleón

A WALK TO THE HERMITAGE OF THE HOLY SPIRIT

with its historic houses. Walk all the way up this street to come to the Plaza de la Constitución. ❾

To return to Eljas retrace steps to the Y junction after the bridge at Fuente Petril. Turn right at this Y junction. The dirt path, lined by walls quickly comes to a very wide Y junction with an agricultural complex ahead. Turn left. ❿ Within 100m is a Y junction but both paths join 50m later. On the left is a copse of trees and ahead is Eljas. Pass Casa Valverde and a campsite on the right. Follow the path as it drops sharply to the right to run alongside the campsite hedge and fence. The path comes to a fenced house with a locked gate yet it has the waymark to the right of the locked gate. Go back a few paces. Turn to look at the house. To the right, hard up by the wall on the right is a tiny, indistinct path with granite boulders. Take this tiny path. ⓫

Walk along with the house on the left for a few metres and keep the wall as a guide. The tiny path quickly establishes itself. There are views of Eljas, ahead and to the left. The path goes through an area of trees, and meadows. It comes to a stream bed with stepping stones. Cross over. Ahead and left, just inside a meadow, is a *chozo* (a traditional round shepherd's hut). The path comes to a T junction with a wide lane. Turn left. ⓬

Follow the lane, ignoring all turnings, as it winds past a boulder, left, with white, green and yellow waymarks. On the right and ahead is Eljas and just below can be seen the top of the multiple signpost we passed earlier. The lane bends right and makes a sweep with the boulder-strewn expanse on the left to come back to the signpost. Turn right to retrace steps back to Eljas.

THE SIERRA DE GATA 3

GPS Points
A Walk to the Hermitage of the Holy Spirit

1. N40° 13' 01.73" W06° 50' 49.16"
2. N40° 13' 05.38" W06° 50' 50.99"
3. N40° 13' 17.01" W06° 50' 51.47"
4. N40° 13' 17.57" W06° 51' 19.27"
5. N40° 13' 23.95" W06° 51' 25.84"
6. N40° 13' 25.43" W06° 51' 34.39"
7. N40° 13' 56.07" W06° 51' 29.76"
8. N40° 13' 30.42" W06° 52' 17.86"
9. N40° 13' 30.25" W06° 52' 45.38"
10. N40° 13' 26.09" W06° 52' 16.88"
11. N40° 13' 23.05" W06° 52' 01.35"
12. N40° 13' 18.50" W06° 51' 50.07"

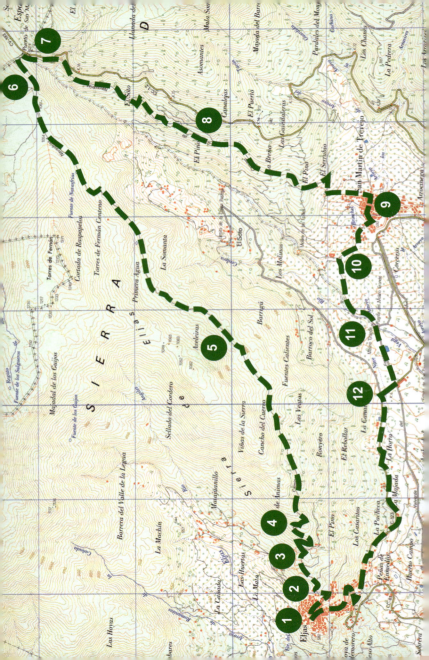

THE SIERRA DE GATA **3**

3 The Walk of the Pass of San Martín

Start: Plaza de la Constitución, Eljas

Finish: Plaza de la Constitución, Eljas

6 hours

18.5 km

Low: 520m
High: 1,058m

Medium-High

Eljas → San Martín de Trevejo → Eljas
Map: IGN 573-111 Eljas 1:25.000

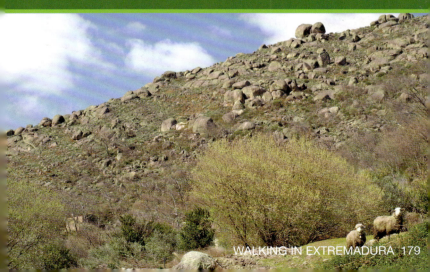

Lane back to Eljas, February

THE WALK OF THE PASS OF SAN MARTÍN

Introduction

This walk follows an ancient communication path, the Camino de Navasfrías, over the Sierra de Gata to the *Puerto de San Martín* (Pass of St. Martin) sometimes confusingly referred to as the *Puerto de Santa Clara* (Pass of St. Claire). It links Extremadura with Castile and León. There are four distinct parts to the walk. The climb out from Eljas is initially quite steep but it levels off to pass through an extensive Pyrenean oak wood. The second part of the walk is a long gentle ascent through wild boulder-strewn moorland to the Pass of San Martín. The next part is downhill all the way to San Martín de Trevejo through woods of Spanish chestnut and Pyrenean oaks. The final part is a return to Eljas via a series of small lanes and a minor road.

There are many opportunities for flower and bird spotting. In spring, the flowers are at their best but I last walked this route in June and the flowers were still spectacular. For a good list of flowers, read the introduction to the Walk of Pico Jálama. On the top of the sierra the landscape is reminiscent of Dartmoor, Devon, England but with extensive areas of pasture. There are many small waterfalls and water chanels and these are good places for observing nature. There is no shade on the second part of the walk once you leave the mountain wood and before you get to the wood from the Pass of San Martín to the village. Do not walk in high summer during mid day and, equally do not walk in mist, fog, rain or poor visibility. Check the weather forecast before setting off. In autumn the colours of the changing leaves in the two extensive woods rival anywhere. Much of the side of the sierra is grazed by cattle. They are not dangerous — there are never any bulls. However, in spring, the cows will have calves. Walk smoothly and quietly without sudden movements or flapping clothing. Do not approach the calves but go around if necessary. They may be curious but tend to move away cautiously to resume the business of the moment — grass munching.

THE SIERRA DE GATA **3**

Directions

With the Town Hall in the Plaza de la Constitution, Eljas, ❶ on the right, walk ahead. At the T junction, turn left up the ramp, then immediately right up Calle de Emigrante. At the T junction with Calle Folnu turn left, then right. Look ahead for a sign saying Calle Cantonis. Go straight up this tiny road to the right of the sign. Turn first right into Calle Orienti, another tiny road but with picturesque, ancient houses. Go straight up this road. Do not take any junctions. At the end of the road is a T junction with Calle Forca, ❷ turn left on to a wider road. Walk ahead to reach the top of the village with vines and olives growing on the right. There are still houses on left. At a Y junction, on the right is a map of walking routes in the area. Turn right on to a concrete track going up. The village is behind and olive and fig fincas are on either side. At a garage on the left, and houses on the right, the track bends left. Continue along the track. On the left are views of the valley and Valverde del Fresno. The sierra lies ahead. On the left, pass a bath with a pipe and running water and a construction with a solid fort-like base. The concrete track ends and becomes rougher but still goes up. Pass a white and yellow waymark on a rock to right. The track goes towards the sierra ahead. Come to small open space. ❸ Ignore the gate on the right. Turn left to a gate with a notice in Spanish, *cierre gracias* (shut thanks). This gate leads into a huge wild grazing area for cows and is an ancient public right of way. A waymark on the right pillar by the gate makes doubly sure of the way. Beyond the gate is a granite-paved path going straight ahead. This is our path all the way to the Pass of San Martín. It is mostly granite-paved, never more than 3m wide, sometimes narrowing to a tiny dirt track and, on occasion disappearing altogether. At these times the waymarks also, helpfully, disappear.

This is a wild, uncultivated part of the sierra but it is not barren. There are white and yellow broom and lavender bushes, foxgloves, ferns and daisies even as late as June but they are low growing

THE WALK OF THE PASS OF SAN MARTÍN

as this is an exposed high sierra. Walk straight ahead on the paved path. After 50m, at a large boulder, there is a definite bend right to start the zig-zags upwards, steadily but not sharply. As the path ascends the views out over the valley on right become more extensive. Already there are birds and hawks to be spotted — depending on when you walk. The path zigs left. ❹ On the right there are low granite agricultural buildings. The going up is relentless, so pace yourself. Pass a tap flowing water into containers for animals, right. The path turns right for another zag. 100m after the turn, there appears to be a Y junction. Keep straight ahead. There is a waymark on a rock to the right. The path bends left and quickly comes to the next bend right but we are almost at the top. Take one last look behind at Eljas and Valverde and the valley as we are about to go over the top to the other side of the sierra.

The walk continues up slightly. Pass a rock on the right with a waymark and a few deciduous oak trees. The view on the right, through the trees and granite outcrops, is south-west towards the plains before Eljas and the Sierra de Olalla. The path becomes flat and the walking is easy. In season the bird song is deafening and the trees are home to many birds including azure winged magpies. As the path narrows and becomes a bit rough, come to a gate. Go through and close it behind you. The walk now goes through the thickest part of the wood with trees on both sides of the path which widens slightly. Come to a gate on left. Ignore it. Ahead on a big boulder on the left is a waymark. Pass another gate tucked in on left. Ignore it. Continue on the path to come to another gate. This gate looks all tied up with wire and rope but the right side simply pushes open. Go through and close it behind you.

Come to a Y junction but ignore the tiny path, right, that plunges into the wood. It is the first of a series of openings, on the right, that lead into the wood that stretches all the way down the side of the sierra. Within the wood are bluebells, ferns, thapsias,

THE SIERRA DE GATA 3

Flowers at over 1000m, May

THE WALK OF THE PASS OF SAN MARTÍN

foxgloves, broom and lush vegetation in season. (If you want to explore the wood, do so, but come back to the path to continue the walk.)

The path comes to where the trees start to thin and there is a gate with a waymark on the right gatepost. Go through and close it behind you. The trees end on the left altogether and the view is of granite boulders and low growing shrubs but trees continue on the right. The path is rough and boulder strewn but the waymarks continue with one on a boulder to the right. Come to an old gatepost with no gate followed by a gate made of bedsprings, usually open. Go through these. There are two little gates, right, and some small outbuildings. (When I walked here last May I met a goatherd with his herd of goats.) Come out to an open meadow but the path is clearly defined by granite paving. There is a meadow and a dry stone wall, right, with views south and an open expanse and the high sierra, left. Ahead is Pico Jálama. Occasionally the path becomes compacted earth but is clear as no grass grows on it. Keep Pico Jálama as a vague point of orientation — it should be ahead and sometimes a bit right. Ahead and sometimes a bit left are jagged outcrops called the Torres de Fermán Centeno. Legend has it that he was a bandit who seized Eljas and Trevejo castles in 1474, terrorised the local people, and hid out in these 'towers'. Below and right, San Martín de Trevejo comes into view nestling in its valley.

The path comes to a large area of pastures and low growing shrubs. It is easy to wander off but keep to the dirt path as it bends slightly right. Cross a stream (in season) with stepping stones. Walk with Pico Jálama directly ahead. After cresting a rise the path drops again and it is visible winding a long way into the distance. The path is dirt or grassy and winds towards the granite outcrops again. Occasional water channels cross the path from left to right. Come to a strange but distinctive area of giant rounded granite boulders, possibly tumbled from the sierra

THE SIERRA DE GATA 3

on the left and eroded over centuries. ❺ The path bends left to go through the middle of the boulders and bends left again. This part of the sierra has a wild, primitive aura but is softened with white and yellow broom and there is a pretty stream with stepping stones. It becomes hard to pick the way but veer left and the paved path appears again to climb up towards the jagged outcrops once more. It is an isolated and solitary place although cattle may be chewing contentedly on the higher slopes.

The path, now very rocky, crosses two water channels and bends decisively to the right. It drops down to a softer meadow area and the rounded boulders are left behind. More channels of water from the left cross the path and tumble down the hillside, right. To the right, below, at the end of a pasture is an interesting formation of boulders and just ahead is a rounded boulder balancing on another boulder. It is a rock-lover's paradise. Pass more water channels — if walking after a lot of rain it might be boggy in places. The path comes to grassy area and swings to the left towards the jagged outcrop. It becomes a tiny dirt path and continues parallel to Pico Jálama. There are now various paths and no waymarks so it is a bit tricky. Keep the Jálama sierra opposite parallel and after 50m the path becomes clear again — it is still a tiny dirt path but then has a few granite paving slabs. It goes up. Come to a grassy area and the path disappears completely. Look for the two biggest boulders opposite. The path is to the left of these where it becomes wide and paved and goes up through another grassy area where it disappears again. Walk straight over this grassy area. San Martín is on the right and the jagged outcrops are on the left and behind.

Over to the right the main road is in view and the Pass of San Martín is not far away. The path comes to a inverted Y junction where it is joined by a path from the left. Continue on the joined path. Walk straight ahead on the dirt track through a very open

THE WALK OF THE PASS OF SAN MARTÍN

area with rounded rocks, grassy pasture, ferns and flowering bushes. Ahead is a fence. Once at the fence, ❻ turn right and follow the path, wide enough to become a track, with the fence on the left. In spring, there are thousands of flowering bushes to the left, mainly halimium commutatum with tall spikes of asphodels — they are quite a surprise as the area is over 1,000m and the sierra is quite exposed. The fence goes off to the left as the track bends right and goes towards the tree-covered hillside ahead. It winds its way down between the flowered, but rocky, side of the sierra, left, and the huge valley sweep to right. Come to the head of the valley with impressive views down. Come to a gate — go through and close it behind you. ❼ There are information boards and signposts on the left; PR-CC 184 Eljas 7.5km, which is the way we have just come and PR-CC 184 5km San Martín, (all downhill) which is the next part of the walk. It is waymarked with white and yellow.

Facing the main road, the CC(CV)-193 turn right to find the track to San Martín. It is granite paved and wide and for the next 4km it runs through a really beautiful Spanish chestnut and Pyrenean oak wood. The trees are the highlight. Last year's leaves and spent chestnut cases lie underfoot. In spring the verges are covered with bluebells, white campion and daisies. There are many butterflies. The views in between the trees on the right are of the side of the sierra we just walked. Only ten minutes into the wood there is a cascading waterfall on the left. The path becomes a bridge here as the water flows under us down to the right and the valley below. Around the waterfall there are many bushes of Spanish heath. Continue down, through alternating oak and chestnut swathes into the deepest part of the woods. Occasional water channels cross the track but these are easily negotiated.

Come to two huge chestnut trees in the middle of the track. ❽ These are the Grandfather and Grandmother chestnut trees and are extremely old. After this the track continues down and the woods stretch ahead, thinning to come to an open rural landscape

Woodland waterfall, May

THE WALK OF THE PASS OF SAN MARTÍN

with San Martín visible below and right. At a T junction turn right, and 50m later, turn left, to drop down into the outskirts of the village. Pass a water trough on the left with clear running water; a good place to 'wash up' before having a rest in San Martín before the last part of the walk. To get to the square, Plaza Mayor, walk ahead and at a Y junction, turn right.

Leave the square by the lane to the left of the church. ❾ Turn right into Calle Corredera. At the T junction turn left to follow the flow of the water in the channel in the road. At a junction past shops on the left, turn right into Camino de Convento. Ignore junctions and walk all the way down as it bends right past an outbuilding, right, with a waymark. Just after an electricity carrier with a waymark, left, is a junction, left, just before the old Convent of San Miguel. At the junction, turn left. ❿ Walk on this wide concrete lane past meadows and flower-filled verges dotted with deciduous oak trees. The sierra is on the right and, left, are views across a wide shallow valley to mountains beyond. After 1km turn right at a junction to cross a stream by a concrete bridge with crenellated sides and wooden railings. ⓫ Over the bridge, on the right, is a mill restored as a modern dwelling. Continue for another 0.6km to make another right turn at a crossroads with agricultural buildings, left. Within 200m there is a T junction. Turn left into the Carretera de Eljas de San Martín de Trevejo. ⓬ It is a quiet back road but does take occasional local traffic. It winds up steadily all the way to Eljas but is shaded by trees and is pretty in spring with flowers in the verges. The view, left, becomes more extensive as the lane goes up. On entering the village follow the road as it winds back up to the square.

THE SIERRA DE GATA 3

GPS Points
The Walk of the Pass of San Martín

1. N40° 13' 01.73" W06° 50' 49.16"
2. N40° 12' 55.84" W06° 50' 39.63"
3. N40° 13' 04.70" W06° 50' 19.41"
4. N40° 13' 03.53" W06° 50' 17.07"
5. N40° 13' 43.86" W06° 48' 33.59"
6. N40° 14' 36.73" W06° 47' 18.78"
7. N40° 14' 46.71" W06° 46' 40.63"
8. N40° 13' 42.25" W06° 47' 20.81"
9. N40° 12' 46.57" W06° 47' 48.02"
10. N40° 12' 58.11" W06° 48' 08.50"
11. N40° 12' 44.07" W06° 48' 38.59"
12. N40° 12' 41.93" W06° 49' 09.69"

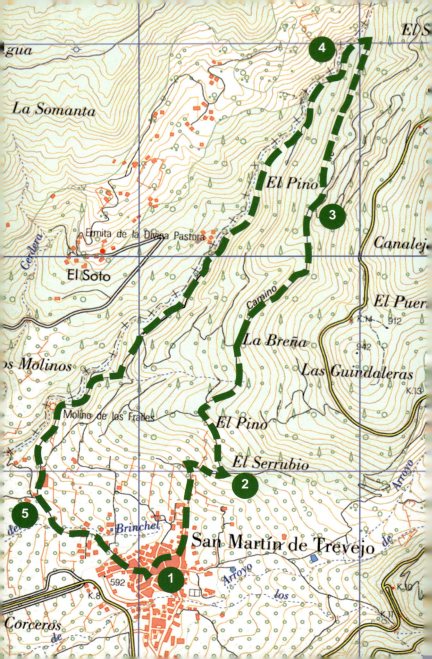

THE SIERRA DE GATA **3**

4 The Walk by the Riverside

Start: Plaza Mayor, S. Martín de Trevejo

Finish: Plaza Mayor, S. Martín de Trevejo

2.5 hours

7 km

Low: 575m
High: 816m

Easy

San Martín de Trevejo → San Martín de Trevejo
Map: IGN 573-III Eljas 1:25.000

Woodland footpath to river, June

THE WALK BY THE RIVERSIDE

Introduction

The first part of this pretty walk goes gently up the old track linking the village of San Martín de Trevejo with a 'pass' to Salamanca province and the villages and towns in the north. In medieval times it must have been like the motorways of today — a fast line of communication. Halfway up the track our walk turns into the woods to follow a route down to the River de Vega. The middle part of the walk is through the woods with the river flowing on the right. It is enchanting all year around. The final part of the walk is past an old convent in the process of being turned into a hotel and restaurant. Most of the walk is through woods and flowers are not profuse but the verges on the lanes back to the village are lush in spring. The trees are the feature of this walk; new leaves in spring, full shade in summer, red-gold in autumn and bare branches in winter. The walk is accompanied by bird song.

Directions

Start in the Plaza Mayor in San Martín de Trevejo. ❶ Walk straight up Calle del General Franco ignoring all junctions left and right. The road bends right. At the very end come to a T junction. Turn left. Walk straight up this wide lane. As it leaves the village, on the right is a water trough with running water. Follow the lane up. On the left, behind, are views of the village with tree-covered hills in the distance. Ignore a tiny turning, left, where the lane turns sharp right for 20m before turning sharp left at a junction. ❷ The lane narrows to become a track and it continues through rural and farming vegetation before it enters a chestnut and deciduous oak wood. This extensive wood harbours many birds and small mammals. What you see and hear depends on when you walk.

After 1.4km since the left turn, come to two huge chestnut trees visible ahead. ❸ These two trees are extremely old yet they are not the oldest in Extremadura. They are known as the Grandfather and Grandmother chestnut trees. About 50m after these chestnut

THE SIERRA DE GATA 3

trees, on the left, is a small path that goes down gently, into the trees. Leave the track and take this path. It is soft compacted earth and is narrow. A lot of last year's leaves may lie underfoot. The wood is deep, close, dark and silent — but for bird song. The path follows in the same direction as the main track for about 10 minutes. Then it bends left, goes up, drops down and crosses a water channel. The path turns left, left again ❹ and drops down more steeply to the river. At the river turn left to follow the path with the river on the right. There are granite boulders in the riverbed and, with the fast flowing water, the effect is very refreshing on hot days. This river never runs dry but the amount of water will be dependent on the rainfall during the previous winter. The path crosses the water channel we crossed earlier just above. Where the sunlight filters through the canopy of leaves there are patchs of flowers, in season.

After passing more water channels the path comes to a Y junction. There is a signpost on the left with two options; left is the SL-CC 208 for San Martín 2.8km, and that path goes up; right is for the Convent of San Miguel 2.9km. This option follows the river and is our path. It becomes tiny and can be boggy (in season) in places. It goes up at times leaving the river below but then comes down to run side-by-side with the water. The view on the right, through the trees, is of meadows with the sierra as a back drop. Come to a turning right to access the water where it is wide enough to paddle or even swim if it is very hot. The trees on the right thin giving more open aspects and views of continuing meadows. On the left there are chestnut trees behind a wall. Vetch, wild roses and honeysuckle tumble down this wall during May and June. A fence starts on the right with a few gates, fincas, outbuildings and gardens. The path widens to become a track which comes to wide lane. There is a white and green waymark on right to remind us we are on the right track.

The going is slightly up but this reveals lovely views on the right of

THE WALK BY THE RIVERSIDE

meadows and mixed trees with the granite-topped sierra above. Come to a tall pine wood with glimpses of terraced gardens on the right; the accessibility of water from the river makes this area fertile. Pass another waymark, right, and signs to indicate that this is a fishing area. There are picturesque old agricultural buildings in granite. The pine wood thins to show olive groves and terraced vineyards, right. Suddenly the spire of the Convent of San Miguel, built in the 15th century, comes into view ahead, left. As the lane bends to left the convent is before us. It is in the process (2012) of being converted into a hospedería (hotel and restaurant), but it has been a project for over three years now. Every time I come to walk here I always think I might, at last, sample the food ... Take some time to explore. On the right there is a structure with a cross in front and an information board written in the Falla language.

Continue the walk past the convent and an old people's home on left. San Martín is very close. Walk ahead to a junction but do not go right. ❺ Continue straight ahead past a waymark on an electricity carrier. The lane is concreted with walls on either side and bends left. On an outbuilding, left, is another waymark. Ignore a turning left, but follow the lane, the Camino del Convento, as it bends right and goes up steeply. Ignore a second turning left. At the crossroad go straight ahead to the main road. At the T junction turn left. Follow the opposite direction of the running water in the channel in the road. Go right at Calle Corredera then left for the square and refreshments.

THE SIERRA DE GATA 3

GPS Points
The Walk by the Riverside

1. N40° 12' 46.94" W06° 47' 47.32"
2. N40° 13' 03.13" W06° 47' 33.44"
3. N40° 13' 42.23" W06° 47' 20.76"
4. N40° 14' 11.18" W06° 47' 09.37"
5. N40° 12' 58.08" W06° 48' 08.43"

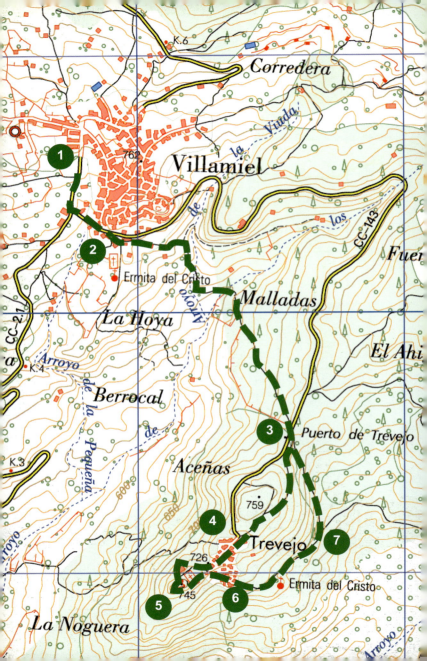

THE SIERRA DE GATA 3

5 The Walk of the Bandit's Castle

Start: Av. de Extremadura, Villamiel

Finish: Av. de Extremadura, Villamiel

2.5 hours

5.8 km

Low: 655m
High: 745m

Easy

Villamiel → Trevejo → Villamiel
Map: IGN 573-III Eljas 1:25.000

Trevejo Castle, June

WALKING IN EXTREMADURA 197

THE WALK OF THE BANDIT'S CASTLE

Introduction

This little walk is not difficult but there are two small up-and-down valleys to walk. However as the route is so short it merits a 'low' rating. The walk can be enjoyed throughout the year as quite a lot is shaded by huge deciduous oak trees. Spring here is glorious. Even if walking as late as June you can still expect to see foxgloves, mallow, yellow and white daisies, clover, viper's bugloss, wild roses, honeysuckle, purple vetch, cow parsleys, white lupins and flowering brambles ready to set fruit for picking in August. If walking in the hot summer months this route is perfect for a 07.00 or a 19.00 start as a pre-breakfast or dinner stroll. The autumn sees the sierra blazing with colour from the falling leaves and in winter the path is dappled with sun because the trees are bare.

The highlight of the walk is Trevejo with its castle which has a very interesting history. It was originally Moorish, built before the 12th century but captured during the reconquest. The Knights of the Order of St. John of Jerusalem rebuilt the castle in the early 15th century. However, in 1474 it was taken by Fermán Centeno who was an infamous bandit and smuggler. The castle saw most activity two centuries later during the 17th century and the border wars with Portugal. The views from the castle are 360 degrees. Take binoculars.

Directions

If driving, follow the signs for Villamiel from Cilleros or Hoyos and enter the village on the CC-21. The road from San Martín is the CC-22. Both these roads meet and become the Avenida de Extremadura. Park there and walk to the bottom of the avenue (south). At a Y junction, on the left is a faded information board about walking routes. ❶ Turn left. A view of Trevejo Castle is ahead and to the right. After walking about 100m come to a multiple junction in Avenida de Trevejo. On the right is a concrete area with trees and stone benches. Here there is a signpost

THE SIERRA DE GATA ③

for a walk; 'Los Lagares 10km 3h *ida* (outbound)' but no other information. However, even though there is no indication, this is our path. ❷

Walk down the tiny granite paved path parallel with the Avenida de Trevejo. Ignore the path immediately on the right. There are walls and a house on either side of our path and various gates to fincas. Ahead is the tree-covered slope of a small sierra. The path drops down and veers right, away from the road. At a junction there is, at last, a reassuring white and red waymark. Ignore the turning, right, and keep on our path. Come to a second waymark on the right as the path winds right. Pass through an area of meadows where there may be cattle or goats grazing. There are many copses of deciduous oaks with flower-filled verges in spring. Occasionally there are painted red arrows indicating the opposite direction. Ignore these.

The path drops down into a valley and crosses over a fast flowing stream, that, in spring, is heard rather than seen, such is the lushness of the vegetation. The path can be a bit boggy here, under the shady trees, but as it bends around to the right it becomes a concrete bridge and crosses over another stream, the Arroyo de la Viuda. The path, now much wider and granite paved in places, bends sharply right and climbs up through copses of trees, mainly oak. It comes out at the CC-143, the minor road from Villamiel to Trevejo. Cross the road. There is a waymark, GR-10 E7 Villamiel-Trevejo. ❸

With the CC-143 behind, look right. Take the little path that bends right and shadows the road for a few hundred metres — there is a waymark on a rock. The path enters a hillside of granite boulders and low growing bushes. It is a little indistinct in places but keep the road on the right, and look for the next waymark. At a Y junction do not go left and down the valley. That is the way to Hoyos and our return comes up that path. Follow the path as

THE WALK OF THE BANDIT'S CASTLE

it bends slightly left away from the road. It is paved and clearly defined. The views on the left out over a valley are tremendous with deeply wooded sierra slopes. Start to climb and pass another waymark on a rock, left. This is an excellent area for hawk spotting. The path narrows and ferns or bushes encroach at times but it is not a jungle. Keep going straight up. At a radio mast the path divides into various paths but all converge to drop into Trevejo via Plaza el Corro. ❹

Walk straight across the square and down Calle Pizarro in the direction of the castle. The village is built in granite and is very pretty. There is a bar and a postbox but no shops that I could see. Come to the hill on which the castle is built but first go to the right to investigate the Church of St. John the Baptist. Next walk around the church to admire the free-standing bell tower and, finally, approach the castle. There is a good information board in Spanish and English.

Walk around the castle to admire the ruins with pulpit towers, coats-of-arms and inscriptions. The path is in reasonable condition but only until you get to the top. ❺ Retrace steps to descend. Don't be tempted to do any climbing down as it is much too high for that. The views are spectacular and the circling birds easy to spot. There are also a lot of flowers, especially mallow and foxglove, in late spring.

On coming down from the castle, before you re-enter the village, there is a giant granite boulder on the right with pine trees growing out from the centre. Just there is a path to the right. ❻ Take this path as it bends left and goes sharply down. At a wide junction ignore the lane on the left. Our path bends left and down and then veers right. This is the oldest part of the village and it is picture-postcard but I am sure living here in the winter is altogether another story. Keep going down and leftish to skirt the bottom of the village. Ignore the next turning right. Come to the edge of the

THE SIERRA DE GATA [3]

Footpath from Villamiel, June

THE WALK OF THE BANDIT'S CASTLE

village. On the right is an information board showing the ancient route from Hoyos to Trevejo. Follow that path now by continuing ahead.

Ignore the path to the left and keep on the paved path as it drops down past the plain and serviceable hermitage, the Ermita del Cristo, on the right. The path continues to drop down through an area of deciduous oaks. There is a sweeping meadow on the right with wooded sierra slopes right and ahead. Come to the boulder area with low growing shrubs we crossed higher up earlier but keep on the path. By two huge chestnut trees is a paved path going left. There is a waymark on a boulder, right. Take this path, left, because this is where we leave the path as it continues another 6km to Hoyos. ❼ Keep on our path as it goes up quite steeply but, in places, granite steps have been laid to help with the ascent. Come to the CC-143 and the waymark. Cross the road to retrace the path back to Villamiel.

THE SIERRA DE GATA 3

GPS Points
The Walk of the Bandit's Castle

1. N40° 11' 15.38" W06° 47' 09.77"
2. N40° 11' 03.36" W06° 47' 03.11"
3. N40° 10' 39.87" W06° 46' 34.63"
4. N40° 10' 26.25" W06° 46' 41.16"
5. N40° 10' 19.06" W06° 46' 51.79"
6. N40° 10' 21.35" W06° 46' 47.07"
7. N40° 10' 27.29" W06° 46' 29.44"

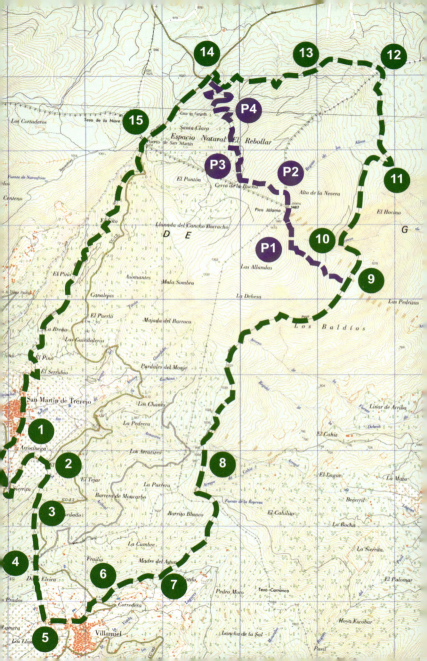

THE SIERRA DE GATA 3

6 The Walk of Pico Jálama

Start: Av. de Chafaril, S. Martín de Trevejo

Finish: Av. de Chafaril, S. Martín de Trevejo

7-8 hours

24.75 km

Low: 610m
High: 1.226m

Medium-High

San Martín de Trevejo → Villamiel → Pass of San Martín → San Martín de Trevejo

Maps: IGN 573-I Navasfrías 1:25.000
IGN 573-III Eljas 1:25.000

Final climb up to Pico Jálama, November

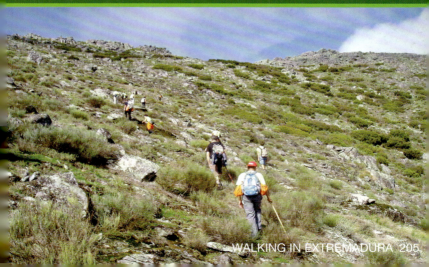

THE WALK OF PICO JÁLAMA

Optional summit route: Time: 7-8 hours
Distance: 23.25 km up and over / 24.85 km out-and-back
Elevation: lowest 610m, highest 1,487m
Difficulty: high

Introduction

This walk will take most of the day but what a great way to spend the time. The main route skirts the mountain named Pico Jálama but an option is to add 240m to the climb and go over the summit. The walk has five distinct parts and the first is a steep ascent of the wooded sierra between San Martín de Trevejo and Villamiel. The next part goes gently upwards through the edge of a forest to come out at a level, open expanse with extensive views. The middle part is along the gently rising ancient Camino del Payo, the footpath linking Villamiel and El Payo in Salamanca province. The route then splits. The main route continues on the footpath to the provincial border, then through a wooded area to the main road, the CC(CV)-193, from El Payo to San Martín. Alternatively, go up and over the Pico Jálama to drop through wooded slopes to the same main road, the CC(CV)-193, or climb the peak from this point, up a less severe zig-zag path, as an out-and-back option. The final part is from the Pass of San Martín back to the village of San Martín de Trevejo via a huge wood of Pyrenean oak and Spanish chestnut. It is gently downhill all the way.

The Pico Jálama is the third highest mountain in the Sierra de Gata but exactly how high it is seems in dispute. The provincial map of Cáceres has it at 1,492m but the local map, IGN 573-III Eljas, has it at 1,487m. Both maps are issued by the Instituto Geográfico Nacional. My own reading was 1,489m with my GPS flat on the top rock. However, the Peña Canchera at 1,592m and the Bolla at 1,519, are higher. While still in the Sierra de Gata, they are further east located in Las Hurdes.

THE SIERRA DE GATA 3

The opportunities for finding wild flowers and spotting wild life and birds is extremely high, in season. Spanish heath, lavender, retama, broom, rosemary, pink and white cistus, mallow, pennyroyal, foxglove, yellow sunrose, esparto grass and hundreds of southern autumn crocus can be enjoyed. There are thousands of low growing bushes of yellow halimium commutatum (a rockrose species) growing at 1,200m. In between the granite on the path you can see paronychia, pimpernel, campanula, tolpis, and stonecrop. There are many small waterfalls and streams which attract birds. Overhead there are hawks and eagles. In spring there are butterflies, especially the small copper and scarce copper. There are rabbits and Iberian hare but I have also seen a pine martin, that nearly frightened me to death as I was walking through the woods near Villamiel. From late spring to early autumn in the middle part of the walk, occasional rustlings can be heard in the undergrowth. There may be snakes but it is almost certain you will not see any as they are shy and timid. However I do not recommend the Pico Jálama option from the south-east to north-west in those months. Leave the wild habitat to its residents during the summer heat. Better to climb the peak in an out-and-back route from the path on the north-west side.

This route is perfect for the fit walker who loves total peace, quiet, empty spaces and panoramic views. There may be danger-loving mountain bikers at weekends but almost no one during the week. I've walked both versions of this route — the summit route with the Almoharín walking group one November and the path route on my own last June. However, do not attempt this walk solo as there is no mobile coverage at the top of the sierra. Do as I say, please, and not as I do — the walk is not dangerous but anyone can have a fall and if I had known there was no mobile coverage I would not have done it alone either. Do not walk in July and August as there are long sections with no shade. Walk from mid-September to mid-June but start by 7.00 in the warmer months. Check the

THE WALK OF PICO JÁLAMA

weather forecast before you set off and avoid wet or foggy days in the winter. Take water and some high-energy foods plus seasonal kit. Take binoculars and a good, old-fashioned compass if you are going up Pico Jálama.

Unusually I have put in a few timings for this walk simply because it is long. It is easy to become disoriented after several hours on the same mountainside and the timings will help.

I have used some road numbers in the directions taken from road signs and maps. The numbers may seem baffling, lack continuity and may even change but I can only do what I can with the information available.

Directions

Park somewhere in the Avenida de Chafaril, San Martín de Trevejo, where there is usually space. Walk south, down the avenue and away from the village. At the main road ❶ the CC-11, turn left and walk up the road as it winds around to give good views of the village below and the Sierra de Gata behind. Keep on the road and pass a picnic area, left, built on a huge outcrop overlooking the village. After another bend in the road come to a crossroads. Ignore the track left, and take the dirt track, right. On the right is a white and red waymark and a signpost, GR-10 E7. ❷ The dirt path winds slightly but goes up and enters a forest of pines and mixed trees; oak, chestnut, poplar and a few beech. There are many flowering bushes. At a Y junction go left. There is a waymark on the left with a small sign that reads, 'Ruta Turistica. Villamiel. Trevejo'. The track is rough but the trees are wonderful. Pass another waymark on a rock but these are not really necessary as the track is clear. At a second Y junction and sign ❸ keep left again. The track winds but does not zig-zag. Consequently it is extremely steep with loose gravel, stones and rocks underfoot.

About 30 minutes after leaving San Martín, the top of the climb

THE SIERRA DE GATA 3

is reached. There is a flat, rocky open space with many flowers. Look right for a view of Eljas with Valverde immediately behind. Cross the open space on the track which enters into a copse. The track is less rough and flat and the walking is very pleasant. Enter another open area with lavender bushes and flowers, followed by yet another copse. The going is slightly up. On the right is an open field with many low retama bushes and an extensive view of the sierra in the distance. Just before entering a third copse pass a white sign on the left. On the other side someone has hand written *bajado peligroso* (dangerous descent) for walkers coming the other way. Certainly, I would not like to do the walk in reverse as the steep descent has too many loose rocks.

Come to a crossroads. ❹ On the right is a cattle grid leading to a huge finca and, left, is a track to a T junction with the CC-11. Keep to the path straight ahead as it goes down through a wooded area. The descent becomes steeper and there are some loose rocks but it is not difficult. Villamiel is close — on my walk last June I heard the church bell strike the hour and I had been walking for 45 minutes. The path bends to the left and divides around a telegraph pole. The right path is less steep. Take care as the going is now steeper and rougher. On the left, ahead, is a good view of Trevejo castle. As the path bends again, Villamiel can also be seen.

Ignore all small turnings and finca entrances to walk ahead to come out to a Y junction. Turn left. At a T junction by a faded information board about walking routes ❺ turn left to walk towards the village. Keep straight on past houses on both sides of the street, Avenida Plaza de Torros. Come to a War Memorial on the left by the main road, the CC-22. Turn left to walk up the hill. Ignore turnings and make for the bus stop, ahead. At a Y junction, if you want to visit the village turn right for centro urbano. To continue the walk, turn left in the direction of San Martín, 8km and El Payo, 18km.

THE WALK OF PICO JÁLAMA

After about 30m there is a track to the left with a sign announcing 'Villamiel' to on-coming traffic. Take this left track as it goes up. It is paved with granite and quickly enters some woods and starts to go up more steeply. There are small water channels on either side of the path with, occasionally, water crossing the track. Look out for butterflies attracted to the water and lush verges. At a little house and low construction on the left, and a water trough and picnic spot on the right, the track comes out on to the main road. Cross straight over the road to continue to walk uphill on the track through a wooded area.

At a Y junction, keep left. As the track goes up there are views to the right especially of Trevejo castle. At the next Y junction keep left again. Come to a cattle grid with two gateposts. Immediately after the cattle grid turn left. ⑥ This is an area of grazing cattle but there are never any bulls — it is a public right of way. At the next junction keep left but go right at the following, indistinct, Y junction. The track breaks up a little and there are various options but continue ahead. The trees become more spaced with areas of grazing between them and finally end at an open area. There are low growing bushes and boulders on the left but views of successive mountain peaks, right. Ahead is the sierra with the Jálama in the distance. Cross a cattle grid which marks the end of this part of the walk. As a guide, the walk up to this point takes around two hours from the start. ⑦

The path ahead is mainly granite paved and over a metre wide but occasionally it is dirt or grass and narrower. It winds very slightly but follows the line, gently but relentlessly upwards, all the way around the Jálama to the other side. The views are to the right, ahead and behind and become more spectacular the higher the path goes. The village in the valley is Acebo and the far off reservoir is Borbollón. On the left is the sierra.

At a Y junction, ignore a track on the right that doubles back and

THE SIERRA DE GATA 3

Going around Pico Jálama, June

THE WALK OF PICO JÁLAMA

down. Keep on the path. On the left is a sign GR-10. There are still a few trees during the first 10 minutes on the path but these become rare. Pass a single radio mast on the left where the area is very open and the walking is easy. There is a waymark on the left. Come to a gate, go through and shut it behind you. There is a sign from the Junta de Extremadura on the left announcing that we are on 'Public Way 9 Jálama' which is reassuring. ❽ It's been 20 minutes since we crossed the last cattle grid.

The path makes a wide sweep to the left, then right. Look ahead to the sierra. The diagonal line that goes up from the bottom left to the top right, where you can see the clump of pine trees, is our path. Water crosses the path. It is a good place to be still, stop and spot birds. Pass a narrow waterfall on the left. The water goes under the path and tumbles down into the valley on the right. This is another good place to stop for a while. It is at the head of the valley with excellent views but there is no shade until one lone oak tree further on.

The drop to the right is considerable but there is a natural low hedge of flowering bushes at the edge of the path. To the left are many bushes and boulders with the high sierra towering above. Water runs in the path at intervals and another waterfall is on the left. Enter the clump of pine trees seen earlier. The path becomes flat and the walking very easy with extensive views ahead, right and behind as the path winds decisively around to the left. The Acebo valley is now behind and hidden from view. Ahead is a different range of mountains. Walk through a low growing copse of pines. To the left are many rocky outcrops. There are hundreds of yellow halimium commutatum bushes growing here at over 1000m and, if walking in May and June they attract butterflies. On the left is the back of the Junta sign announcing the path to people walking in the opposite direction so we are now through the 'official' path. The time taken to walk between the Junta signs is about one hour.

THE SIERRA DE GATA 3

On the right come to a house with the roof fallen in. **9** If you want to climb the Pico Jálama from this side, south-east to north-west, this is the point of orientation. Directions follow now.

Keeping the ruined house behind you start walking up the mountain with Pico Jálama slightly to the right. As you climb higher it gets steeper but an old sheep track crosses the way up. **P1** Pick up this sheep track and turn right as it follows the side of the mountain to the summit, zig-zagging only occasionally. It is extremely steep. Once at the top have a rest and admire the 360 degrees view. The wind farms on the horizon, west, are in Portugal. The area is dotted with huge granite boulders and low growing shrubs — it is not barren. Follow the path, north-west, down the other side **P2** to come to the *Pozo de la Nieve* (Well of Snows) called 'La Nevera'. It is an ice house made of granite and hundreds of years old. There is an information board in Spanish, but with diagrams, explaining how and why ice houses were made and used. Walk due west through low-growing vegetation using cairns of small rocks as waymarks to pick up the downward going zig-zag path **P3** that goes north and drops down to wider zig-zags **P4** through pine woods to arrive at the CC(CV)-193 and the rendezvous with walkers going the longer way around.)

For those not walking up the Pico Jálama, continue ahead on the path. Look left for a terrific view of Pico Jálama. On the right are two striking outcrops of rock with another ruined house. Spanish heath grows profusely on this side of the sierra and the deep pink flowers bloom throughout the spring. The path bends slightly left then straightens to go ahead fairly flat with easy walking. As the path swings left again it starts to go up. Ahead is the face of the sierra with, to the right, what looks like a wall going up. This is the path: it follows around the head of a deep valley at the bottom of which is the reservoir and dam of Cervigona. As the path bends very sharply to the right **10** it passes a high waterfall on the left,

THE WALK OF PICO JÁLAMA

the Arroyo de los Hocinos, whose water falls over the path (use the stepping stones) and under it to cascade down the valley on the right. The area is lush with bushes and flowers and shade. The path is now about a metre wide and continues to follow the line around the sierra. It is not dangerous in any way but there is nothing to stop you falling off the edge — if you get dizzy with heights do not look down. Keep left and don't go near the edge.

On the left the height of the sierra has lessened and there are many bushes among the boulders. The going is gently upwards, then level, narrow and lined with bushes. Ahead is a view of El Payo, in Salamanca. The path goes all the way to the village, however, we will turn off before then. At a lone oak on the right, look right for a view of a defensive tower outlined on the top of its mountain. Just before a ruined building on the left is a small path. A red cross is painted on a rock on either side. Do not go that way and ignore another path, left, that goes towards the house. Our path becomes wider, rougher, bends right and goes down. It bends further right with bushes and pine trees on either side. After about 10 minutes the path bends decisively left ❶❶ and El Payo comes into closer view.

The path is flat or going down gently and goes over a stream hidden by vegetation. Come to a wide open area with slate and small rocks on the right and a single large stone on the left. Ignore everything and go straight on. The path comes to two gateposts with a cattle grid. ❶❷ Cross this. Enter the Castile and León Autonomous Region's Salamanca province. Immediately there is a T junction with a track. Turn left. It is an hour since the last time check at the Junta board and ruined house.

The track comes to a pretty area of chestnut, oak, pine, other deciduous trees and flowering bushes. It goes up slightly and bends right. Come to a junction with a track going right. Ignore this as our track will go more-or-less straight towards the

THE SIERRA DE GATA 3

CC(CV)-193 road. There is a sign, almost hidden by bushes on the left. The area used to be an old Wolfram mine but has now been reclaimed for public enjoyment. There are many stones scattered around. Further on the left is another sign indicating the delights to be enjoyed in the area and there is an overgrown picnic site. It certainly looks like nature has reclaimed the site in her own way. Walk straight ahead on the track which is quite stony but as it goes up the vegetation encroaches again and the stones are left behind.

Pass through a metal swing barrier and keep to the track ahead. On the left is a signpost 'Mirador 600m'. I think we've probably seen enough views by now but, if you want to detour to see the view, come back to this point to continue the walk. The track goes up and down through woods and has areas where water crosses from the left. At a Y junction do not go down to the right but stay on the track. **13** Another track joins ours and the two go forward together. As the track curves right, the views on the right, of wooded sierra slopes with rocky outcrops, are impressive. The track becomes more grassy and passes what looks like a landslide on the right. It bends more sharply right and goes up slightly but the pine wood is shady with carpets of fern beneath the trees. The area is full of bird song. A view of the other side of El Payo is on the right.

Come to a T junction with another track. The choice is left and up, or right and down. Go right and down. Ahead is a view of a high and bleak sierra but all around us there is abundant vegetation. The CC(CV)-193 comes into view below. At a Y junction take the lane that goes left. At the next Y junction go right and down. Ahead there are road signs. Pass through another low metal swing barrier. Follow the lane around to the right to cross a cattle grid between two gateposts and reach the CC(CV)-193. An hour since the time check at the last cattle grid. At this point there is a sign for Pozo de la Nieve 'La Nevera' 2800m (that's 2.8km in distance and

THE WALK OF PICO JÁLAMA

not 2,800m high). This is the ice house just below Pico Jálama. Those walking the peak from south-east to north-west should come out on to the road at this point as well. **14** For those who didn't fancy the climb from the other side, but find they still have the energy, follow the out-and-back zig-zag track to the summit from this point.

Now that we are all together, turn left on to the road. There are pine and oak woods on both sides, flowers and views, but there may not be many cars — it is a quiet road. Walk for around 15 minutes until the signposts at the Pass of San Martín on the right of the road. Cross the road to get to them. **15** Our route is the PR-CC 184 all the way, through glorious chestnut and oak woods, gently downhill to San Martín de Trevejo, 5km. The full description of the route is to be found near the end of the Walk of the Pass of San Martín but just follow the path. At the village outskirts, pass a water trough on the left with clear water running from pipes. This is a good place to 'wash up' before finding a café or bar and a long drink.

To get back to the car walk straight down the road. At a Y junction, right goes to the Plaza Mayor. Go left. At the T junction turn left, then first right into Calle del Guardia. At the next Y junction turn left, downhill, then turn right and enter Calle Chafaril.

THE SIERRA DE GATA **3**

GPS Points
The Walk of Pico Jálama

1. N40° 12' 35.92" W06° 47' 44.41"
2. N40° 12' 26.91" W06° 47' 26.44"
3. N40° 12' 06.50" W06° 47' 31.60"
4. N40° 11' 44.60" W06° 47' 30.40"
5. N40° 11' 17.98" W06° 47' 22.60"
6. N40° 11' 41.30" W06° 46' 16.60"
7. N40° 12' 09.40" W06° 45' 51.70"
8. N40° 12' 36.10" W06° 46' 01.90"
9. N40° 13' 46.40" W06° 44' 47.10"
10. N40° 14' 03.00" W06° 44' 51.15"
11. N40° 14' 38.79" W06° 44' 26.01"
12. N40° 15' 21.21" W06° 44' 31.15
13. N40° 15' 24.10" W06° 44' 57.90"
14. N40° 15' 17.40" W06° 46' 04.36"
15. N40° 14' 46.30" W06° 46' 39.50"

Pico Jálama option
- P1 N40° 14' 06.76" W06° 45' 24.36"
- P2 N40° 14' 28.27" W06° 45' 24.97"
- P3 N40° 14' 44.73" W06° 45' 54.31"
- P4 N40° 15' 00.34" W06° 46' 02.97"

WALKING IN EXTREMADURA 217

Mist in the Jaranda Valley, March

The Sierra de Gredos and La Vera

1	The Walk of Yuste Monastery	226
2	The Walk of the Mountain View	238
3	The Walk of the Four Rivers	244

INTRODUCTION

The Sierra de Gredos and La Vera

The Sierra de Gredos lies on the north-eastern border of Extremadura with Castile and León and much of it has been declared a regional park. Its highest point — Pico Almanzor, at 2,592m — lies outside Extremadura in Ávila province. The highest peaks within Extremadura lie to the north-west of Tornavacas on the border and attain heights of over 2,400m.

With the mountains come the valleys, carved out by fast-flowing rivers in beds of granite boulders worn smooth over thousands of years. These rivers do not run dry because in the summer months they are fed by melt waters from snow drifts which can lie on the Gredos for up to six months of the year. The rivers are known as gargantas which can be translated as 'throat' but also as 'torrent' or 'narrow pass between mountains'. The rivers, in their high-sided, tree-clad valleys set against high mountains are one of loveliest features of the area. Many rivers have natural pools and these are wonderful for observing nature, but popular swimming places during the summer.

Two of the largest rivers, the Ambroz and the Jerte, have carved out deep valleys that offer excellent walking experiences and more on that later. La Vera, translated as 'edge' or 'border', is a distinct area in the Sierra de Gredos. It lies north of the River Tiétar and on the north-eastern edge of Extremadura. It has many small, historic villages, some, like Garganta de Olla, with perfectly preserved 17th century houses. The area also has thriving towns geared up for walking tourism but most of the brochures and guides are in Spanish. Many villages and towns in the area have *de la Vera* (of the Vera) added to their names, proud of their location within such a special region.

You will find much to delight you if you are a lover of birds, wild animals, lush spring flowers, plant life, trees and, in autumn, glorious foliage in yellow, orange and red. Walkers tied to July and

THE SIERRA DE GREDOS AND LA VERA

August for holidays can walk each day, early or late, and spend the hotter hours by the cool waters of a river, or plan an all-day walk in a deep oak and pine forest, or climb up into the breeze that blows on the higher paths. It's a wonderful place to walk.

On a historical note the area is associated with Charles V (of the Holy Roman Empire) and I (of Spain), ruler of half the world, 1500-1558. Charles became old and gouty before his time and decided to retire, without actually abdicating, leaving his son, Phillip II, to rule Spain, the Netherlands and the New World while, Ferdinand, the younger brother of Charles, got the Holy Roman Empire. Charles retired at Yuste Monastery but before the monks were ready for him he travelled from Tornavacas, over the mountains, to wait in the castle at Jarandilla for nine months. He then travelled from the castle to the monastery where he died within two years. These two journeys are commemorated every year in celebration walks complete with re-enactments and historical costume. Thousands of walkers join in from all over Europe.

Practical information

Getting around the area is probably best done by car. However, from a base such as Garganta de Olla, Cuacos de Yuste, Jarandilla or Losar there are sufficient walks to occupy a week right from the doorstep. In addition, the No. 904 bus links the towns and villages of La Vera with Madrid. With a small amount of planning a car can be unnecessary. The following web site is only in Spanish but it does work well, will give you timetables, and sell you tickets. http://www.samar.es

All of the towns and villages offer a variety of accommodation. Choose between a castle or a campsite in Jarandilla, casa rurales in tiny villages or large hotels in towns such as Losar. I have only stayed at the Parador in Jarandilla which sounds extravagant but is not. The 15th century castle is atmospheric but the service is

INTRODUCTION

modern, polite and English is spoken with pleasure. Reassuringly, they are not fazed by walking boots, sticks, maps, hats and rucksacks in Reception nor countryside-battered cars in the car park.

Parador de Jarandilla de la Vera
Avda. Garcia Prieto, 1
10450 Jarandilla de la Vera, Cáceres
www.parador.es/en/parador-de-jarandilla-de-la-vera

In Garganta de Olla, the Café-Bar La Serrana in the square, serves good tapas. The Café-Bar Tsunami, opposite, also serves good food. They speak some English, cater for walking groups, and run a budget hostel, Pensión El Salvador.

Café-Bar Tsunami
Plaza Mayor, 2 – 10412 Garganta de Olla, Cáceres
www.casachoni.com

Other walks

There are plenty of other walks in this area as it is a favourite weekend spot for escapees from Madrid and life in the city. Most of the routes are waymarked and towns and villages have information boards with line drawings and brief instructions. Tourist offices usually have someone with a knowledge of English and they are friendly and helpful. Most give away leaflets with basic maps and directions in Spanish. Losar offers two routes in English. However, with an essential IGN map you can plot the route before you set off.

In Garganta there is the Route of the Friars, low rated, circular, and 18km. The walk to the Cave of La Serrana, 15km and circular is medium rated. The Route of the Writers is shorter at 6.5km, circular and with a low rating. All routes are waymarked.

In Jarandilla there is a route I have not yet walked, to the Jaranda Bridge which is 8km away. The information board has the walk

Ambroz Forest, November

INTRODUCTION

at 15.5km each way so check where it goes before you set out. The walk from Jarandilla to Yuste Monastery, commemorating the route Charles V took on his retirement, passes through Aldeanueva and Cuacos. It is a round trip of 24km. There is a walk north along the River Jaranda to Guijo de Santa Barbara taking the old Camino de San Francisco al Guijo. It is marked on the map, IGN 599-II Jarandilla de la Vera 1:25.000. It is 7km there and back. Once at Guijo the signposted and waymarked route to the *Refugio de Nuestra Señora de las Nieves* (Hermitage of Our Lady of Snows) is a stunning 11km total out-and-back walk up to 1,468m. This walk goes along the east side of the Jaranda Valley and is rated high. On the west side is another 8km total out-and-back walk called El Trabuquete only rising to 1,112m. Somewhere, behind the hermitage there is a 2.5km joining path making a 12km circular walk. I still haven't found the joining path. Guijo also offers a less strenuous circular walk of 5km passing streams south-east of the village.

In Losar, the tourist office is very organised with information on eight different walks ranging from 5km up to 22km. Three walks are rated low, three are medium and two are high. Local guides are recommended for walks going high into the mountains. In any event plot them on an IGN map first and establish the distances securely. Some distances are one-way only and if you want to get back that distance needs to be double. It sounds obvious but not all information is consistent.

Further afield, but still in the Sierra de Gredos, there is the world-famous Valley of Ambroz. Every November up to 10,000 walkers from all over Europe turn up to see the enormous chestnut, oak and terebinth forests ablaze with autumn colours. The route is linear, starting near Baños de Montemayor at La Garganta, passing through Hervás and Gargantilla before finishing in Segura de Toro. It is 25km but shorter out-and-back walks can be done. It is a medium rated walk with a few steep hills. Hervás has a good tourist office with information on walking in the area. They speak English.

In the Jerte Valley there are lovely walks along the river. I can recommend a route, starting at the Emperor Charles campsite just south-west of Jerte on the N-110, going into the woods to a natural phenomenon called Los Pilones. This is where granite boulders have been swirled around on top of granite bedrock by the water and over millennia have created deep, round pools. Or walk further along this route to the *La Garganta de los Infiernos* (Narrow pass of Hell) where this wonderful river crashes over boulders in a beautiful natural setting. Rated medium. Ask at the tourist office for directions but the route is signposted from the campsite.

Finally, for walkers who want a real challenge start at Tornavacas and walk over three peaks, including a climb over the Cuenda de los Infiernos at 1,822m, to arrive 32km later at Jarandilla de la Vera. You will be walking in the footsteps of the local men who fought for the honour of carrying Charles V in a sedan chair on his way to the castle in Jarandilla. The first time I walked this route I almost didn't carry myself — never mind another person. It is, however, a spectacular day-long walk.

A last word: always check the weather forecast before setting out for the mountains — for obvious reasons.

Maps

Map: IGN 599-1 Aldeanueva de la Vera 1:25.000

Map: IGN 599-II Jarandilla de la Vera 1:25.000

or

Map: IGN 599 Jaraíz de la Vera 1:50.000

Map: IGN 576 Tornavacas 1:50.000

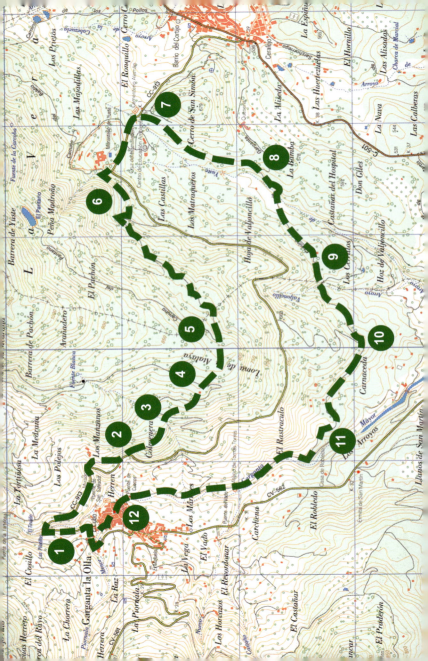

THE SIERRA DE GREDOS AND LA VERA **4**

1 The Walk of Yuste Monastery

Start: Ctra. de Cuacos, Garganta de Olla

Finish: Ctra. de Cuacos, Garganta de Olla

4 hours

13 km

Low: 506m
High: 810m

Easy with Medium stretches

Garganta de Olla → Yuste → Garganta de Olla
Maps: IGN 599-1 Garganta de Olla 1:25.000
IGN 599 Jaraíz de la Vera 1:50.000

Towards Yuste, June

THE WALK OF YUSTE MONASTERY

Introduction

This walk goes from the pretty historical village of Garganta de Olla over the Lomo de la Atalaya to Yuste Monastery and back on a lower track. The first part of the walk climbs out from the village and passes through several areas of granite, flowering bushes and deciduous oak woods to come to spectacular views of high peaks in the Sierra de Gredos. The next part of the walk drops down to Yuste Monastery nestling in oak woods. The return follows a gently downward track through oak woods and dramatic areas of granite, cherry orchards and raspberry farms. The final part shadows the Garganta Mayor, a river that never runs dry, even during the hottest summer.

Garganta de Olla (*olla* means pot, and the village certainly sits in a pot surrounded by tree-covered mountains) is an ancient village with granite houses with wooden framework upper stories built to overhang the narrow streets. Many of the houses date from the 17th and 18th centuries. There is a good information board in English at the entrance to the village coming from Jairíz, but additional information boards around the village are only in Spanish.

Yuste is a Hieronymite Monastery (following the Rule of St. Jerome) but its claim to fame is that Charles V chose the monastery as his place of retirement. He said the area reminded him "forever of spring". The Monastery is open every day except Monday from 10.00-19.00 and in winter 10.00-16.00. Visitors can see the private rooms of Charles V and inspect the church. It does not take long, but is of interest to history lovers and some information is in English. There are toilets, a picnic area, and a machine selling bottled water.

The walk is waymarked throughout but establishing the path at the start is tricky. It is a walk surrounded by high mountains and there are opportunities to spot birds of prey – but it is the mountain

THE SIERRA DE GREDOS AND LA VERA

views that make the walk so enjoyable. There are butterflies in spring and summer. I have seen Apollo and Camberwell Beauty, but there are also many varieties I do not recognise. This walk can be enjoyed all year but parts are not shaded so an early start is essential in summer. There are water stops but take the usual summer kit. In winter the distant mountains will be snow-covered. Spring and autumn, as always, are the best times to walk.

I have used the most up-to-date road numbers I can find, but frustratingly, they vary from map to map.

Directions

Garganta de Olla is a small village and can be reached from Cuacos de Yuste on the EX-391 (CC-913). Park on the right just after the bridge that crosses the Garganta Mayor. ❶ If coming from Jaraíz de la Vera on the CV-173 (CV562) at the entrance to the historic centre of the village there is a 'no entry' sign. Turn left into Carretera de Cuacos at a sign for Yuste Monastery. Follow this road for about 300m and park on the left where the road bends right and crosses the Garganta Mayor. This area of the river has natural pools, right, and a waterfall 100m in the woods on the opposite side of the bridge from the pools. After the walk on hot days swimming here is almost obligatory. In winter, when the water is high, the falls are worth seeing.

Cross the bridge and follow the road as it bends to the right and goes up. Ignore all junctions as the road winds slightly and climbs steadily leaving the village in its valley, below and right. The mountain slopes are covered with deciduous oaks and chestnuts and, even in summer, the effect is cool and green. After 1.8km come to a statue, right, overlooking the village. It is of a woman with a crossbow and a sword. 'The Legend of La Serrana' recounts her story in the tradition of medieval Romance poetry. This super-human woman lived in a cave in the mountains and

THE WALK OF YUSTE MONASTERY

captured local men for her own purposes. She then killed them and stacked their bones in her cave.

Directly opposite the statue is a rough track with a sign for 'Mirador de la Serrana', Leave the road to go up this track. Pass an area of flowering bushes, fern and oak trees and an open space. Come to a fence made of wooden poles, left, and walk through a gap in the fence – there is no gate. The track meets the road again. At this point, on the left, is a concrete path and a sign to the right of it with a white and yellow waymark and 'Yuste 1 hour and 40 minutes' (SL)PR-CC 80. Do not take the concrete path. With the concrete path, left, and the sign, right, just to the left of the sign is the tiniest footpath imaginable. ❷ It is partly hidden by lavender bushes, cistus and broom but look for it — it is certainly there.

The path, dirt but with a few granite slabs and encroached by bushes and oak saplings, goes straight up for 10m then bends right to run parallel with the road below. After about 75m it is very insubstantial for a few steps. Take care. The path bends left just after this, moves away from the road and as it goes up it gets clearer. Keep on the path and do not take any other paths or tracks. The path enters an oak copse, winds and goes up. Through the trees there are glimpses of the village below — we have climbed steadily from the start. About 300m from the start of the path there is a white and yellow waymark on a rock to the right. From this point on there are wooden poles, rocks and trees with waymarks. There are a lot of them and I won't mention them all. The path leaves the trees and zig-zags a little to ease the climb. Pass over huge flat granite rocks but be careful because they are slippery when wet. Walk ahead, parallel with the village, below right. As the climb continues an oak copse comes into view ahead. This is a point of orientation.

Reach a series of flat granite rocks like a wide path on the right.

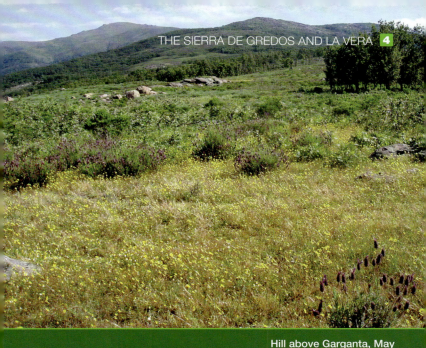

THE SIERRA DE GREDOS AND LA VERA 4

Hill above Garganta, May

Waters falls down over the granite — how much water depends on the time of year and previous rainfall. Walk towards a wooden waymark. Opposite the water is another wooden waymark. Cross over at this point. Walk towards the copse, enter and, following the waymarks, leave the copse to cross a small lane. ❸ Continue on the other side of the lane by a waymark post. Enter a deeper wood. Walk ahead on the dirt footpath and cross a boggy area using the stepping stones. The path hugs the edge of the wood. The majority of trees are left. The path comes out at the top of a succession of granite water troughs in an open area. The water exits a pipe and flows from trough to trough and there are a dozen troughs. The water is cold and drinkable. Refill those water bottles.

Leave the area with the granite troughs, behind and left, and go straight up. As the climb continues a radio mast comes into view.

THE WALK OF YUSTE MONASTERY

Make for the mast. Come out from the wood and pass an area of low growing bushes. The path goes slightly left and crosses another loop of the small lane. Continue left to negotiate granite boulders. The radio mast is about 150m to the right. The path goes up and zig-zags to the right putting the radio mast directly ahead. As the climb continues smaller masts can be seen. Pass all the masts, right, with just one electricity carrier on the left. Enter an oak copse with low growing oaks and cross the third loop of the small lane ❹ to pick up a waymark immediately opposite. The dirt path winds through oak saplings, broom, lavender and a few mature oaks. The climb is very gradual and Garganta de Olla can still be seen way below and behind. At the top of the climb the expanse is more open with granite rocks, low flowering bushes and small oak saplings. A copse of larger oaks lie on the left, as the path bears left. As we cross the highest point of the walk, the Lomo de la Atalaya, stunning mountain views emerge, left and ahead.

The path drops down and the mountain peaks lie ahead. On the right are views of Cuacos and Jairíz. At a T junction, left is a rough track and right is a concrete track. Turn right on the concrete track that descends. ❺ The verges are lush with bushes and wild flowers, in season. During the autumn the changing colour of the trees makes the view from here phenomenal. The concrete on the track ends abruptly at a cattle grid. Cross the grid and walk ahead on the track, now rough, as it enters an oak wood and winds downwards. As the track leaves the wood the view ahead, right, is of the villages of the area: from the left, Guijo de Santa Barbara, Jarandilla, Aldeanueva, Cuacos, and Jaraíz on the extreme right. These villages are all set in tree-covered slopes against the backdrop of mountain peaks — spectacular walking country. The eagle-eyed will be able to see Yuste Monastery below to the left, half hidden by trees.

At a multiple junction with two small paths going left, ignore them

Garganta Mayor waterfall, June

THE WALK OF YUSTE MONASTERY

to keep right on the main track. It becomes concrete once more within 30m and descends steeply. The track bends round to the right quite sharply and reveals three waymarks painted on the left edge of the track. ❻ These indicate to turn left, off the concrete track, and pick up a path that turns sharply left and left again in a U-turn. The path plunges into an oak wood. Waymarks are painted on tree trunks. The path winds up and down and is a bit rough in places with granite boulders to negotiate but nothing is dangerous. At a vague Y junction there is a waymark. Go left. The path comes out from the wood, but very soon enters another. To the right, below, are glimpses of a tarmac road. Pick up a well-made dry stone wall on the right. The path shadows this wall and continues ahead almost straight and drops down to arrive at Yuste.

After exploring, leave with the monastery behind and on the left. Walk down the tarmac road — do not take the concrete track to the right. In the wall, on the left, is a doorway with a metal grille through which can be seen the monastery's garden. Follow the road as it winds down past a wood on the right and the monastery walls, left. Set within the wall, left, is the huge coat-of-arms of Charles V. The road comes to an ancient stone cross, Cruz de Humilladero, right. ❼ Look at the cross. Over on the right is a wall. To the left of the wall is a footpath. This is our path. (Just before we take this path, continue on the road for a further 50m. On the left is the German Cemetery. This peaceful olive grove is the resting place of German servicemen whose ships were sunk in Spanish waters or whose planes came down in Spanish territory during the two world wars. Retrace steps to the path by the cross.)

Within a few metres there is a Y junction with an electricity carrier and a waymark, white, red and yellow. The waymark is on the right. Take the path, right, and enter a wooded area. Keep the wall on the right as a guide as the path follows the wall, sometimes closely, sometimes further away, but always visible. To the other

THE SIERRA DE GREDOS AND LA VERA 4

side of the wall is an extensive wood. The path goes through flowering bushes, flowers, trees and quite lush vegetation. Follow the waymarks on tree trunks. Come out from the trees rather abruptly into an area where new trees have been planted before plunging back into the woods. Below and right are glimpses of the raspberry tunnels which make this area famous. Cross over and pick up the path slightly left. It goes through another oak wood. The raspberry tunnels are ahead, right. After about 300m in the wood come out to a T junction. Go right. The track sweeps left and down. **8**

The track descends and zig-zags and passes over a small stream. Once over the bridge the track winds and goes up and the trees fall behind. Pass the raspberry tunnels, left, and continue upwards. There are fincas of olive and fig dotted around so ignore turnings left and right that access them. Enter an oak copse. Ignore junctions and turnings. Reach a T junction with a waymark on a rock on the left. Go right and down. **9** The track winds, crosses a stream bed and goes up slightly. Pass an agricultural building, right, and enter another oak copse. To the left is a panoramic view of tree-covered hills and some of the villages we saw from higher up. Pass an open area of flat granite rocks with low flowering bushes. At an inverted Y junction go right and slightly up. Pass enormous flat granite rocks — it is as if the earth has become granite and is quite distinctive. At a Y junction turn left and down. **10** The track is wide and a bit rough and as it winds down it passes cherry orchards, right. As it bends right, and just before it enters a copse, the tops of the village houses come into view. At another Y junction keep straight on — the left turning has a white and red cross painted on it. **11**

On the left, within a wood, the Garganta Mayor runs alongside the track. At times the water is very close and there are places to enter the wood and go up to the water. Pass a stream running across the track from the right where there is a water channel. Many

THE WALK OF YUSTE MONASTERY

cherry trees overhang the path. It has been known for walkers to sample the delicious sun-warmed juicy cherries in June. Pass weekend houses and just after an impressive house, left, turn left to cross the river by an 18th century bridge, ⑫ the Puente de Cuacos, with a granite cross and inscription, right. The inscription is indistinct and its meaning seems to be lost today.

Once over the bridge, there is an information board (Spanish only) to the left. Turn right to go straight up the hill. The left turning also goes to the village centre but our way is more picturesque. Turn left into Calle San Lucas and walk ahead, ignoring junctions, to get the corner of the 16th century Church of San Lorenzo. Turn left to go behind the church. At the T junction with Calle Portal turn right to stand in front of the church. If it is open, look inside. On leaving the church, with it on the right, go straight down Calle Gradas by the ramp or the steps. Walk ahead for refreshments and to explore the village.

To return to the car from the square walk up Calle Gradas and take the first left into Calle Llana. Ignore all junctions and walk straight ahead. At a Y junction go left down Calle Piornala towards an open area at the end of the village. Turn right, then left up a concrete track to join the Carretera de Cuacos, Turn right. The car is 500m ahead. If it is summer, change into swimming kit and cool off in the Garganta Mayor.

GPS Points
The Walk of Yuste Monastery

1. N40° 07' 03.07" W05° 46' 40.35"
2. N40° 06' 41.40" W05° 46' 12.02"
3. N40° 06' 31.37" W05° 45' 54.84"
4. N40° 06' 20.61" W05° 45' 43.34"
5. N40° 06' 15.69" W05° 45' 26.83"
6. N40° 06' 44.30" W05° 44' 41.82"
7. N40° 06' 39.08" W05° 44' 03.34"
8. N40° 06' 05.50" W05° 44' 22.23"
9. N40° 05' 44.64" W05° 45' 02.92"
10. N40° 05' 35.43" W05° 45' 26.12"
11. N40° 05' 42.92" W05° 45' 59.57"
12. N40° 06' 39.81" W05° 46' 26.81"

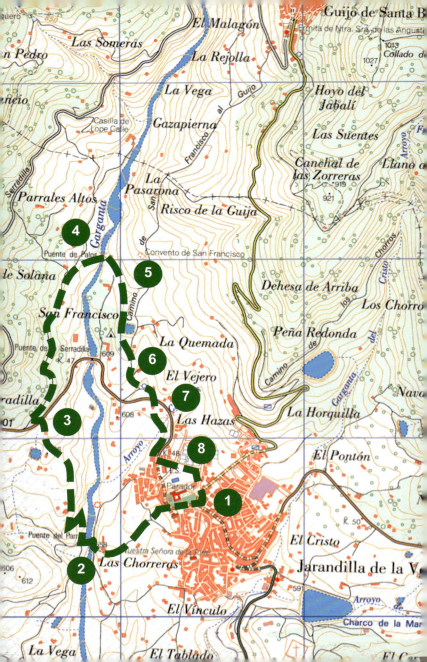

THE SIERRA DE GREDOS AND LA VERA 4

2 The Walk of the Mountain View

Start: Parador car park, Jarandilla

Finish: Parador car park, Jarandilla

1.5 hours

5 km

Low: 560m
High: 665m

Easy

Jarandilla de la Vera → Jarandilla de la Vera
Map: IGN 599-II Jarandilla de la Vera 1:25.000

Puente del Parrel, Jarandilla, December

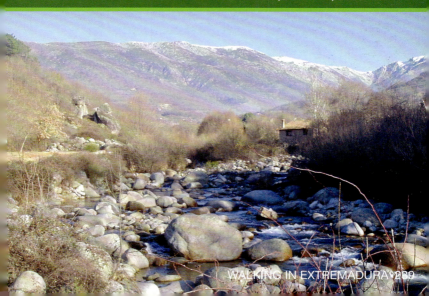

THE WALK OF THE MOUNTAIN VIEW

Introduction

Everyone can do this lovely little walk but there is one medium climb of 1km from the first bridge. It crosses the Garganta de Jaranda twice; once by the *Puente del Parral* (Bridge of Untended Vines) and once by the *Puente de Palos* (Bridge of Sticks). It goes gently uphill, through pine and deciduous oak woods to give lovely views of the mountain village of Guijo de Santa Barbara with high peaks of the Sierra de Gredos behind. The walk back to the town is through more oak woods. It is perfect all year around and can even be walked in the height of summer, early or late. In winter the mountain behind Guijo usually has snow and, I think, looks very pretty.

The EX-203 appears as the C-501 on the map, IGN 599-II Jarandilla de la Vera 1:25.000.

Directions

Start from the Parador car park in Jarandilla. ❶ With your back to the car park, turn right and walk all the way around the wall, through the pretty little park where the tourist office hut is located, keeping right. On the left is the main road, the EX-203, and over the road is a pink sign, Ruta el Emperador. This refers to the 12km walk to Aldeanueva, Cuacos and Yuste Monastery. It commemorates the journey Carlos V made from the parador, then a castle, to his retirement at Yuste. If you want to do that walk another day, just follow the pink signs. (Today, this walk follows the signs until the first bridge.) Cross the road at the crossing, then turn right. Just ahead, left, is the Church of Santa María de la Torre. As the pavement ends, turn left into Plaza Soledad to pass the church keeping it on the right and go straight down Cuesta de los Carros with houses on both sides. At the T junction, turn right. The lane becomes a smaller track and cobbled. It goes down steeply. Take care in the wet — the cobbles can be slippery. At the bottom of the track take the first right to cross over the bridge. ❷

THE SIERRA DE GREDOS AND LA VERA 4

The Garganta de Jaranda never runs dry but how much water is in it depends on the time of year. In summer, this area is popular for swimming and there is a restaurant on the left.

Once over the bridge, pass the leisure area on the riverbank, right, and take the concrete lane, right. It goes sharply up almost at once and bends left then right. On a rock, left, is a white and green waymark, the first of regular waymarks along the walk. The lane is lined by trees but there are good views of Jarandilla, right. The concrete lane gives way to compacted earth and the oak trees become thicker. As the lane winds higher Jarandilla falls back. Ahead are high mountains. Come to a white and green banded waymark post, right. Our compacted earth lane joins a tarmac lane from behind and left. There is another junction as well. On the right is a white and green cross. Do not go right. Ahead is a waymark. Go ahead. Within 100m the lane comes to a main road. ❸ There is a signpost, SL-CC 56 Jarandilla 30mins and Puente del Parrel 10 minutes (back) but we go forward and cross the road. Straight ahead is a gap in the woods and a signpost. Walk on the footpath through the woods.

Within 10m the path joins a larger track at a vague T junction. Turn right. Walk through deep oak woods. The track is wide, smooth and goes in and out of trees. Walking is easy which allows for looking at the mountain view as Guijo de Santa Barbara becomes visible ahead. Pass a tumbledown agricultural building, right and a waymark, left. Come to a Y junction but ignore the left turning. The track starts to descend towards an area with a few picturesque disused buildings, right. There is a waymark and signpost on the left. Turn right down a small dirt path between the buildings. ❹ It is lined with dry stone walls, has boulders in the path and is rough but within metres it comes to the second bridge of the walk. It is made of a huge granite pillar with wooden boards and wooden poles for hand rails. There is an information board to the left, only in Spanish, and a white and yellow waymark.

THE WALK OF THE MOUNTAIN VIEW

The crystal clear water lies in pools between giant boulders and, in summer, this is another popular swimming area. Cross over the bridge and turn right. All around are granite boulders and flowering bushes and wild flowers, in season. The path is not immediately obvious. Keep the river below on the right and pick the way closest to the river. In 50m there is a white and yellow waymark on a boulder, left, and the path becomes a little clearer. Stay on the rough, boulder-strewn path until it bears left at a white and yellow and a white and green waymark on a boulder, left. The path quickly comes to a fence on a low dry stone wall across the path but a waymark indicates left. Turn left on to a clear footpath. ❺ Keep the wall and fence on the right. On the left are wonderful mountain views. The path leaves the river and enters into successive copses of deciduous oaks. The fence drops back, the path becomes wider and the trees get thicker. Sunlight filters through the trees and flowers grow abundantly in the wood — even in July there is something to see.

As the path comes out from the trees there are olive groves and a few cherry trees. Come to a concrete path at a Y junction. ❻ Ignore left and up, and go down and right. On a telegraph carrier, right, there are three sets of waymarks, White and yellow, white and green and white and red. (The white and red waymarks go to Guijo de Santa Barbara along the old Camino de San Fransisco al Guijo, 7km there and back.) Ahead are the twin towers of the parador. Come to a T junction with another signpost. Take the left turning. This comes to the EX-203. ❼ Cross over and walk ahead on a lane that bends right. At the T junction turn left. At the open space, ❽ turn left to come to the EX-203 once more. Turn right and walk for 300m. Turn left to walk through the park and come back to the parador car park on the right.

THE SIERRA DE GREDOS AND LA VERA 4

GPS Points
The Walk of the Mountain View

1. N40° 07' 45.33" W05° 39" 39.07"
2. N40° 07' 35.58" W05° 40' 02.03"
3. N40° 07' 57.85" W05° 40' 14.07"
4. N40° 08" 28.39" W05° 40' 06.42"
5. N40° 08' 25.24" W05° 40' 01.09"
6. N40° 08' 06.45" W05° 39' 55.12"
7. N40° 08' 02.49" W05° 39' 49.92"
8. N40° 07' 55.86" W05° 39' 48.57"

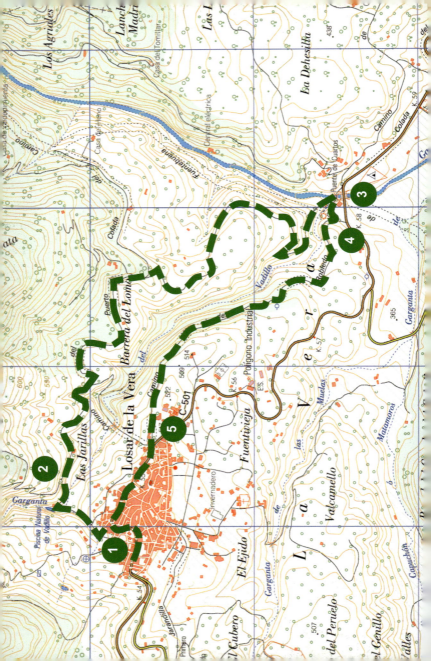

THE SIERRA DE GREDOS AND LA VERA 4

3 The Walk of the Four Rivers

Start: Plaza Viñuela, Losar de la Vera

Finish: Plaza Viñuela, Losar de la Vera

2.5 hours

7.5 km

Low: 360m
High: 550m

Mostly Easy

Losar de la Vera → Losar de la Vera
Map: IGN 599-II Jarandilla de la Vera 1:25.000

Walking above Losar de la Vera, July

THE WALK OF THE FOUR RIVERS

Introduction

This walk never strays from a small concrete lane that runs from Losar, through successive copses of Pyrenean oaks and pines, down to Puente Cuartos, a 19th century bridge. At that point it crosses the Garganta de Cuartos and its meeting with three smaller rivers; the Vadillo, the Valle and the Matamoros. As they combine they flow into the River Tiétar which in turn meets the River Tajo in Monfragüe National Park. The return is just as lovely, passing through a long stretch of pine woods. Along the way are views of the spectacular mountains of the Sierra de Gredos, with some peaks attaining over 2,270m. The verges of the lane are flower-filled in spring as are the meadows on the lower slopes of the sierra. The trees shelter many birds and hawks circle overhead, looking for food. I saw two booted eagles last May and nearly collided with a tree in my excitement of looking up and walking at the same time. The meeting point of the rivers is an area of many granite boulders eroded smooth over thousands of years. It is a lovely area especially during autumn, winter and spring. In summer it can be busy as it is a popular swimming area with restaurants and cafés, only one of which stays open all year.

The best times to walk are spring, for the flowers, and autumn, for the colours of the deciduous oak woods. However this walk can be enjoyed in summer, even in August, by walking early. The trees shade the lane before the sun gets high and the swimming is wonderful. I know this from experience. In winter the mountains in the distance are usually snow-covered and the rivers are higher and more dramatic. Walking with an extra jumper on is no problem. It is a good walk year-round.

Directions

If coming in to Losar on the minor road from the junction on the Navalmoral de la Mata to Jarandilla road, the EX-119, or coming directly from Jarandilla on the EX-203, both roads become the

THE SIERRA DE GREDOS AND LA VERA **4**

Avenida de Carlos V where there should be room to park. Walk ahead and as the road bends left come to Plaza de Viñuela with a small park and fountain on the right. Pass the tourist office hut, Town Hall, Police Station and an information board about routes in the area, all on the left. **❶** Keep on the road as it bends right. At a multiple junction with Calle Cervantes turn first left down Calle la Piscina. At the end of this road come to some trees. Walk ahead and come to a signpost; Refugio del Berezo 2 hours 58 minutes, Piscina 6 minutes, with white and yellow waymarks. Turn right on to a lane that drops down steeply through an area of trees. Cross a small bridge over a fast-flowing river to come to the area of the natural swimming pool and, in summer, there is an open-air café.

Continue the walk uphill with a U turn to the right. The lane is steep with views of Losar on the right. Come to a crossroads with signposts. **❷** Left is the Camino la Sierra and the way to the refugio. (There is also a walk which loops around the valley you can see ahead and follows the line of a river; it is a good, medium-rated walk of 8km). Also left is small lane going up. Ahead is Camino el Lomo. Walk ahead on Camino el Lomo. Continue on this lane, ignoring all junctions, as it winds its way gently down to the meeting of the four rivers. On the left are views of the high sierras and mountain peaks of the Sierra de Gredos. Right are views of Losar and, later, farming country. The lane wanders in and out of deciduous oak copses and passes the occasional weekend house with olive, fig or vine fincas.

As the walk progresses the small village of Robledillo de la Vera comes in to view ahead. Don't forget to look behind for views as well. In the middle of two weekend houses is a dirt track going right with a signpost; GR-111 with a white and red waymark. This is not our track. Keep on the lane and continue ahead. Left is a white, red and green waymark but they are positioned on the right of the concrete pillar so ignore the turning, left, and keep ahead. The lane starts to wind down more sharply with a large oak wood

THE WALK OF THE FOUR RIVERS

stretching down the side of the valley, left, as it plunges down to the river below. At a Y junction there is a signpost, left, for the GR-111 but we go right and keep on the lane. Ahead, left, the modern bridge which carries the EX-203 by the old one can be seen. The lane zig-zags and after a bend, left, a café is ahead. Pass the café with it on the right, turn right and come to a metal bridge over the Vadillo. Cross it to explore the old bridge. On the EX-203 is an information board about the four rivers (the Vadillo is marked Vahillo) and the bridge. ❸

On leaving the area walk to the metal bridge. With the EX-203 ahead and the metal bridge behind look directly ahead to the wall. There is a signpost, Puente de Cuartos, left, and SL-CC 57 Losar 55 minutes, right. Turn right on a concrete lane to walk uphill past a residential centre for school children who come to learn about Nature, right. Reach a crossroads. Turn right. ❹ There is a white and green waymark on a road sign 10m away, right. The lane goes up and winds in and out of copses of oaks. Pass a picnic area on the left with granite benches and a table made out of a millstone. There is a fountain but the water is not treated. Enter into an area of huge pine trees, chestnuts and oaks stretching down to the deep river valley, right. In between the trees are glimpses of mountain peaks. The trees fall back and the views become open towards the mountains, right, while on the left is a profusion of Spanish heath and granite boulders on a much lower hillside.

The lane comes to the outskirts of Losar. ❺ Return to the square by keeping on the lane as it becomes the Avenida de Extremadura and passes many small gardens and parks with topiary features. Losar is famed for its gardens. Pass an impressive fountain, left, with coats-of-arms carved in stone, but the water has not been cleared for drinking. Avenida de Extremadura becomes Calle de Cervantes. As the road bends left. Come back to the turning for the swimming pool down Calle la Piscina, but follow the road, left, to come back to the square and time to explore Losar.

THE SIERRA DE GREDOS AND LA VERA **4**

GPS Points
The Walk of the Four Rivers

1. N40° 07' 19.71" W05° 36' 25.58"
2. N40° 07' 32.87" W05° 36' 11.98"
3. N40° 06' 38.94" W05° 34' 55.60"
4. N40° 06' 40.59" W05° 35' 00.84"
5. N40° 07' 15.32" W05° 35' 54.96"

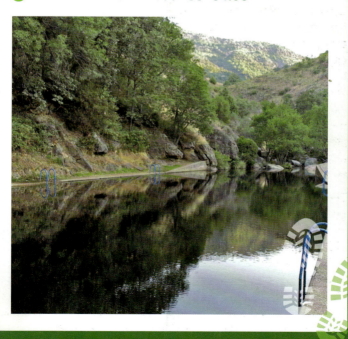

River Tajo, Monfragüe, June

Monfragüe National Park

1	A Walk into Monfragüe	256
2	The Walk of the Mediterranean Oasis	262
3	The Route of the English	268

INTRODUCTION

Monfragüe National Park

Monfragüe is very often referred to as the 'Heart of Extremadura' and it is easy to see why. It is small: a strip of 7km by 30km where the River Tiétar meets the mighty River Tajo, the longest river on the Iberian Peninsular. The Tajo is known outside Spain by its Roman name, Tagus. Monfragüe is 18,000 hectares, an area of dense Mediterranean forest, mainly oak, but also copses of alder and terebinth, surrounded by extensive dehesa: holm oak and pasture. There are thousands of cistus and lavender bushes and the park is beautiful in spring. The combination of water and forest and the absence of large population centres means that the wild life, especially birds, are undisturbed.

The park is famous for birds. It is home to more birds of prey than anywhere else in Europe. Hundreds of bird watchers visit in spring during the breeding season. Short-toed, Bonelli's, booted, Spanish Imperial and golden eagles can be seen. There are vultures: Black, Griffon and Egyptian and there are black storks and eagle owls. Even for the non-enthusiast it is impossible to go to the Salto del Gitano (Gipsy's Leap) and not see birds. Kingfishers and cormorants hunt on the water and many birds such as the azure winged magpies have their home here. There are chances of seeing fox, genet, deer, wild boar, Iberian hare and rabbit in the wooded pastures but other animals may be more timid.

There is not much trace of ancient human activity in the park but there are caves, some with paintings dating back 5,000 years. There is evidence of the Roman occupation in granite paved tracks and ancient wells. Monfragüe Castle, perched high on a commanding cliff top, is Moorish dating from the 12th century. The bridge, Puente del Cardenal, that joins the road between Trujillo and Plasencia is medieval. However, man has stepped lightly here leaving Nature well in command.

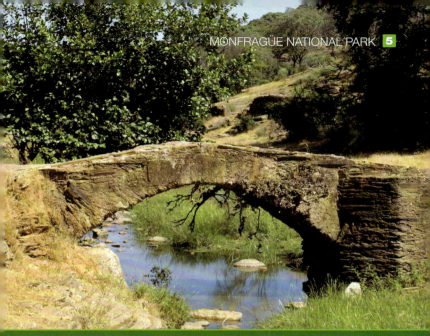

MONFRAGÜE NATIONAL PARK 5

Ancient footbridge, between Romangordo and Albalat, July

Practical Information

Once in Extremadura, getting to Monfragüe by car is easy; follow the signs from Navalmoral de la Mata, Plasencia, Cáceres or Trujillo. The park is very well signposted. It can also be reached by train from Madrid or Cáceres as the park has its own railway station but the station is isolated and you may have to arrange a taxi from nearby Malpartida de Plasencia.

Villareal de San Carlos is the only centre in Monfragüe. It was originally a village. The local inhabitants, despite considerable protests over the years, have, gradually, given way to information centres, interpretation centres, cafés, bars, restaurants and shops selling maps, books and souvenirs. It is a good place to park, gather information and start, or finish, walks. However, if you visit in the winter months, on a week day, you may find everything

INTRODUCTION

closed except for the interpretation centre and the small shop selling souvenirs. Luckily, the shop sells drinks, sandwiches and toasted rolls.

There are towns dotted around the edge of the park; Serradilla, Torrejón El Rubio, Serrejón, Romangordo, Casas de Miravete and Jaraicejo and each offers a good variety of accommodation and services. In Jaraicejo, Gertjan and Elly, an English-speaking Dutch couple offer luxury self-catering bungalows in the beautiful holm oak dehesa. Gertjan is well known as a nature/bird photographer and offers private bird guiding tours — not only in Monfragüe but other walking locations with good bird spotting opportunities. Elly speaks five languages and you can be sure of a warm welcome from them both.

Finca las Abubillas
www.extremadura-spain.co.uk

Other Walks

The area is not mountainous and the low, rocky hills are not challenging — the fitness level to walk here can be fairly low. The walk up to Monfragüe Castle is steep, with steps, but the climb is short. Most of the park is closed to walkers as the wild life must be undisturbed but the park is popular in spring and at weekends. The routes open for walking can get crowded. If you prefer the chance to walk quietly and see wildlife, walk mid-week. I walked here last July on a Monday. Not only did I see Griffon Vultures but as I sat very still by a natural spring under cover of trees a small herd of deer came up to drink. It was a magic moment.

From Villareal de San Carlos there are many waymarked walks — almost over waymarked — that allow for a good walking experience. There are routes to the best bird spotting locations, to the castle, to various viewpoints, to bridges, to dams and to villages. Most are low rated and circular or out-and-back. Some guide books are confusing and list out-and-back distances as only one way (4km when it should be 8km) and sometimes they list just one way (and it is one way). There is no consistency and the more you cross-reference the more confusing it gets. Check the length of any route you want to walk with the interpretation centre before you set out.

Romangordo is a pretty village that offers good walks with maps, route descriptions and waymarks. Plot the route on map IGN 652 Jaraicejo 1:50.000 before you start because not all signposts point in the right direction and waymarks have a habit of stopping just when they would be most useful. Never-the-less, wherever you end up, you can always just turn around. An out-and-back walk can be just as rewarding as the circular route.

In 2009 the GR113 was established as the *Camino Natural del Tajo* (the Nature Way of the Tajo) running along the entire 1,095km of the river. There are red signposts in Monfragüe and white and red waymarks to indicate the route and its stages. I have walked stages around the historical bridge of Albalat, 1537, near Romangordo, which incorporates the Cañada Real del Puerto de Miravete, but not the entire route through Monfragüe ... yet. The signposts are excellent with GR 113 and the stage number clearly marked, plus the places the stage connects and the distance. An outstanding example of how route signage should work.

Maps

Map: IGN 623 Malpartida de Plasencia 1:50.000

Map: IGN 651 Serradilla 1:50.000

Map: IGN 652 Jaraicejo 1:50.000

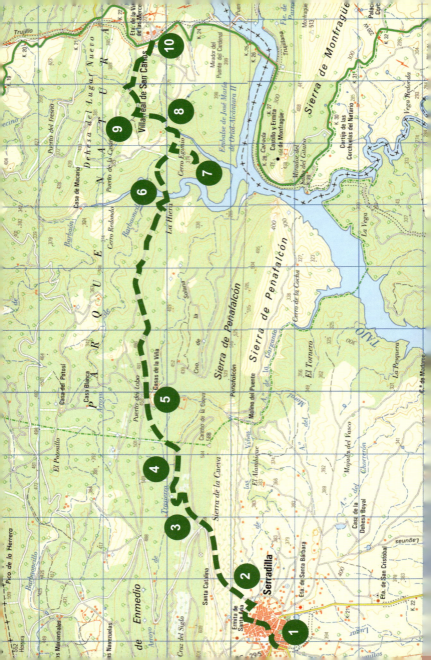

MONFRAGÜE NATIONAL PARK 5

1 A Walk into Monfragüe

Start: Serradilla

Finish: Villareal de San Carlos

4 hours

14 km

Low: 240m
High: 560m

Easy

Serradilla → Villareal de San Carlos

Maps: IGN 623 Malpartida de Plasencia 1:50.000
IGN 651 Serradilla 1:50.000

Entering the pine woods, February

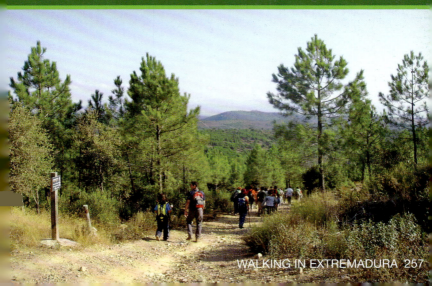

WALKING IN EXTREMADURA 257

A WALK INTO MONFRAGÜE

Introduction

There is nothing quite like going somewhere for the first time and arriving on foot. It gives a completely different perspective to the experience of discovering a new place. This easy walk starts in Serradilla, with gentle ups-and-downs, through varied scenery, into the heart of Monfragüe. The route, on tracks and footpaths, winds through extensive forests, but it is well signposted and waymarked. The trees are mainly pine but there are also cork and holm oaks and mixed deciduous trees. There are many low growing flowering bushes: lavender, cistus, broom and retama and, along the small streams there are opportunities to spot flowers, dragonflies and butterflies, in season. At all times along this walk there are excellent chances to see birds of prey overhead. Take binoculars.

Spring is probably the best time to experience the full beauty of Monfragüe with the rivers high after the winter rain, the trees in full leaf, the cistus white with flowers and the birds busy feeding their young. During the summer, early or late in the day, are best times to walk. The autumn and winter are quieter but the deciduous trees can turn the hillsides very pretty with colour before the leaves fall.

The walk is linear. If there is no spare driver willing to meet walkers at the other end (and pass the time waiting by doing a small walk from Villareal), it might be best to arrange a taxi while in Serradilla to meet you.

Directions

Start the walk from the village of Serradilla to the west of Monfragüe. Coming in from the signs on the N-630, the Carretera de Serradilla becomes the Calle de los Cuatro Lobos at the western edge of the village. Park near the Guardia Civil building. This is also where the village bus stop is located. ❶ Cross the Paseo de Extremadura, turn right, then take the first left to walk

MONFRAGÜE NATIONAL PARK 5

through the village to the pretty square with the Town Hall, on the left. Leave the square by the lane diagonally opposite. Walk on to the large church, left. The Church of the Assumption is famous for its Baroque altarpiece crafted in 1749. If you want to see it and the church is not open, ask for the key at the Town Hall. Coming out from the church, turn left, at the T junction is a sign for the *fuente* (fountain), turn left and at the Y junction go right to come to the fountain.

Take the wide track on the left of the fountain and start up the hill. ❷ Keep to the track. At first it goes up quite sharply but then bends to the right and levels off to gently ascend the side of the hill. The track is stony but still wide and has pine trees and flowering bushes, especially cistus, to the left. Look right for a view of the village and the dehesa covered plains stretching into the distance. As the track climbs higher it gets narrower to become a path and the stones give way to slate paving. After about 20 minutes the path comes to the top of the climb, makes a sharp U-turn left, and reaches a road. From this point on the route is signposted and waymarked. The signpost reads *Itinerario Marrón* (brown route) and if anyone fails to understand that the words are underlined in thick brown paint. Do not cross the road but turn right and, ignoring an immediate track, right, walk ahead for 100m to a bend with a multi junction. ❸

On the right are two tracks. Take the second one. It is clear, wide and descends slightly through deep pine woods. It also has a signpost, left, indicating it is the brown route. Come to a sharp bend left but no junction — it remains a single track. Reach a turning to the right. Take this turning. ❹ The track winds downwards but before too long it ascends again and comes out from the woods. As the views become more open the other side of the valley can be seen. As the track continues the old Moorish castle of Monfragüe can be seen in the distance but this view is lost as the track descends once more.

A WALK INTO MONFRAGÜE

Come to a junction of several tracks crossing a bigger lane. This area is *Puerto del Lobo* (Pass of the Wolf) ❺ Take the right hand bigger lane and ignore any junctions. This is a very pleasant stretch of wooded hillside. The lane starts to descend and narrows back to a path. The path continues to meander over the pretty hillside with flowering bushes, trees and open views. The path bends left, then right, to come to a concrete bridge with metal railings over a tributary of the River Tajo. ❻

Once over the bridge the path turns, left, on through much gentler slopes with open views and deciduous trees among the pines. It winds right to come to a meeting point of four different routes. The *Cerro* (Hill) Gimio — marked Egimio on the map for some reason — is just a short climb away. ❼ It is worth making the detour for the view. The path winding up to the top is waymarked. Once at the top there are remains of walls from a Moorish lookout tower built on foundations dating back to the Bronze Age. There is a spectacular view over the River Tajo and an excellent place to spot birds. The castle, on the opposite bank, is impressive. Descend the hill to return to the meeting point of the four different routes.

Here there are route options but our walk now leaves the brown route. Pick up the green route, which comes from Villareal de San Carlos to the hill we have just climbed. Pass through gentle low hills with soft vegetation and a variety of trees. The path winds and, at times, is a bit insubstantial with small granite rocks but this does not present much of a challenge. ❽ A small stream flowing into the Tajo appears on the right and keep it right as the path continues ahead. This is a good place for the nature lover to explore but it depends on the water level. Pass a stone bridge constructed in rural style but do not cross over it. Cross the stream further on at a second bridge. ❾ Follow the path as it winds over the last ridge to drop into Villareal de San Carlos and a welcome drink in one of the bars. ❿

GPS Points
A Walk into Monfragüe

1. N 39° 49' 38.40" W 06° 08' 38.60"
2. N 39° 49' 50.70" W 06° 08' 11.40"
3. N 39° 50' 15.40" W 06° 07' 20.60"
4. N 39° 50' 29.50" W 06° 07' 00.40"
5. N 39° 50' 47.50" W 06° 05' 51.90"
6. N 39° 50' 42.10" W 06° 03' 37.50"
7. N 39° 50' 28.50" W 06° 03' 13.30"
8. N 39° 50' 42.60" W 06° 03' 07.60"
9. N 39° 50' 58.10" W 06° 02' 41.50"
10. N 39° 50' 49.92" W 06° 01' 50.83"

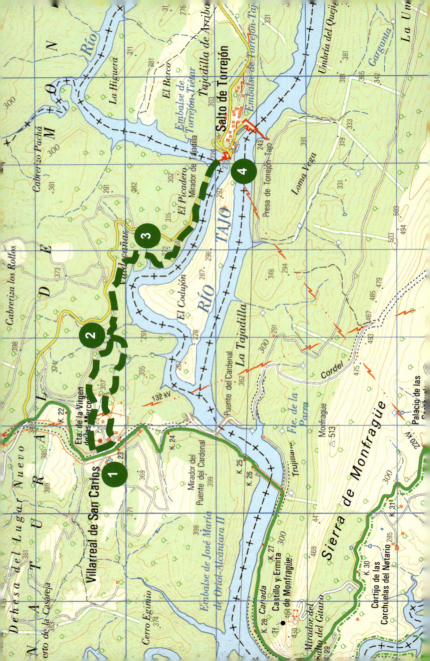

MONFRAGÜE NATIONAL PARK 5

2 The Walk of the Mediterranean Oasis

Start: Villareal de San Carlos

Finish: Villareal de San Carlos

2.5 hours

8.5 km

Low: 215m
High: 315m

Easy

Villareal de San Carlos → Villareal de San Carlos
Maps: IGN 623 Malpartida de Plasencia 1:50.000
IGN 651 Serradilla 1:50.000

Griffon vultures opposite the viewing point at Tajadilla, July

THE WALK OF THE MEDITERRANEAN OASIS

Information

This walk is one of many options from Villareal de San Carlos and is signposted as the walk of *Fuente de los Tres Caños, Mirador de la Tajadilla, Presas de Torrejón* (Fountain of Three Spouts, Viewpoint of Tajadilla, Dams of Torrejón) which is just too long a title. It is waymarked throughout with yellow bands on wooden posts. I've chosen to include this walk, rather than another, because it passes several small streams, crossed by nine wooden bridges. These areas are good for exploring nature, over and above the constant soaring birds of prey. Additionally the path passes through two distinct areas of natural springs where deciduous trees, mainly alder, have created two shady copses attracting wild life, especially during the hotter months. It is in one of these that I sat quietly last July while a deer came to drink.

Near the end of the walk out is a picnic area shaded by trees. This is another good place for wildlife. Last spring I watched as five deer munched grass under the trees. Here the Tajadilla viewpoint looks towards a high cliff on the other side of the River Tiétar where a colony of Griffon Vultures live. A few metres further on is the first of the two Torrejón dams. The one at the end of this walk creates the reservoir on the River Tiétar. The other dam creates a reservoir on the River Tajo.

The walk can be enjoyed all year but it is better while the streams still run as they do dry up during summer. There is no shade on the stretch that gives wonderful views of a horseshoe bend in the River Tiétar, so start very early or late in summer. Rest in the two shaded oasis and wait for wild life. Take binoculars.

Directions

Park in the free car park at Villareal and walk ahead to the only main road in the village. On the left is the interpretation centre where they speak English and are happy to talk about all aspects of walking in Monfragüe. Continue down the road. At the end, on the right is a handy toilet block but we turn left at the yellow *ruta* (route) sign. ❶ There is a dry stone wall on the right as we walk uphill on a compacted earth track. At the signpost for the fountain, viewpoint and dam, turn right where the wall ends and leave the track. The path is rough but winds through a pretty area of tall cistus and low hills covered in vegetation. On the left are hills covered in low flowering bushes. Right are meadows and dehesa. Pass two signposts in red for the GR 113 but follow the sign for the fountain. Continue through this pretty area as the path criss-crosses a stream with three bridges in succession.

Start to climb out from the trees into classic dehesa. Cross another bridge and climb up a long, gentle slope that gives the first views of the River Tiétar, right, and the dam, ahead. Follow the path as it winds up and down. At a T junction, ❷ turn right and descend steeply in to the first shady copse with the Alisar fountain flowing in the shade. The area is described as a '... green Mediterranean oasis for birds on hot days ...' However, people should not drink the water.

Continue steeply upwards through tall cistus bushes as the river below bends in a horseshoe backed by slopes and hills covered in trees. Cross a bridge and enter the second shady copse. This is the fountain with three spouts but, again, it is not recommended that people drink the water. It was here I saw the deer. Just after the copse is a junction. Do not turn left but go sharply down and right to come to a signposted viewing point. Keep on the path as it continues, left, and cross another bridge. The path is now tiny but clear as it goes up and down through cistus bushes with the river below and right.

Cross the seventh bridge (who's counting?) and the path bends right to come down to a meadow area with a stream. ❸ Depending on the time of year the stream could be quite wide and

THE WALK OF THE MEDITERRANEAN OASIS

there are notices advising walkers not to stray off the path. Cross the stream by a bridge and climb up into dehesa. Ahead the dam can clearly be seen. The path gets more rocky as it gets closer to the dam. Cross the last bridge and climb up the slate steps to reach the road, the EX-389 ❹ and the Tajadilla viewing point. Spend some time looking at the area including the Griffon Vultures on the cliff top opposite and birds attracted to the reservoir. Watch for other wildlife.

Retrace the path to the junction after the Alisar fountain. (❷, again) Here there is an option to return to Villareal by a north route. I think the south route is much prettier, which is left at the junction to retrace the out-bound route. To return by the north route, go straight ahead on a wide track that goes up and down through dehesa. The track has no shade but passes through two steep verges which reduce as the track climbs upward to give open views across the dehesa. Reach a small road. Cross over and drop down to the car park at Villareal.

MONFRAGÜE NATIONAL PARK 5

GPS Points
The Walk of the Mediterranean Oasis

1. N39° 50' 53.10" W06° 01' 52.70"
2. N39° 50' 50.40" W06° 00' 54.90"
3. N39° 50' 38.34" W06° 00' 14.08"
4. N39° 50' 19.62" W05° 59' 45.35"

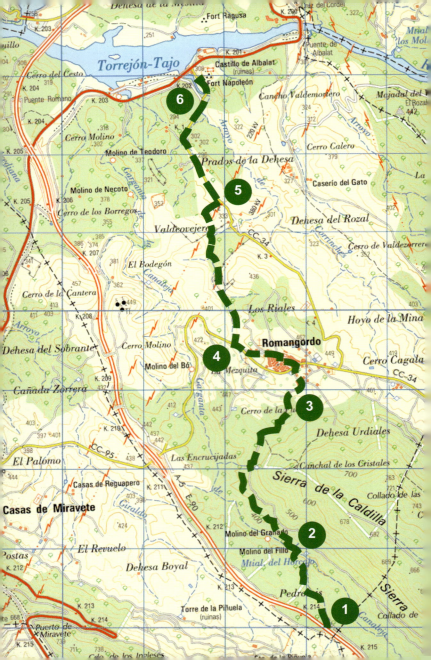

MONFRAGÜE NATIONAL PARK 5

3 The Route of the English

Start: A5 underpass junc. 210 on E-90/A5

Finish: Fort Napoleon, Romangordo

4 hours

10.3 km

Low: 255m
High: 472m

Easy

A5 underpass → Romangordo → Fort Napoleon

Maps: IGN 652 Jaraicejo 1:50.000 or
IGN 652-I Serrejón 1:25.000
IGN 652-III Jaraicejo 1:25.000

Cross of Retamar, Romangordo, July

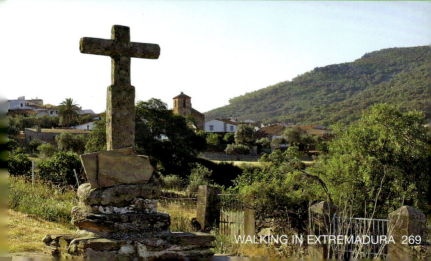

WALKING IN EXTREMADURA 269

THE ROUTE OF THE ENGLISH

Information

This historic walk follows the route taken by English soldiers before the Battle of Romangordo in 1812 during the Peninsular War. It has two distinct parts. The first is through a very pretty wooded valley with the Canaleja stream running along the bottom, to Romangordo. It is 5.30km long. The second part, at a distance of 5km, is from Romangordo, near meadows where the Corrinches stream flows, to Fort Napoleon, commanding a view over the River Tajo. The whole route is well waymarked with illustrated boards with quotes from people involved in the battle – in Spanish. There are many opportunities to see birds including eagles and hawks and, in spring there are many wild flowers especially along the banks of the two streams. In May the cistus bushes are heavy with white flowers and their sweet scent fills the valley air.

A brief explanation is needed as to why this walk is known as the Route of the English. During the Peninsula War, or the Spanish War of Independence as it is known in Spain, Extremadura saw a great many manoeuvres, skirmishes, tactical retreats and decisive battles. The war lasted from 1808-1812 and had the Spanish, Portuguese and British on one side and the French on the other. To cut a long historical story short, Napoleon, for complicated reasons, wanted to invade Portugal but had also been asked to arbitrate between two Spanish kings. Carlos IV, originally abdicated in favour of his son, the disastrous Fernando VII, but changed his mind. He wanted his throne back but Fernando did not want to revert to being king-in-waiting. Napoleon took them both into custody and set his own brother, Joseph, on the Spanish throne. A bad native ruler is always preferred to an efficient foreigner and the Spanish rebelled.

This route follows that taken by the Duke of Wellington's forces on the 19th May when the decisive Battle of Romangordo was fought. The French had entrenched themselves in the area since

MONFRAGÜE NATIONAL PARK 5

Romangordo, May

THE ROUTE OF THE ENGLISH

1809 and had built two forts, Napoleon and Ragusa, on either side of the River Tajo to protect a pontoon bridge and keep supply lines open. Wellington wanted the French dislodged, the forts destroyed and the bridge captured. He came to the village of Casas de Miravete to put the final touches to his plans, ate a dish of onions cooked the local way and promptly fell ill with Spanish tummy. That did not stop him ordering General Rowland Hill into the field with 3,500 troops. It was a brilliant and audacious operation — to move the troops in and out of a valley in order to surprise the French. Victory was complete. The Battle of Romangordo led to the Battle of Salamanca and the liberation of Madrid. If you want more information Sir W.F.P. Napier's account is excellent but there is simply no room here for a longer history: www.romangordo.info/historia/napier/surprise.htm

The Route of the English is traditionally walked on the Saturday closest to 19th May accompanied with weapons, re-enactments and pyrotechnics at the fort. On that day an additional 6.40km is walked through a pine forest, up and over the Sierra del Frontal. The rest of the year the gates at either end of this forest are locked — it is private property.

There is an interpretation centre for the walk in Romangordo. It is open Friday, Saturday and Sunday, 10.00-13.00 and 17.00-20.00 and has an exhibition in Spanish and English. Phone: 0034 626613841. There are various options for enjoying this walk, dependent on the flexibility of your transport and how much of the route you want to walk. A taxi can be organised from Julio Camacho Sanchez, Plaza de Constitución, 7, 10350 Almarez. Phone: 0034 927 544291. I have spoken with him and, although he doesn't speak English he regularly transports walkers to the start, or picks them up at the finish. The centre will give you help to book his services if you need it.

Directions

MONFRAGÜE NATIONAL PARK 5

To reach the start, leave the E-90/A5 at junction 210 signposted for Casas de Miravete, Romangordo and Higuera. If coming from the north, turn right on to the sliproad to get off the motorway, turn right at the junction (with the motorway overhead, left,) then turn first left down a compacted earth lane. If coming from the south, turn right on to the sliproad to get off the motorway, turn left at the junction to go under the motorway, then do not turn first left (that is the sliproad back to the motorway) turn second left on to a dirt lane. Follow this lane for 3km as it passes under the motorway once, then twice. After the second time the lane comes to a multiple junction. Ignore both turnings right and carry straight ahead. The lane passes under the motorway for the third time. Park off-lane — there is plenty of space around — but be aware that the area is isolated. Do not worry about the proximity of the A5, it will not disturb your enjoyment of the walk.

With the underpass behind you, look left. There is a woodland path. Turn left on to this path. ❶ On the right is an information board with a map. Follow the little footpath through the eucalyptus wood; it goes up and down and winds around but the main direction is forward. There are two points of orientation: a sierra high on the right and a small stream in the valley also on the right. The path shadows both of these. In addition the route is waymarked with clever little rounded rectangles of wood, painted red, that hang off trees and bushes at eye-level — very environmentally friendly and less of an eyesore than splashes of paint on rocks. The wood is intensely pretty with many flowering bushes especially cistus and lavender. The path passes occasional open areas on the right where it is easy to get near to the stream to look more closely for water-loving plant and wild life. Just after the second of these open areas it is possible to miss the path. At an indistinct Y junction the path goes up and to the left. Look for the two red waymarks in quick succession. As the path climbs up, quite steeply, it leaves the stream completely quite a long way

THE ROUTE OF THE ENGLISH

down in the valley. The path continues to shadow the sierra on the right. Pass an information board about Sir John Thomas Jones on the right and continue upwards.

After a small clearing the path drops down again. Pass an area with a lots of pale lacy lichens on fallen branches and twigs — they may not be flowers but are very pretty. On the right there are good views of the sierra clad in holm oaks and eucalyptus. On the left the trees are thinning slightly but the flowering bushes continue. The path drops down sharply in a series of zig-zags but watch for exposed tree roots that can trip you up. The stream is below, right, and the path comes to a wooden bridge to cross the stream.
❷ There is another information board on the right concerning a message from General Hill to Wellington.

The path bends left and goes up in zig-zags. It is a little insubstantial in places and there are exposed tree roots but follow the red waymarks and take it easy. The path widens to become a track — it is at least 2m wide — and there are eucalyptus trees on both sides. The track winds its way gently upwards. On the left, across the motorway, are views of the village of Casas de Miravete beyond a deep valley covered in mixed deciduous and evergreen trees and cistus bushes. Turn right, then left at the Y junction but the track is still going up. Pass another information board on the right with quotes from Sir William F.P. Napier. Another track comes from the right to join our track. Continue ahead. The eucalyptus trees are behind and the dominant tree is now holm oak.

Pass a lovely cork oak wood on both sides of the track. The going is flat and the view, between the oaks, on the left continues. Pass a small white building on the right. To the left of the building is a tap with running water. It is safe to drink. The track is wide enough to be a lane. Ignore all turnings and junctions but keep on the lane as Romangordo comes in to view ahead and on the left. The lane, flanked by tumbling honeysuckle, drops down to wind its way into

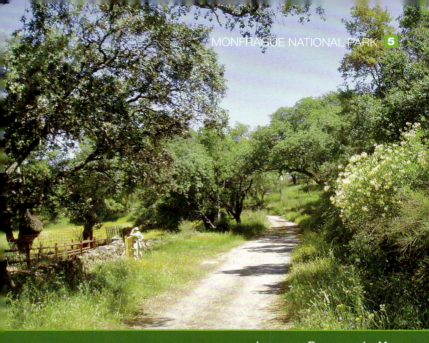

Lane near Romangordo, May

the village. The view of Romangordo is very romantic with olive trees in flower-filled meadows in the foreground and the pretty little red-roofed houses and huge church beyond. It sits in Monfragüe National Park and is deeply rural with many birds. Come to a wide crossroads. ❸ Turn right. At a second crossroads, turn left. Pass benches and running water with a granite pool on the left, then more benches on the right. Walk straight ahead to enter the village proper. At a wide crossroads, walk straight on, slightly uphill, to reach to the main road. Go straight over the main road to walk straight on. Ignore two turnings right and one left to go next left. At the Y junction, turn right. At the next Y junction with Calle Hornos turn right and immediately left into Travesia Llanillo and straight up, on the left, is the Plaza de España.

Romangordo is an interesting little village with a commemorative

THE ROUTE OF THE ENGLISH

plaque in the square honouring the English and Portuguese who fell in the battle. I saw it unveiled on 19th May 2012, the battle's 200th anniversary. Stop a while to explore the 15th century Church of Santa Catalina and the village or take refreshment in one of the bars before continuing the walk.

With the church behind you leave the square by the corner directly opposite. Walk all the way down the road, passing Casa de Potal on the left. There is a junction with Calle Alta on the right but ignore it. Come to an open area with a multiple junction. Turn left and down, past the interpretation centre on the left. Walk down the hill. Ignore the left turn. At the Y junction, turn left. Ahead the ancient Cruz de Retamar is visible. Pass the cross and the road drops down to join a road. Turn right in the direction of Navalmoral de la Mata and Trujillo.

Within 50m turn right on to a path at a waymark with a quote from Captain John Patterson. ❹ The path is earth and lined with flowers, vegetation and trees. Follow this path as it goes up and down and winds slightly until you come to a junction. Turn right, to reach the CC-34, a very quiet, pretty lane with flower-filled verges in spring. ❺ Turn left to walk on the lane. On either side are meadows with trees. The Corrinches stream flows through the meadows, right. Reach a point where the stream passes under the lane. Continue until the waymark below the hill up to Fort Napoleon. On the right is a gate. Go through and close it behind you. Follow the footpath up for the inconsequential ruins of the fort but a spectacular view of the River Tajo. ❻

MONFRAGÜE NATIONAL PARK 5

GPS Points
The Route of the English

1. N39° 42' 42.96" W05° 41' 44.55"
2. N39° 43' 19.73" W05° 42' 09.55"
3. N39° 44' 17.93" W05° 42' 01.68"
4. N39° 44' 38.83" W05° 42' 25.16"
5. N39° 45' 36.38" W05° 42' 28.54"
6. N39° 46' 32.91" W05° 42' 34.30"

Guadalupe, September

Las Villuercas

1	The Walk of the Hermitages	286
2	The Pilgrimage Route of Isabel the Catholic	294
3	The Hunting Route of Alfonso XI	302

INTRODUCTION

Las Villuercas

Las Villuercas is made up of multiple sierras which give the area a barren and mountainous aspect yet with a distinct beauty; grand and remote. Walkers with a medium level of fitness will find the routes here inspiring, stunning and satisfying. The area is higher and less populated than the Sierra de Montánchez but lower and more accessible than the Sierra de Gredos. Las Villuercas lies at the south-eastern edge of Cáceres province, rising to a high point at Pico Villuercas, 1,589m, which can be seen from the Hunting Route of Alfonso XI. A series of deep valleys run in parallel to the sierras. This distinct formation has led to different ecosystems with varied micro-climates. The rugged mountains are softened in places by deciduous and coniferous forests, with trees so typical of Extremadura: Pyrenean and holm oaks, Spanish chestnut and pine. The valleys are altogether different: more lush with abundant vegetation. This habitat gives Las Villuercas a prolific wildlife, including red deer, wild boar, otter, Iberian hare, rabbits and, in the most untouched and least accessible areas, the Iberian lynx.

Along with the neighbouring areas of Ibores and Jara, Las Villuercas was designated by UNESCO as a Geopark in 2009. Quite apart from the surrounding natural environment, it is an important zone for breeding birds and it is now, rightly, protected. Walking here during the spring and summer months can result in rich rewards for bird lovers. Among species to be spotted are the Booted and the Short-toed eagle, the Egyptian vulture, the black stork and the alpine swift. More common is the lesser spotted woodpecker, the coal tit and numerous song birds.

Surprisingly, both mountains and valleys are covered with flowering bushes of lavender, cistus, broom, thyme, Spanish heath and heather throughout the spring. There are countless wild flowers along the paths and river valleys for up to six months of the year. Between April and May look out, especially, for violets and a small

Guadalupe Monastery, September

variety of orchids but by early summer it is the foxgloves that are rampant. The air is crystal clear and the views are fantastic. The Sierra de Gredos, way to the north, and the Montes de Toledo in the east, are visible from the higher paths.

The reason why walkers need at least a medium level of fitness to walk here is because the uphill climbs, while not severe, are long. Stamina is needed. It helps if you have a sense of direction as well. The shorter of the three routes featured is circular and waymarked. The two longer routes are linear. Although easy to follow, the paths in the woods may become confusing as older paths become disused or new ones are created. Should you get lost for ten minutes it will not matter if you remember the general direction in which you are heading. An old-fashioned compass or a GPS is handy but using the sun as a guide is just as good. You can walk

INTRODUCTION

almost all-year round but take extra water in the summer and pace yourself on the uphill climbs. Watch the weather forecast during the autumn for possible rain or mist, both of which could make the longer routes more difficult and less enjoyable. There may be snow in the winter. A sprinkling is pretty. Heavy snow is nice to look at and photograph but, be safe — walk here another day.

Practical Information

Guadalupe, a UNESCO World Heritage Site since 1993, is the most visited place in Las Villuercas and with 2,000 inhabitants it is also the most populous. The dominant feature of the town is the impressive Hieronymite Monastery, which grew from a small 14th century building erected to house the shrine of Our Lady of Guadalupe. Tradition has it that the statue of Our Lady originated in Andalucia and when the Moors invaded in the 700s the statue was taken north, to safety. The fleeing monks only got as far as Extremadura when it became obvious they were not going fast enough. The statue was buried in a field only to be rediscovered 600 years later after a local man had a dream. Our Lady became the patron of Extremadura, Spain and Mexico. Pilgrims started arriving in 1326 and today thousands still make the journey every year. The town is always bustling and busy with a real international feel. Many pilgrims come from South America. The church is open to all but a guided tour is the only way to visit the monastery. It is conducted in rapid Spanish. My pleas for audio-guides in different languages have, so far, been resisted. If you are keen, and it is very impressive, read up about it before you take the tour.

If arriving in Guadalupe by car, from the EX-102 (Trujillo/Mérida/Toledo) or EX-118/380 (Navalmoral de la Mata/Madrid), it is worth finding the car park via the roundabout south-east of the town where all roads converge. Follow the signs for Guadalupe and the car park is on the left of the Carretera de Guadalupe as it bends to the right after the bus park also on the right. Parking in Guadalupe itself is extremely limited and the best streets are tiny. Use the car park — it's free.

I've never stayed in Guadalupe's hotels or casa rurales so cannot make any personal recommendations. There is plenty of accommodation ranging from the grand Parador to a large campsite. The Hospedería, part of the monastery, is also a hotel with surprisingly reasonable rates and they keep up the age-old tradition of giving a warm welcome to walkers. They do speak English but the web site is, so far, only in Spanish.

Hospedería del Real Monasterio, Plaza de Juan Carlos I.
www.hotelhospederiamonasterioguadalupe.com

The restaurants and cafés in the main plaza in Guadalupe are perfectly fine, and good places from which to people-watch, and no one place is either outstanding or terrible, but 'Restaurante Las Villuercas' (shut Tuesdays) in the Plaza de Santa María does do great tapas. For something a bit different walk around the monastery to the left, keep going, then walk up the huge flight of granite steps to the Hospedería. Eat in the fantastic cloister of the monastery itself for only a few euros more than eating in the plaza.

Apart from Logrosán, Cañamero and Alía, other towns are considerably smaller with less than 700 inhabitants. They are charming places to visit but are quite remote. Some of the roads in and out of the villages, especially Navezuelas, need driving skills and nerves of steel. Don't let that put you off — just take care.

Transport can be varied, patchy or non-existent but Guadalupe does have an efficient taxi service. This following incredibly long link has information on everything to do with Guadalupe including bus timetables: http://oficinadeturismoguadalupe.blogspot.com/2010/11/horario-de-monumentos.html

but, you guessed, it's in Spanish.

INTRODUCTION

Other walks

Apart from the routes in this chapter, everything else, either printed or on the internet, is, at the time of writing, in Spanish. There are other walks in the area with many different starting and finishing points but I have only described the ones I have walked so far. This is an area I am discovering more about. The tourist office in Guadalupe is the best place to find out about more walks. The tourist officer, Rocío, is friendly, charming and speaks English. More importantly she is very helpful. In particular there is a route called 'La Ruta de los Molinos' (the Route of the Mills, 20km, requiring a medium level of fitness and 5 hours) that looks good but, so far, I've not walked it. All the route instructions are in Spanish and the map is a vague line drawing. If you are going to walk it plot the route on maps IGN 707-I Berzocana 1:25.000 and IGN 707-II Guadalupe 1:25.000 before you go.

The Tourist Office, Plaza de Santa María, Guadalupe.
Phone: 0034 927 154128.

This web site relates to medieval pilgrim routes into Guadalupe. They are, naturally, linear but they are being waymarked and revived. The information on the site is currently in Spanish. However, there's a facility to download GPS points and so some sense might be made of the routes by experienced walkers.
www.itinere1337.com/

Cañamero, famous for its wines, has waymarked routes and stunning scenery. Just outside Cañamero, going towards Guadalupe, is a deep, dramatic valley carved out by the River Ruecas. The routes are centred around the river, the ruins of Anchanat Castle perched high above, and the Hermitage of Santa Ana south of the town. Ask for maps and information at the Town Hall in Cañamero.

Although the Geopark was created in 2009 the official mapping of

LAS VILLUERCAS 6

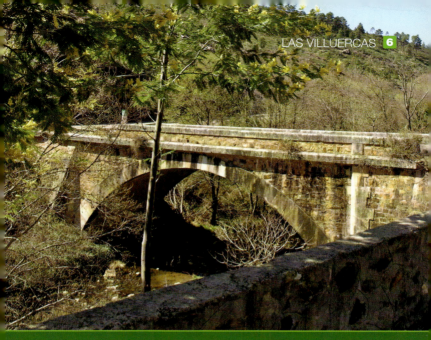

Near Cañamero, April

walks is a slow process. There is a web site with an English option but, at the time of writing, it is in its infancy.
www.geoparquevilluercas.es

Maps

The smaller maps are better for this area:

Map: IGN 707-I Berzocana 1:25.000

Map: IGN 707-II Guadalupe 1:25.000

Map: IGN 707-III Logrosán 1:25.000

Map: IGN 707-IV Collado de Martín Blasco 1:25.000 (optional)

or

Map: IGN 707 Logrosán 1:50.000

and for the tip of Navezuelas for the Hunting Route of Alfonso XI;

Map: IGN 681 Castañar de Ibor 1:50.000 (dated 1956)

LAS VILLUERCAS 6

1 The Walk of the Hermitages

Start: Guadalupe

Finish: Guadalupe

2.5 hours plus stops

10 km

Low: 558m
High: 763m

Easy to Medium

Guadalupe → Guadalupe
Maps: IGN 707-11 Guadalupe 1:25.000 or
IGN 707 Logrosán 1:50.000

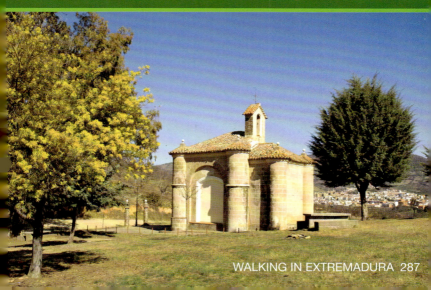
The Hermitage of San Blas, April

WALKING IN EXTREMADURA 287

THE WALK OF THE HERMITAGES

Introduction

This little walk takes in breathtaking views, diverse countryside and plenty of history with good information boards at various points along the route in both Spanish and English. In medieval times Guadalupe was a popular place of pilgrimage. It seems that all paths led to the town and the famous Marian shrine. As pilgrims drew closer to Guadalupe, they could stop to pray and give thanks for their safe journey at one of the three hermitages outside the town. The Humilladero can be seen near the end of the Hunting Route of Alfonso XI. Those of San Blas and Santa Catalina are featured in this walk.

San Blas is the patron saint of throats and his feast is celebrated on February 3rd. He was tortured with iron combs used for wool-carding and beheaded in Armenia in 316, but he's very popular in Spain. Spanish shepherds tie red ribbons around the necks of new-born lambs to keep foxes from attacking them by the throat and people with sore throats very often use red ribbons in favour of Strepsils. Santa Catalina is the patron saint of learned women and schoolgirls. I feel both hermitages have been over-restored during the last century but the essence of them, their place within the countryside, and the views of Guadalupe from their grounds still evoke a feeling of past pilgrimages.

The dominant feature of the first part of the walk is the Viaduct of Guadalupe. This structure was destined to carry a railway line. It was built in concrete and finished in 1959 but was never commissioned. Plans for its use were abandoned in 1962. The views from the top of the viaduct are impressive but if you suffer from vertigo don't look straight down — it's 58m high.

The view towards Pico Agudo, 1,093m, is on the left for most of the middle part of the walk. The pine woods are cool and shady and the walk passes through several of these woods. The sight and sound of the River Guadalupe is refreshing towards the end.

LAS VILLUERCAS 6

Views of Guadalupe itself are, of course, almost constant. The walk ends through the most historic route into the town where the information boards come thick and fast. For history lovers especially, this route is very rewarding.

The walk, although short, does have a climb of 205m — but not all at once. It can be enjoyed all year around. However, there are sections without shade and so the walk is not suitable for high summer at noon.

Directions

Start from the Plaza de Santa María in Guadalupe with the monastery and the fountain behind you. ❶ Walk straight ahead down Calle Gregorio López. At the end of the road is a signpost for Navalmoral de la Mata going left. Ignore this. Go straight ahead down a small road, Calle Ángel Marina. After a few metres it bears left. The road comes to a multiple junction but keep straight on for the Avenida Juan Pablo II. As the avenue bears left, past a children's playground, there is a good view of the viaduct the route crosses shortly. On the right there is a small compacted earth track going down rather steeply. This is our track. ❷ There is an information board to the left to make doubly sure of the way. The view to the left is of olive fincas but ahead there are tree-covered hills. The track bears right, then left and comes to a T junction within a few minutes. Ignore a tunnel, left, which goes back towards the town and go right to the viaduct. Its width is much greater than you might suppose and it's also very long. The views from both sides are worth taking some time over.

Once over the viaduct go straight ahead on the completely flat broad track. The countryside is mainly of pine trees and flowering bushes but there are still some olive fincas. The track is crossed by an ancient bridge called the Puente de Palomo and within metres after the bridge is a crossroads. Take the small, rough path going

THE WALK OF THE HERMITAGES

up on the right. ❸ A little way up the steep path is another path on the right. Ignore this. There is a white and yellow waymark on stones on the left to keep us left. As the path continues upwards it enters an area of many chestnut trees through which, on the right, are good views of Guadalupe. The path levels off, goes down and then continues upward. Ahead and on the left, at a distance of about 300m the pretty Hermitage of San Blas can already been seen. The path descends a little and comes to a T junction. Admire the view of Guadalupe and then turn left to go up to the hermitage.

Enter the grounds by the middle gateway as the other two gates are usually locked. There are views all around and the medieval pilgrims must have been quite pleased at the sight of Guadalupe, below. The hermitage itself is a lovely shape but has a strange modern cladding. After exploring, leave the grounds via the main gateway. The path we came up on continues left, but there is a small path going straight on directly opposite the main gateway. ❹ Take this path.

The rough, uneven and narrow path has walls on either side. Ahead is a view of Pico Agudo with its slopes covered in trees and bushes and an imposing granite outcrop at the summit. The path goes up slightly and enters an area of many pine and chestnut tree copses. Reach a T junction and there is a helpful arrow pointing left. Go left. As the path continues, Guadalupe appears to the right and below because the path has been climbing steadily for some time. At the Y junction turn right. Look back. What a view.

The path continues up and enters another copse of pines. At a second Y junction go right. The left path drops down into the wood and may be a good place to rest in the shade but to continue the walk use the right hand path. It gets rougher and continues upward. On the right are pines and cistus. On the left are more pines, cistus, mimosas, thyme and heather. There

LAS VILLUERCAS 6

are delightful splashes of colour all along the valley below Pico Agudo. Hidden in the bushes are bee hives — the *Miles Flores Miel* (thousand flowers honey) is sold in Guadalupe. Ignore a small path going back on itself on the right and stay on the path ahead. It continues sharply up and snakes to the right past a new house on the left. On a pine tree trunk on the right is a waymark. The view to the right is of Guadalupe with a range of high mountains in the Sierra de Guadalupe in the distance. The Hermitage of Santa Catalina can be seen ahead and to the right.

At a T junction this walk meets that of the Pilgrimage Route of Isabel the Catholic. **5** From here to Guadalupe the route is the same. Turn right and walk towards the hermitage. After 100m there is a turning, left, that goes up to the Palace of Mirabel which is now a private house. Continue on the path to the Hermitage of Santa Catalina and explore the building, grounds and views. (To the left of Guadalupe the naked eye can just about make out the Hermitage of Humilladero.) There are many chestnut trees in the area.

Leave the hermitage and turn left to continue towards Guadalupe. The path becomes a wider compacted earth lane. Behind is Pico Agudo, to the left is the Sierra de Guadalupe and ahead beyond the town as far as the eye can see there is peak after peak of the mountains of Las Villuercas and the Montes de Toledo. The lane winds downwards and is flanked by many flowering bushes and trees, mainly pine. The pines become a denser wood. In spring there are butterflies, especially the Orange Tip, attracted by the flowering bushes. The lane loops downward **6** but, at times, there are paths through the woods that cut off the loops. These are clear because the lane below can be seen before leaving the lane above.

As the lane drops the woods thin. Just after a green radio mast on the left is a small turning, also left, where there is a wooden picket fence and a metal gate. Go there for an excellent view of Guadalupe unimpeded by trees. Return to the lane as it goes

THE WALK OF THE HERMITAGES

down and bends left. To the right the scene is peaceful and rural, dominated by the last view of Pico Agudo. The lane goes down more steeply with a junction, right, but stay on the lane ahead. As the descent continues, a stream runs into a ditch on the right of the lane. At the valley bottom go straight ahead to cross Puente de Cañamero ❼ over the River Guadalupe where the stream from the ditch joins the river. This is a quiet place to watch for birds and butterflies. Once over the bridge follow the lane to the right, uphill. The lane joins the CC-712 to Guadalupe after about 200m. Turn right and walk along the verge. Ahead is the viaduct from the start of the walk. After about 20m, there is a small path on the left. ❽ Cross the road and take this path. On the right is a man-made channel carrying water and on the left pass a (drinking) water fountain with animal drinking troughs.

The outskirts of Guadalupe are ahead. At the Y junction take the road on the right and follow it all the way up. Dead ahead is an old pilgrim cross. Turn right into Calle Tinte. At the top of the road is the Arco del Tinte, pass under and keep going up the road. At the top of the road is a Y junction. Take the left turning and ahead is the Fuente de Tres Chorros where travel-stained pilgrims washed before entering the monastery. Turn left into Calle Seville and the ancient, historic part of Guadalupe. Walk through the Arco de Seville and enter the square in front of the monastery once more.

LAS VILLUERCAS 6

GPS Points
The Walk of the Hermitages

1. N 39° 27' 07.65" W 05° 19' 38.54"
2. N 39° 26' 54.16" W 05° 19' 15.82"
3. N 39° 26' 17.70" W 05° 19' 09.83"
4. N 39° 26' 08.52" W 05° 19' 32.14"
5. N 39° 26' 12.84" W 05° 20' 30.85"
6. N 39° 26' 30.91" W 05° 20' 19.37"
7. N 39° 26' 39.51" W 05° 19' 50.01"
8. N 39° 26' 42.37" W 05° 19' 43.71"

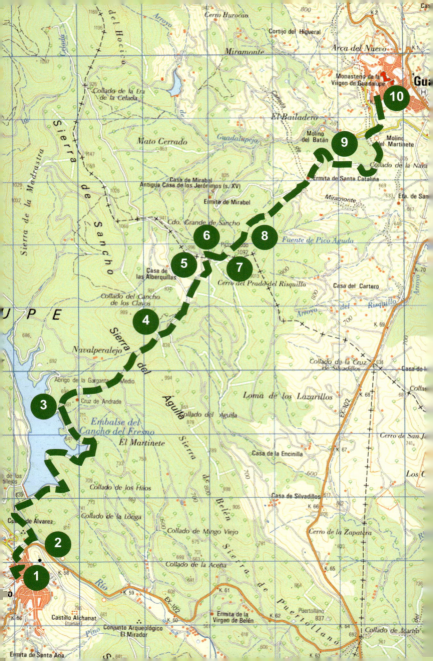

LAS VILLUERCAS 6

2. The Pilgrimage Route of Isabel the Catholic

Start: Cañamero

Finish: Guadalupe

4 hours

13.5 km

Low: 561m
High: 988m

Medium

Cañamero → Guadalupe
Map: IGN 707 Logrosán 1:50.000

In the woods, Cañamero, February

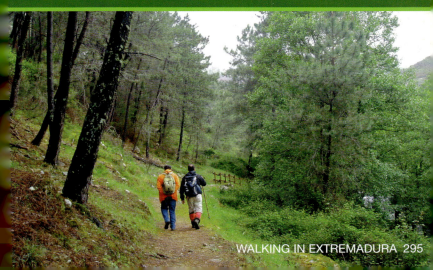

WALKING IN EXTREMADURA 295

THE PILGRIMAGE ROUTE OF ISABEL THE CATHOLIC

Introduction

A pretty route, with bird spotting opportunities and long stretches of flower-lined paths in the lower parts of Las Villuercas. This walk is named after Isabel of Castile. When she visited the monastery at Guadalupe she came this way to rest in the Palace of Mirabel, still marked on the map as the 'Casa de Mirabel, Antigua Casa de los Jeronimos s.XV'. However, I doubt she walked. The route was also used by ordinary pilgrims and they did walk. It is an enjoyable route because of the variations in the landscape and the views. It starts in the main street of Cañamero, a town large enough for a bus service to Guadalupe, and with cafés, bars and restaurants. As the route is linear either start with a bus from Guadalupe or return by bus to Cañamero. Check the times of buses using the link in the introduction and plan your walk accordingly. For the really fit, with time to spare, walk out and back and get the views in both directions.

The route itself is waymarked, albeit haphazardly, but it progresses unfailingly in a north-easterly direction. It climbs gently from the start but, after twenty minutes, the pretty stretch along the side of a huge reservoir is flat. The route then climbs up rather unrelentingly over a bleak mountainside until it enters a more wooded area. From then on the way is almost level or downhill. The views are lovely. The walking in the woods, especially under the pine trees with cistus, lavender and heather lining the path, is quite magical. Don't rush it. This walk is less spectacular than the Hunting Route of Alfonso XI, the other linear one described for Las Villuercas, but I think it is prettier. It is also less demanding; the highest point is 252m less, and the climb from lowest to highest point is also less, but medium fitness is still needed as some of the climbs are long.

LAS VILLUERCAS 6

Directions

Start at the Guadalupe end of Cañamero in the main Calle Pablo García Garrido. Looking towards Guadalupe, take the small road on the left, sign-posted Berzocana 13 kms. There is a sign on the right of this road indicating the 'Ruta de Isabel la Católica' but it's very faded. ❶ Within a few metres there is a narrow concrete path bearing right. It descends sharply. Take this path. It passes a big white house on the right. By the house is a telegraph pole with the white and red waymark of the route. Follow the path down as it enters an area of trees. Ahead, to the right is a small path running alongside a water pipe carried on a bridge. To the left is a small farm building usually with some goats. Just before the farm, on the left is a bridge and a second footbridge crossing a small stream. Cross either bridge to put the farm on the right. The path is now made of soft earth and enters a wooded area.

On the right above there are huge granite mountains whose lower slopes are covered in vegetation and flowering bushes. Below the River Ruecas flows through the woods. There is a junction where a path forks back, left. Ignore this. Our path continues straight on but a few metres later, as the main path continues ahead, there is a little path to the right. Take this path. It has a wooden fence on its right side. It drops down gently to a picnic area. The shaded river banks are full of wild flowers for up to six months of the year. Especially lovely are the intensely coloured violets. Cross the river by the bridge on the right. ❷ Turn left up the rough stone steps to find the path which becomes very narrow and is lined with cistus bushes. It goes up gently but continuously. Opposite the river on the left, and now below, are the hills of the Sierra de la Madrila covered with trees.

The path continues up and leads to a huge reservoir off to the right, the Presa Cancho del Fresno. To the left is a road over the dam but take the wide earth track to the right. Keeping the

THE PILGRIMAGE ROUTE OF ISABEL THE CATHOLIC

water on the left, walk nearly halfway around the reservoir. This part of the walk could take an hour but is very undemanding and peaceful. The wooded area on the right, especially at the start of the walk around the water, is a good place for song birds, and listen out for the woodpeckers.

As the wide track goes around the reservoir, at nearly the halfway point is a small path to the right with a signpost made of planks of wood, some fallen. The lettering is indistinct (at the time of writing) but this is the sign for the Ruta de Isabel la Católica. ❸ Take this small path to the right that goes uphill from the beginning. It goes through bracken and cistus bushes but the aspect is quite open. It widens out but continues directly ahead and upward. Look back for a view of the reservoir and the dam. Stay on the path and keep going up. Eventually there is a granite pilgrim cross, the Cross of Andrade, and another indistinct signpost. No matter; the ancient cross is the waymark. At this point the path is visible a long way ahead as it climbs upwards through the valley in the distance and the Sierra del Aguila. Look out for eagles.

At the top of the climb the path disappears under a scree of rocks and boulders brought down by an avalanche many years ago. Cross carefully; some of the rocks still move but I've done it four times now and it is all right. The path is now rocky, narrow and winding but enters a wonderful scenic stretch with high mountains on the left. Look up for possible sightings of birds of prey. On the right are deciduous and pine trees and flowering bushes. The path winds out from the high valley and becomes flatter as it meets a track at a T junction. Either go straight ahead through dense bushes, or, make this short detour: turn right for 100m, turn left at the next T junction, walk another 100m and turn left at the third T junction to pick up a wider track that the short cut also joins. ❹ Don't worry if it seems confusing — these are woodland tracks. Keep to the directions and check the GPS at this point if necessary. Ignore the next two junctions, right, and keep on the

LAS VILLUERCAS 6

track. There is a long stretch of easy, gentle walking and the trees thin and give way to more open meadows. 5

At the Y junction keep right. The track comes to a large, substantial fence which is recent and encloses a private area of land which includes the *Castaño Abuelo* (the Grandfather Chestnut Tree), a spectacular specimen allegedly first recorded in the 14th century. 6 Formerly the track continued ahead but turn right for a path that follows the fence until the path bears slightly right again and leaves the fence behind. There is a small path, left. 7 Take this left path and enter a wooded area once more. At the Y junction turn left. 8 The path is very clear. It does bend about but do not take any other junctions — keep going forward. Follow it down into a pretty stretch of flowering bushes and shady trees. Continue through a large wood of deciduous oaks and chestnuts. At certain times of the year, when the trees are not in leaf it is possible to get glimpses of the Palace of Mirabel which is now a private house with the status of a Historic Artistic Monument.

The path comes out to run along the side of a fence with distant views of Guadalupe on the left. At a junction there is a path on the right. This is where the Walk of the Hermitages joins this route into Guadalupe. After 100m there is a turning, left, that goes up to the Palace of Mirabel. Continue right towards the Hermitage of Santa Catalina. The path becomes a wider compacted earth lane. Behind is the Pico Agudo, to the left is the Sierra de Guadalupe. Ahead beyond the town the peaks of the mountains of Las Villuercas and the Montes de Toledo are visible.

The lane winds downwards and is flanked by many flowering bushes and trees, mainly pine. They become denser and the bird song louder. In spring there are butterflies, especially the Orange Tip, attracted by the flowering bushes. The pine wood is shady, cool and dark. The lane loops downward but, at times, there are paths through the woods that cut off the loops. These are clear

THE PILGRIMAGE ROUTE OF ISABEL THE CATHOLIC

because the lane below can be seen before leaving the lane above.

As the lane drops the woods thin. Just after a green radio mast on the left is a small turning, also left, where there is a wooden picket fence and a metal gate. Go there for an excellent view of Guadalupe unimpeded by trees. Return to the lane as it goes down and bends left. It goes down more steeply with a junction, right, but stay on the lane ahead. As the descent continues, a stream runs into a ditch on the right of the lane. At the valley bottom go straight ahead to cross Puente de Cañamero over the River Guadalupe where the stream from the ditch joins the river. This is a quiet place to watch for birds and butterflies. Once over the bridge follow the lane to the right, uphill. It joins the road from Guadalupe, the CC-712, after about 200m. ❾ Turn right and walk along the verge. Ahead is the Viaduct de Guadalupe. After another 20m, there is a small path on the left. Cross the road and take this path.

The outskirts of Guadalupe are ahead. ❿ At the Y junction take the right road and follow it all the way up. Dead ahead is an ancient pilgrim cross. Turn right into Calle Tinte. At the top of the road is the Arco del Tinte, pass under and keep going up the road. At the top of the road is a Y junction. Take the left turning and ahead is the medieval Fuente de Tres Chorros where pilgrims washed before entering the monastery. Turn left into Calle Seville and the ancient, historic part of Guadalupe. Walk through the Arco de Seville and enter the Plaza. As befits one who has just completed the pilgrim route, visit the monastery church. It's amazing.

LAS VILLUERCAS 6

GPS Points: The Pilgrimage Route of Isabel the Catholic

1. N 39° 23' 02.96" W 05° 23' 24.13"
2. N 39° 23' 19.80" W 05° 23' 24.50"
3. N 39° 24' 16.60" W 05° 23' 05.10"
4. N 39° 24' 52.64" W 05° 21' 53.37
5. N 39° 25' 11.60" W 05° 21' 43.40"
6. N 39° 25' 36.80" W 05° 21' 34.80"
7. N 39° 25' 35.00" W 05° 21' 29.70"
8. N 39° 25' 35.10" W 05° 21' 22.90"
9. N 39° 26' 40.85" W 05° 19' 49.13"
10. N 39° 26' 57.50" W 05° 19' 46.6"

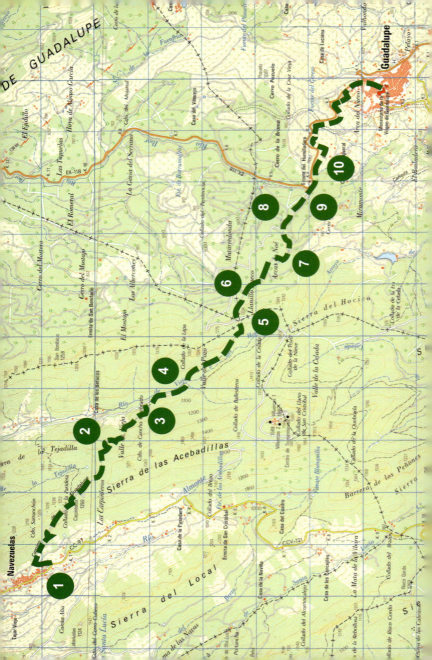

LAS VILLUERCAS 6

3 The Hunting Route of Alfonso XI

Start: Navezuelas

Finish: Guadalupe

5-6 hours

16.5 km

Low: 695m
High: 1.240m

Medium-High

Navezuelas → Guadalupe
Maps: IGN 707 Logrosán 1:50.000 and for the tip of Navezuelas IGN 681 Castañar de Ibor 1:50.000 (dated 1956)

Starting from Navezuelas, October

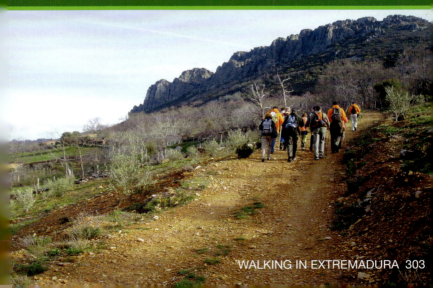

WALKING IN EXTREMADURA 303

THE HUNTING ROUTE OF ALFONSO XI

Introduction

An easy to follow route, with plenty of bird-watching, through oak and pine woods across the natural, high and deserted part of Las Villuercas. This spectacular walk follows the old hunting route favoured by King Alfonso XI who liked to hunt bears. That's probably why there are none left here. However, the king died aged only 27 in 1885 so may not have been totally responsible for the extinction of bears in the area. The walk starts in the small mountain village of Navezuelas which nestles almost in the middle of the Sierra de las Villuercas. Approach the village via the CC-21 (CV-121) signposted to Berzocana from Cañamero on the Logrosán/Guadalupe road N-401. There are other approaches but all are equally alarming. The walk is linear so it's best to arrange to be dropped off in Navezuelas and picked up in Guadalupe. The person not doing the walk, however, will have plenty to see and do in Guadalupe, possibly the Walk of the Hermitages, so the wait for the walkers will not be boring. Alternatively, drive to Guadalupe and get a taxi to Navezuelas. There are no buses.

The route itself is not difficult to find and follow: it progresses unfailingly in a south-easterly direction. It is a little more demanding than the other linear walk, the Pilgrimage Route of Isabel the Catholic, as it starts higher, goes higher and is longer. It climbs up almost from the start and goes up and down four mountains — but none of them hard for a walker with a medium-good level of fitness. The views are, of course, brilliant. The path travels through several woods of mainly pine, oak, chestnut and other deciduous trees. There are flowers in the spring specially along the river valley and the meadow edges on the long approach to Guadalupe. There are birds everywhere. Take binoculars.

LAS VILLUERCAS **6**

Directions

Start at the southern edge of the village of Navezuelas at the southern end of Calle Francisco Pizarro where there is a map and information board of the route. ❶ The village is tiny so there will not be a problem determining this location. Climb from the village along a gravel and earth path that goes up gently towards an imposing rocky outcrop. The path loops to the right. The village falls away and to the right. Behind the village a long string of mountain peaks look impressive. In spring, flowering bushes are a delightful feature of this walk. The gravel and earth path narrows and is lined with shrubs and small trees. The path becomes more rocky but it continues upward. Keep going. Pace yourself. Don't forget to look around and behind for the view.

After 2.3km, the path widens out and the trees fall away to reveal panoramic views. The highest point of the route is reached with a helpful information board as a landmark: 'Collado de la Pariera' 1,240m. The views out over the landscape are fantastic. To the north lies the Sierra de Gredos. All around are the parallel mountain ranges of Las Villuercas: some barren and austere, some covered in trees and vegetation. What you can see in the way of birds and flowers depends on the time of year you are walking.

Continue along the narrow path on top of the ridge. The way is reasonably flat, but it is rocky. The path enters an ancient deciduous oak wood which must give welcome shelter during the summer — but I love walking here in the winter. The wood has a quiet mystery about it. There are glimpses of the Sierra de Gredos behind. The path crosses a section where it is impeded by rocks brought down several years ago during the winter rains, however, they are easy to cross. The going is very slightly downhill.

You come to a small information sign; 'Collado de los Ajos' 1,220m. Follow the path as it winds along the top of this ridge with other mountain tops, trees, bushes, views and unspoiled nature

THE HUNTING ROUTE OF ALFONSO XI

all around. Feel the silence. This is a lovely stretch of the walk. The path starts to zig-zag ❷ and go downhill steeply into the Valle del Viejas.

The path joins a small road at a Y junction and merges with it. ❸ Turn right on the path-road. After following the path-road for about 10 minutes the path leaves the road and turns left. It very quickly drops down and crosses the River Viejas to the left, over a wooden bridge. ❹ Cross this bridge. Walk up the path with the river down and on the right. There are chances to see small birds here and examine the flowers more closely. In less than 5 minutes there is a small granite house with a garden on the left.

Continue on and the path goes up slightly. There is a point at which the path goes forward but take a small path to the left. It is very narrow, lined with bushes and small trees and climbs up. You cannot miss it as there are no other junctions at this stage. Keep going up through the bushes and trees. The river valley, backed by the Sierra de la Acebadillas, is to the right. Eventually, at the top of the climb, there are huge granite outcrops from which there is a view across the valley behind towards peaks that include Pico Villuercas at 1,589m.

Continue on the path, still going up, to a small road. ❺ Cross this road straight over. Ahead is a broad but very steep, very rocky track going downhill. Go down this track but, be careful, the scree is rolling. Halfway down the hill, turn right onto a wide track, into a deciduous oak wood. The turning is signposted. ❻

The track is earth underfoot and runs through the wood. It is cool in summer but a lovely space at any time of the year. There are many other paths that criss-cross the track but stay straight ahead. The oaks start to give way to occasional pines, then the track, now narrower and a path once more, enters into a deep pine wood. Soon Guadalupe is visible ahead in the distance and to the right.

The path down to Guadalupe, February

THE HUNTING ROUTE OF ALFONSO XI

You will come to a series of junctions within the wood but always choose the path that is more straight ahead than the others. After 1km of walking in the wood there is a broad junction. ❼ Go ahead on the broad track and then take the first right along a small path. Don't worry if you miss this path as the broad track ends up in the same place as the small path, but the path is nicer. At a T junction with a straight track through the woods, turn left then first right. ❽ The track goes downhill. Ignore any turnings. It broadens out and ends at a gate where there is a small road. Go through the gate and turn right along the small road. ❾

Walk along this small road with the pine wood on the right. At the roundabout, where the road joins the EX-118 Carretera de Navalmoral, the 15th century Hermitage del Humilladero is on the left. ❿ Look right. A signpost shows the way to the footpath to Guadalupe. The footpath follows the line of the road and the valley. It is a pretty, open view with Guadalupe, ahead and on the right. In February pretty almond blossoms line the path. Follow it around to the right.

Keep going. Although Guadalupe looks near it does take another hour to get to the square. Enter Guadalupe via Calle de Matarrol and continue on Calle Caño de Abajo, Calle Real and Calle Nueva de los Capellanes. At last, relax and have a cold drink in one of the many café bars in front of the monastery.

LAS VILLUERCAS 6

GPS Points
The Hunting Route of Alfonso XI

1. N39° 30' 25.10" W05° 26' 07.50"
2. N39° 29' 55.59" W05° 24' 37.38"
3. N39° 29' 20.54" W05° 23' 49.77"
4. N39° 29' 12.80" W05° 23' 45.90"
5. N39° 28' 33.30" W05° 22' 46.00"
6. N39° 28' 35.50" W05° 22' 36.25"
7. N39° 28' 29.85" W05° 22' 23.93"
8. N39° 28' 19.10" W05° 22' 02.16"
9. N39° 28' 06.40" W05° 21' 25.70"
10. N39° 27' 52.42" W05° 20' 59.93"

Calle las Palomas, Trujillo

City Walks

1. The Walk of the Roman Citizen — 316
2. A Walk in a Renaissance City — 326
3. A Walk with the Conquistadores — 336

INTRODUCTION

City Walks

Although most walkers come to Extremadura for the countryside, you are bound to be tempted to visit one of the historic cities featured in this chapter; Mérida, Cáceres and Trujillo. As with any city, it is possible to waste time and exhaust yourself wandering around, finding some things by accident yet missing grander sights. My walks will take you on a route past the best there is to see with a minimal retracing of footsteps. However, they are neither architectural guides nor historical tours. My contribution is in the route planning so that you can concentrate on the sights.

In recent years Extremadura has made a big push to adorn all buildings of historical interest with information boards in English. Mérida's signage is good but the signage in Cáceres is patchy. Trujillo's efforts are excellent. Much can be understood and appreciated through the new signage and, consequently, that information need not be repeated here. For those of you who still want more, reasonable guide books in English are available and most tourist offices have someone who can speak English. The small amount of historical information that I have included in this chapter has been taken from many sources, mainly Spanish, but from no one special place.

A very brief history follows in order to increase the enjoyment of the walks.

The tribes of Extremadura were conquered by the Romans around 200 B.C. However, the indigenous peoples were not fully subjugated until c.50 B.C. Extremadura, along with modern Portugal, became Lusitania, the westernmost province of the Roman Empire. In 410, with the fall of the empire, the Christian Visigoths ruled but they enjoyed power only until 711 when the Moors invaded. They held sway in Extremadura for 500 years. In the late 12th century the Christians united to launch a serious campaign at reconquest. Led by three generations of the same

The Bishop's Palace, Cáceres

royal family — that of Galicia, León, Castile and Toledo — the Christians came from the north, which the Moors had never conquered, from Portugal, and from the new Military Orders.

During 62 long years of fighting cities in Extremadura were conquered, lost, reconquered and, finally, held. It wasn't all warfare though; one Christian king, Alfonso IX, somehow made time to father a minimum of 22 children (the exact figure is unknown) by at least six women. He also founded the University of Salamanca in 1215.

Victory brought rich rewards for the conquerors. The military orders and individual knights were awarded land and noble titles according to their bravery. They settled down to build fortified houses and palaces, govern, marry into each other's families, fight

INTRODUCTION

with each other, raise children and see their cities grow prosperous through commerce, crafts and markets.

In 1469 Isabel of Castile married Ferdinand of Aragon; a move towards uniting the various crowns of Spain. However the kingdom of Castile had a succession dispute in 1474. The power struggle was between Juana, possible daughter of Henry IV, and Henry's half-sister, Isabel. Knights chose sides, sharpened swords and prayed they backed the winner. Isabel won. She rewarded her supporters in the usual way with land and titles.

The discovery of the New World in 1492 brought untold wealth into Extremadura and changed the balance of power. Formerly established noble families gave way to previously impoverished adventure-seekers who arrived back from exploits on the other side of the world with fabulous amounts of gold. Those who didn't die in the New World settled down to enjoy their wealth but most of the New World money went straight through Spain to fight religious wars in Europe.

The Peninsular War, 1808-1812, ravaged Extremadura and the bridges over the River Guadiana and River Tajo were as important to the Duke of Wellington as they had been to the Romans ...

That's where I will leave the history because this is a book on walking and my pages are running out. However, as you walk the cities, especially on winter days when there is no one else around, it is very easy to feel enveloped by the atmosphere of thousands of years of history and you may want to know more. Sadly, a good book in English on the history of Extremadura waits to be written.

Practical information

Public monuments in cities are open 7 days a week, usually from 10.00-14.00 and from 16.00-20.00 but evening closing times can be earlier in winter, or an hour later in summer. Museums are usually shut Sunday afternoons and all day Monday. In all the

CITY WALKS

cities time your walk well. If you are going to see everything, work around the lunch break.

All cities have a wide range of accommodation and eating places so it is best you do your own research. The main squares are always great places for a drink and to watch the world go by, but for something a bit special seek out hidden spots in the walled cities, or in the smaller squares. For car parking, see the individual walks.

Other walks

Mérida has information boards on a Walk of the Roman Waters at 22km. The Via de la Plata runs through both Mérida and Cáceres and some out-and-back routes can be walked. See the chapter on Roman Waters for further information on a circular walk from Mérida to Proserpina reservoir. Further walking can be done in Cáceres outside the city walls. In Trujillo there are a few places of interest to the south of the city. Additionally the cities of Plasencia, Coria, Guadalupe and Badajoz will reward inquisitive walkers.

Maps

Use the maps in the book but because they are small they cannot show the name of every road. Follow the directions and road names in the text as they are the best guide. City maps are available from the tourist offices. Some are excellent. Some are confusing. Trujillo gives out two different maps and they are just that — different.

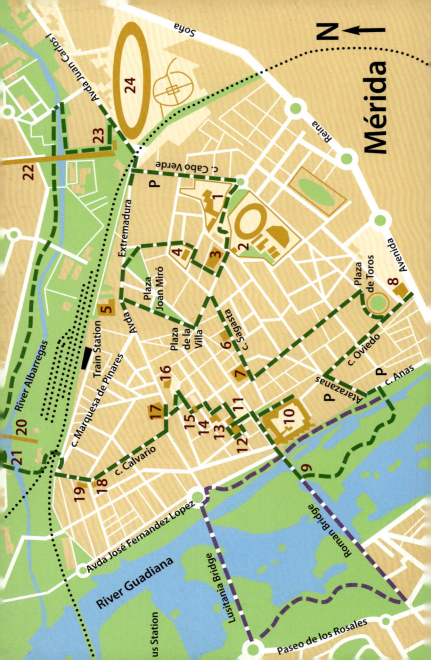

CITY WALKS 7

1 The Walk of the Roman Citizen

Start: the car park in Calle Cabo Verde, Mérida

Finish: Car park in C. Cabo Verde, Mérida

3 hours

8 km

Low: 210m
High: 234m

Easy

1 The Walk of the Two Bridges

Start: Calle de Anas (by the slope to the River Guadiana)

Finish: the eastern end of the Roman bridge by the Alcazaba

1.5 hours

3.5 km

Low: 210m
High: 234m

Easy

WALKING IN EXTREMADURA 317

THE WALK OF THE ROMAN CITIZEN

Introduction

Mérida, as Emerita Augusta, was the Roman capital of the Lusitania province, geographically important as the best place to cross the River Guadiana. The Roman bridge and city were built to last and we can still see impressive evidence of that two millennia later. Visigoth remains are mostly in museums but they are quite beautiful. The Moors left an outstanding fortress designed to defend the bridge over the River Guadiana. The Christians have left impressive churches, but only one palace from Renaissance times. Mérida was chosen to be the capital of Extremadura in 1983. Ten years later it was declared a UNESCO World Heritage Site.

The historical sights are spread out over the city and they are very impressive. However, I've resisted the urge to write superlative adjectives because you can fill them in for yourself as you walk. All the numbered sights on the map for this walk have information boards in English (except the Visigoth Museum). For the enthusiast, multi-tickets can be bought from the ticket office near the entrance to the theatre, to see six monuments. Each full-fee ticket gets a substantial 80-page information booklet in English. Reduced price ticket holders can buy a booklet in the tourist shop by the entrance to the theatre for €1.00.

The walk can be extended by including The Walk of the Two Bridges, a loop around the modern Lusitania bridge and returning by the Roman bridge. That walk is especially enjoyable in the autumn when the trees turn red, or the winter, when the Guadiana is high and the wintering birds live in the reeds on the central island.

Mérida has a train and bus station. If arriving by train start the walk at the Church of Santa Eulalia. **(5)** If arriving by bus start at the western end of the Lusitania bridge. If arriving by car, park in one of three places on the route; Calle Cabo Verde (paying), Calle Atarazanas (paying) or Calle Anas (free). Wherever you park you

CITY WALKS 7

The Forum

THE WALK OF THE ROMAN CITIZEN

can start the walk at that point as the route is circular.

Read the chapter introduction for opening times and tickets. However, in August Mérida hosts the world-famous Classical Theatre and the Roman theatre will be closed in the evenings for performances so, unless you have a ticket for the play, plan your visit earlier. It will also be helpful to read the introduction to the chapter on Roman Waters.

Directions

Numbers refer to the numbers on the map.

Start at the car park in Calle Cabo Verde easily reached from the direction of the E-90/A5 by following the pink signs for the Theatre and Amphitheatre. The modern building to the right as you leave the car park on foot houses exhibitions relating to the city, a café, toilets and a tourist office with friendly officers who speak English. On leaving the building turn right to walk up Calle Cabo Verde. Ignore all junctions to arrive at a roundabout with a statue and a small park, to the right and across the road. At the roundabout turn right. To the right, beyond the fence, is the Casa del Anfiteatro. **(1)** The road comes to an open square. On the left, behind the hedge is the Roman theatre and amphitheatre. **(2)** Right, is the entrance to the Casa del Anfiteatro. Ahead is a modern statue and behind this, right, is the ticket office.

Turn around from the ticket office and walk across the square. The joint entrance for the theatre and amphitheatre is on the left. Prepare to be amazed and allow at least an hour, maybe more. On leaving the theatre walk ahead and cross the road. The tourist train stop is on the left and the Roman Museum **(3)** is right. Walk ahead down Calle José Ramón Melida. Pass equally nice cafés on the left. Turn right immediately after the museum down a few steps into Travestia del Museo. Walk ahead, ignoring all junctions. Come to a T junction, turn right, then first left. Within 50m on the left is

CITY WALKS 7

the site of the Roman Snow Wells. **(4)** The site has a walkway into it and it's free. Come out from the site turn left and continue straight down the road. At the crossroads walk ahead. At the junction, cross the road, left, and enter the park. Walk diagonally through the park, direction left.

Leave the park and turn left on the Avenida de Extremadura. Ahead is the Church of Santa Eulalia. **(5)** Eulalia is the Patron Saint of Mérida. Follow the road to opposite the church and use the crossing to reach the church. Just outside the church is the Temple of Marte. After visiting the church and grounds leave by the main entrance, cross the road by the crossing, turn left a few metres, and turn right to walk up Rambla Martir Santa Eulalia. Ignore all junctions but cross the road to walk in the small park on the left. At the top of the park pass a statue of Santa Eulalia, left, cross the road ahead and come to an open space with a statue, fountain, pond and building with clock tower. This is the start of the main shopping area. Turn first left up a short hill, into Calle José Ramón Melida. Do not take any junctions but walk ahead. The museum will come into view once more.

At the pink directional signs on the left, turn right into Calle Sagasta. Pass nice cafés and restaurants and ignore all junctions. After about 200m, on the right, there is a Sacred Site in the City Centre **(6)** with the ruins of a lovely temple once attributed to Diana. Continue down the same street. Within 150m, also on the right, is an architectural time-capsule known as The Forum. It encompasses Roman, Visigoth, Moorish and Renaissance features all within the same building. **(7)** It is worth exploring properly and you can walk all around.

To visit Mitre House **(8)** turn left up Calle de los Maestros and, ignoring all junctions walk up to the bullring. Turn right to walk around the bullring to find the house behind. On leaving the house pass the bullring on the right to walk all the way down Calle

THE WALK OF THE ROMAN CITIZEN

Oviedo to the T junction with Calle Atarazanas. Turn left to pass the car park on the right and an alternative place to start the walk. With the car park on the right, follow the road as it bears left. This road leads to free car parking stretching all along Calle Anas ahead. Just as the road bears left, on the right is a zig-zag ramp that drops down to the pretty tree-filled parks, the Guadiana and the Roman bridge. **(9)** Take the ramp.

For walkers doing the Walk of the Two Bridges turn right at the bottom of the ramp, walk straight ahead on the path, under the Roman bridge to arrive at the modern Lusitania bridge. Walk up to road level, negotiate the crossings at the roundabout and turn left to take the footpath over the bridge. This part of the walk gives excellent views of the full length of the Roman bridge. Once over the Lusitania bridge, turn left into the park, walk with the Guadiana on the left to come to the Roman bridge. Turn left on to the bridge and walk towards the Alcazaba. **(10)**

For walkers not doing the extra circuit, turn left at the bottom of the ramp and turn right immediately to cross a part of the river on a footbridge. Over the footbridge turn right, choose a path through the park and walk towards the Roman bridge. Come to a ramp leading up to the bridge. Take the ramp, turn right on the bridge and walk to the Alcazaba.

On the approach to the Alcazaba the entrance is on the right. To the left is a roundabout with a copy of the famous statue of Romulus, Remus and the She-Wolf. With the Alcazaba on the right walk up the road. Pass a small park, right, with a monument to all the sister cities of Mérida in the world. At a slender Y junction ignore the left road and walk ahead to come to a fountain and gardens. Turn right to continue to walk around the Alcazaba and explore the walls. Retrace steps to come back past the fountain on the right. Cross the road and enter the main square, the Plaza de España, ahead. **(11)** This is a good place to stop for a drink.

The Aqueduct of Milagros, July

The square is pretty but not Roman. However, the north-west side has some notable buildings. On the far left is the Co-cathedral de Santa María. **(12)** To the right of the church is the only palace left in Mérida, the Mendoza Palace. It is now a hotel. **(13)**

Leave the square by walking around the hotel restaurant and turning left down Calle Santa Julia. Walk straight down this road, ignore the little turning left and come to the former Church of Santa Clara which now houses the Visigoth Museum. **(14)** Leave the museum and walk straight ahead down the small road. At a crossroads, right goes towards the shops, ahead goes to the empty Convent of Immaculate Conception and left is the magnificent Trajan Arch. **(15)** Walk under the arch. This is now part of the famous Via de la Plata, Way of St. James.

Turn right into Plaza de la Constitutión. On the opposite side of the

THE WALK OF THE ROMAN CITIZEN

square is the former Convent Hospital of Jesus of Nazareth **(16)** with its historical gardens, now a Parador. Leave the square on the left down Travestia de Almendralejo. At the T junction go across the road. Turn right to look the facade of the Church of Our Lady of Carmen, left. **(17)** With your back to the church, turn right into Calle Almendralejo and, ignoring junctions, walk ahead. On the left is an on-going archeological excavation. At a Y junction go right down Calle Calvario. Walk all the way down, then up this tree-lined street ignoring junctions. Pass a tiny shrine on the left to Santa María Virgen de la Amargura. Just after the shrine, also left, is the Monumental Fountain. **(18)** This is followed by a site explaining how Romans brought water here from Proserpina. **(19)** There is also an information board and map showing various routes relating to the Roman waters: The Walk of the Waters.

Reach a crossroads. Go straight on towards the railway line that can be seen ahead. At the T junction with the main road and the railway turn right to cross the road by the crossing. Turn right to take the footpath down to use the underpass to go below the railway to come out into a park with, on the right, the fabulous Aqueduct de Milagros, **(20)** which brought water from Proserpina to the city. Explore the area. Cross the River Albarregas by using the small Roman bridge **(21)** on the left, or use the bridge beyond the aqueduct. In any event, cross the river, turn right and walk along the footpath through the park with the river on the right.

Come to a main road. Use the crossing to walk straight ahead into another park. Keep walking ahead to reach the Rabo de Buey-San Lázaro Aqueduct **(22)**. This is much longer than the previous aqueduct but not so high. Cross another road and explore the area. The aqueduct is solidly built and has an arch for traffic and another for pedestrians. Walk through the pedestrian arch and after 50m turn right on to a path. On the left is open ground but on the right is the aqueduct. Follow the path. At the river turn left, then right, across a blue bridge over the river. Once over the

CITY WALKS **7**

The Aqueduct of Rabo de Buey-San Lázaro, July

bridge turn right to walk back to the aqueduct. At the aqueduct turn left and walk all the way up the path with the aqueduct on the right. At the junction with a main road there is an excavation of Thermal Sites. **(23)**

Turn left and after 50m use the crossing to cross the road and continue left to find the Roman Circus **(24)** on the right within 100m. Leaving the circus, turn left and walk along the left side of the road. Ignore the junction, left, but walk ahead to cross under the railway line by using the underpass. Turn first left after the underpass. Cross the road. Turn left again then first right to come to the bottom of Calle Cabo Verde and the car park is within 100m.

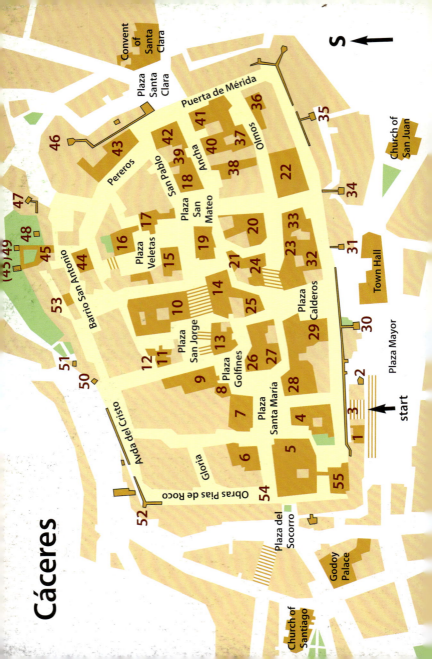

CITY WALKS 7

2 A Walk in a Renaissance City

Start: Plaza Mayor, Cáceres

Finish: Plaza Mayor, Cáceres

1.5 hours

3 km

Low: 431m
High: 464m

Easy

The Convent of San Pedro

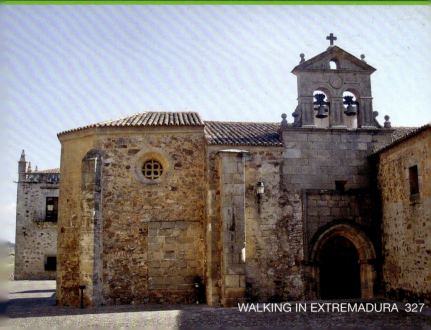

A WALK IN A RENAISSANCE CITY

Introduction

The walled city of Cáceres looks rather austere as there is an almost total absence of trees or any of the softening vegetation we might expect in a city today. That's the whole point. Cáceres is not a city of today. It is, essentially, a 16th century city. Today it is among the most beautiful examples of medieval cities to be found anywhere in the world. Indeed, in 1986 Cáceres was declared a UNESCO World Heritage Site.

The train and bus stations are on the opposite side of the modern city, about an hour's walk away. If arriving by car, park outside the walled city. There are free car parks to the south-west around the Hospital San Pedro de Alcántara, a 10 minute walk away. The nearest paying car park is the multi-storey Obispo Garlaza just behind the Plaza Mayor.

Read the chapter introduction for opening times for monuments. There is a small charge to enter the Bujaco Tower exhibition and the churches. Unfortunately, Cáceres has patchy signage in Spanish, never mind English, however, there is a good book in reasonable English that covers historical information for the enthusiast. 'Cáceres Heritage of Mankind' Ediciones Turimagen ISBN: 84-922397-9-4. It is sold in local bookshops.

Directions

Numbers refer to the numbers on the map.

Start in the Plaza Mayor. Look towards the steps going up to the Star Arch. **(3)** From the left you can see the tower of the Palace of Toledo-Moctezuma, **(55)** the Bujaco Tower **(1)** and the Peace Hermitage next to it, the back of the Bishop's Palace, **(4)** the tower of the Co-cathedral of Santa María, **(7)** the side of Ribera House, **(29)** the General's Wife's House, **(32)** and the Grass Tower. **(30)** Walk towards the Bujaco Tower. **(1)** Go up the steps and turn left to visit the tower and the exhibition if you want to. Next, look to the right to see the Pulpit Tower. **(2)** Then look at the Star Arch. **(3)** This was originally called the New Gate and was built in the 14th century. It was remodelled 400 years later to become what we can see today. Walk under the arch. You have now entered the walled city of Cáceres.

Walk along the narrow street straight ahead into the wide, open Plaza de Santa María. This is the centre of one of the oldest and noblest parts of the city. Turn around. The building in front of you is the Bishop's Palace. **(4)** Turn right to see the Ovando Palace. **(5)** Turn right again to see the Carvajal Palace **(6)** in the corner. Walk towards it to look down a side road to the right to see the 12th century round tower. There is free entry to go inside the palace for the interpretation centre. The best part is the enclosed garden at the back of the palace. It gives an idea of what lies behind most of the facades within the city. The next building to look at is the Co-cathedral of Santa María. **(7)** There is a small admission fee to go into the church. Just outside the co-cathedral is a statue of San Pedro de Alcántara.

Keeping left, walk on to the next open space, past the Palace of the Provincial Council on the left, **(8)** into Plaza de los Golfínes. Look at the Lower Golfínes Palace **(9)** on the left. This building is pretty spectacular and has great character. Ferdinand and Isabel stayed in this palace during their 1477 and 1479 visits to Cáceres. As such, the palace carries the blazon of the Catholic Monarchs. The tower proudly carries the inscription 'This is the house of the Golfínes'. Very grand, especially when you consider the family had a bigger palace higher up in the city.

Walk ahead. Just before Plaza de San Jorge, on the left, is Cuesta del Marquise which goes down to the old Jewish Quarter. We will go there later but for now make a slight detour to the House of Durán de la Roche **(11)** on the right. Just next door, also on the right, is the Yusuf Al Borch Arabic Museum showing Moorish

A WALK IN A RENAISSANCE CITY

cultural life. **(12)** Go back to Plaza de San Jorge and look up at the Jesuit Church **(10)** which dominates the square. The chuch has an exhibition inside and there is an entrance fee — but the view from the tower is worth it. After leaving the church, return to the square. Visit the little shops or take time to sit down. There are public toilets at the end of the shops and a small shady garden.

Walk up a few steps of Cuesta de la Compañia on the right of the square and visit Becerra House. **(13)** The building is now the MCCB Foundation named after Doña Mercedes Calles and her husband Carlos Ballestero. Mercedes was born in Cáceres in 1915. She wanted her city to benefit from her legacy and the building is filled with her collections of furniture, paintings, glass, antiques and jewellery. It's free but they do take donations. Continue up the steps of Cuesta de la Compañia. Pass Calle de la Manga on the right. Turn next right and in the corner on the right is the House of the Sun. **(14)** This house gets its name from the coat of arms of the Solís family who built the house. Retrace the few steps back to Cuesta de la Compañia and continue it upwards to enter Plaza de las Veletas on the left.

Starting from the left is the magnificent Cáceres-Ovando Mansion **(15)** also called The House of Storks. It is currently a Military Museum. The building opposite and in the corner is the Veletas Palace. **(16)** It was built on the site of the old Moorish citadel. Below the courtyard there is the original cistern complete with horse-shoe arches with reused Roman pillars. Only the cistern in Cordova is larger in Spain. The palace has been the Cáceres Museum since 1933 (shut Mondays) and it's free. See the cistern if nothing else. To the right of the Veletas Palace is the small Convent of San Pedro. **(17)** It houses a community of cloistered nuns of the Order of St. Clare. If you do the walk early on a Sunday morning you can sit on the granite ledge at the side of Plaza de San Mateo and hear the nuns sing Mass at 09.00.

CITY WALKS **7**

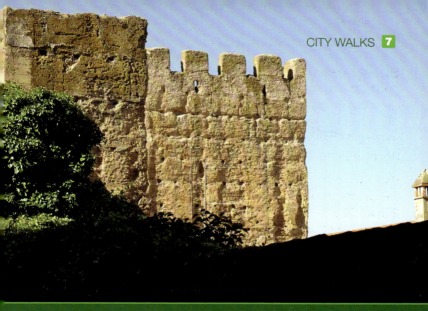

The Tower of El Aver or La Ved

Walking ahead into Plaza de San Mateo, the very large building on the left is the 15th century Ulloa Mansion **(18)**. The building is currently the Cáceres School of Fine Arts. Directly opposite the mansion is the Church of San Mateo **(19)** which was built at the highest point of the city. To the left of the church is the ivy-covered Sande House and Tower. **(20)** The tower is now a restaurant. Next door is Sande House known as the House of the Eagle **(21)** as the eagle was the heraldic device of the Sande family.

Retrace the route to Plaza de San Mateo. The final side of the square is a new hotel. The jury is still out as to its aesthetic qualifications. With the hotel on the left and the restaurant on the right, walk down Calle Condes. The house on the left at the end is the Upper Golfínes Palace. **(22)** It actually incorporates 17 other houses and fronts on to three streets. Built in the 15th century, this is a strong and easily defended house. During the Civil War it served as an early HQ for General Franco.

A WALK IN A RENAISSANCE CITY

Turn right down Cuestra de Aldana. The house on the left is the Moorish House. **(23)** It is the only example of the *Mudéjar* style (Moorish-Christian) in the walled city of Cáceres. Further down the street, on the right is the House of Aldana **(24)** which is now a restaurant. Going down the steps, also on the right, is the House of the Monkey. **(25)** This house gets its name from the stone monkey set on a handrail on the staircase in the inner courtyard. The facade has an impressive coat-of-arms and cheeky gargoyles.

Just after this house turn right and walk left around the building. This is a convent. Continue along the street to re-enter the Plaza de Santa María. The house next to the convent but facing into the square is the House of the Dukes of Valencia. **(26)** Next door is the Moraga House. **(27)** It is now an exhibition centre and shop showing the work of Extremeño craftspeople. The last building in the square and the last one of this circular walk is the Mayoralgo Palace. **(28)** Above the door and between the two windows at the top is the magnificent Blázquez-Mayoralgo coat of arms. Walk ahead. You are now back at the Star Arch where you can finish the walk.

To see more do not exit but turn left to go up the hill. As you walk the city walls will be on your right for most of the time. On the left is the Ribera House. **(29)** This house is currently used by the University in Cáceres. Opposite, is a break in the city walls and a viewing point. To the right is the Grass Tower **(30)** dating from Moorish times. To the left is the Oven Tower. **(31)** Although the base of this tower uses Roman stones, it dates from the same period as the Grass Tower. The main city oven was attached to the wall at the corner of this tower and so it gets its name. Just across the street is the General's Wife's House. **(32)** The house gets its name from the 18th century when its owner, Maria Cayetana Vicenta de Ovando married Lieutenant General Don Vicente Francisco de Ovando Rol. She became the 'General's Wife'. The drum machicolation above the doorway is a reminder that these

CITY WALKS

houses were defensive.

Further on, also to the left is the Palace of the Counts of Adenero **(33)**. Notice the doorway. It is not the usual style of city doorway and was constructed after an Italian design. Opposite and to the right is the Postern and Tower of Santa Ana. **(34)** After the reconquest this was a side entrance to the city. The defensive tower is hard to see unless you go through to the other side and look back. Retrace your steps through the postern and turn left, then right to continue up the road. The walls to the right are very old. The tower of El Aver or La Ved **(35)** can be glimpsed over the wall opposite the entrance to the Golfín Restaurant. This tower is from the Moorish fortress constructed between the 12th and 13th century. It has a Roman base.

The street bends around to the left into Puerta de Mérida. Turn first left into Olmos. On the right is a tourist office. On the left is the Hospital of San Antonio. **(36)** Today a community of nuns from the Order of St. Jerome live here and they sell delicious sweets. On the right is the House of Ovando-Perero **(37)** now part of the Parador and the Olmos entrance to the House of Lorenzo Fernándo de Ulloa **(38)** one of the many houses the family owned. At the end of Olmos turn right to walk into Plaza de San Mateo once more.

Turn right down Calle Ancha. On the left is the Parades-Saavedra House. **(39)** The house displays many different styles of architecture as over the years the facade has changed. Opposite is the Mansion of the Knight Commander of Alcuéscar otherwise known as the house of the Marquis of Torreorgaz. It has been a Parador **(40)** since 1989. You can go inside and look around the public rooms and courtyard. At the bottom of Calle Ancha turn right and walk a few paces to see the Knight's Hospital. **(41)** This is a beautiful little building with charming windows. It was only used as a hospital for a short while and is now a private house. A

A WALK IN A RENAISSANCE CITY

bit further on and opposite are the scanty remains of the Gate of Mérida facing towards that city.

Retrace your steps to see the House of Sánchez-Paredes **(40)** opposite Plaza de Santa Clara. If you want to make a detour to walk into the square you will see the Convent of Santa Clara. This has always been a convent and is currently the home of a community of Clare nuns. They make sweets which can be purchased through the door in the square. If you look down Calle Torremochada you can see the tower of the same name. From the House of Sánchez-Paredes walk ahead into a very small square. In front of you is the House of Pereros **(43)**. This house has an inner courtyard that can be visited where family coats of arms are on display. Walk down Calle Pereros to the left of the house. As the street bends to the left you can see the back view of the Veletas Palace and the gardens. These connect to the House of Horses **(44)** which houses the Fine Art Museum.

Turn right to enter Barrio de San Antonio and the Jewish Quarter. The houses here are much smaller and are painted white. Walk into the square. Turn left. Just past the square, on the right is the Tower of the Wells **(45)** and a free exhibition centre. The guides speak English and are very knowledgeable. The view of the city walls and towers is especially good from the top of the Well Tower. Stand facing the city, from the left and on the left, you can see the following; the Mochada Tower **(46)** (which you also might have seen from Plaza de Santa Clara), the Albarrana Tower **(47)** and the Adosada Tower. **(48)** The Coraja Tower **(49)** is part of the same defensive system as the Well Tower. On the right you can see a glimpse of the Christ Arch and Tower **(50)** which is the oldest gate in the city, It is made of Roman stones and probably dates from the 3rd century. The Tower of the Gate of Concejo **(51)** is just outside the arch. On the far right you can see the top of the Ochavada Tower. **(52)** A pretty impressive array of defensive towers.

Come out from the exhibition, turn right and come to the Hermitage of San Antonio, right. **(53)** This was a Jewish synagogue but with the expulsion of the Jews it became a Christian hermitage dedicated to St. Anthony. Walk ahead along a tiny lane. Turn right, then left to go downhill. On the right is the Arch and Tower of Christ or the River Gate. **(50)** The arch is very nice but I think it looks better from the other side. In any event to get a close-up view of the Concejo **(51)** you need to walk through the arch. It was, of course, a defensive tower for people using the arch to get water. Walk along the Avenida del Cristo. As the street bears left there is just a glimpse of the Ochavada Tower. **(52)** Walk up the Obras Pías de Roco to come to the Espadero Tower and the Coria Gate. **(54)** The gate was originally Roman and got its name from the city it faced — even though the city is about 70km away. The gate was demolished as part of 'progress' in 1879. It was defended by two towers whose remains can be seen incorporated into nearby houses.

If you want to make a detour go through the gate and turn right into Plaza de Socorro. Go down the steps and at the crossroads with Calle de Caleros turn left. On the right is the Church of Santiago. Across the street on the left of the church is the Godoy Palace. Walk around the building and see the top of the King's Tower. Return to Plaza de Socorro and turn right.

Walk straight ahead from the Coria Gate. At the top of the street turn left and there is the splendid Palace of Toledo-Moctezuma. **(55)** Juan Cano de Saavedra, of the Toledo family, was a captain for Hernan Cortés during the conquest of Mexico. Once the conflict was over Juan married Isabel de Moctezuma the daughter of the last Aztec Emperor. One of their grandsons Juan de Toledo Moctezuma married Mariana de Carvajal y Toledo. There is evidence to suggest that they built this house. Walk ahead to return to the Star Arch and well-deserved refreshments in the square.

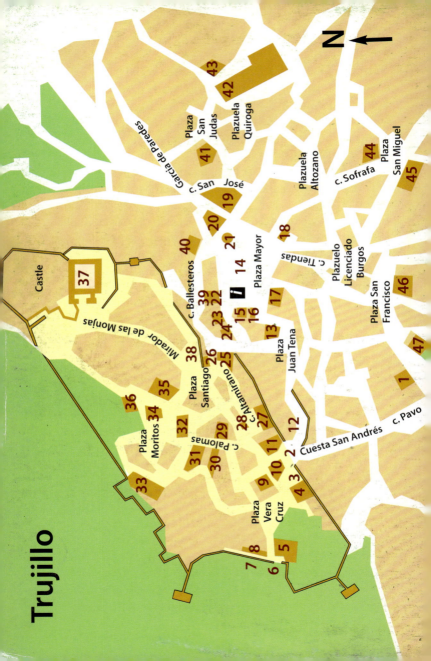

CITY WALKS 7

3 A Walk with the Conquistadores

Start: Town Hall, Trujillo

Finish: Town Hall, Trujillo

3 hours

6 km

Low: 520m
High: 579m

Easy

Stronghold of Luis Chaves from the Gate of Santiago

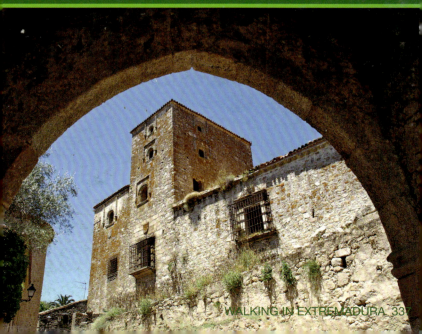

A WALK WITH THE CONQUISTADORES

Introduction

Conquistadores! The word invites divided opinion: men, heroic yet brutal, brave yet greedy, determined yet demented in their search for riches. Trujillo is forever linked with a handful of men who, five centuries ago, left their homes to conquer lands in the newly discovered Americas. Whatever judgements we may make today about their actions, one thing is clear, the looted treasures from one world built a fabulous city in another: Trujillo: City of the Conquistadores.

Trujillo has no train station but has a good bus station with links to Madrid. If arriving by bus it is a short walk to the starting point — less than 10 minutes. If arriving by car, do not drive into the walled city as you will get stuck. If coming to the city on the EX-381 from Montánchez there is free parking near the park on the right, in Avenida de Peru. There is a paying underground car park at the bottom of Calle Jacinto Ruíz de Mendoza opposite the Town Hall, the starting point for the walk.

Trujillo has excellent information boards in English at every number on the map in this book which makes this city walk extremely rewarding. It also means that the directions are just that — directions — and not long historical explanations. Most people begin to explore Trujillo from the Plaza Mayor where the tourist office is located. I think that's a real shame and we are not going to do that. Although the office sells multi-tickets for entry to monuments my walk is structured so that you do not need a ticket for anything until after you get to the tourist office. Do not go there first. Follow the walk. Now ... go back in time eight centuries, pick a side and attack the city properly.

Directions

Numbers refer to the numbers on the map. All defensive arches in the old city walls originally had wooden gates. These have

CITY WALKS 7

Trujillo houses

A WALK WITH THE CONQUISTADORES

long gone but the arches remain. Confusingly they are known as *puertas* (gates). The one exception is the Arch of Triumph which is called an arch for a special reason.

Start at the Town Hall which is also known as the *Alhóndiga* (Public Granary). **(1)** Look inside for the ground floor patio, old bell from the Church of Santiago and free toilets. Go up the staircase. The bust of Diego Garcia de Parades, a local hero, is on the first landing. From there, turn right up the stairs to enter a municipal office. Ask to view the meeting room. It is probably the most beautiful in Extremadura. It is free — but only avaliable during office hours.

Leave the Town Hall and turn right. Take the first right into Calle del Pavo. Walk straight up the old cobbled road. As the road bends to the right, ahead, up a very steep hill, Cuesta de San Andrés, we can see the Gate of San Andrés. **(2)** Imagine fighting your way up here — at least the decisive battle was fought in January and the armies did not have the summer heat to contend with as well as the gradient.

Just before the Gate of San Andrés, to the right, is a part of the city wall. We will come back here shortly. Walk through the gate and enter the Plaza de los Descalzos, **(3)** and the oldest part of Trujillo. Look left. The building painted white is the beautiful Palace of Chaves-Mendoza. **(4)** With the palace on the left, walk clockwise around the square. The road bears around to the right to come to two triangular parks with a path through the middle. Take this path. On the left, pass a gate for the palace, and, second left, is an imposing entrance for the Fortress of the Bejaranos. **(5)**

Walk back from the fortress entrance and continue left. The white walls in front of us are the City of the Dead and we are in the Plaza de la Vera Cruz. Walk on and keep the fortress on the left. Enter Calle del Arco del Triunfo. Follow around to the left, then right. Ahead is the gate the fortress defended. In 1232, during the

Christian onslaught this gate was the first in the city to give way. Legend tells us that the Virgin appeared to the flagging Christian troops urging them on to 'one last try' and the gate gave way. The Christians entered the city triumphantly. In commemoration of this miracle the gate was renamed the Arch of Triumph **(6)** and an image of the Virgin was installed above the gate.

Walk through the arch to leave the city. After about 20m there is a small path to the right to walk for a short distance to look at the defensive walls **(7)** as an attacking army might see them. Return to the city through the arch. Follow the road left, then right, where, on the left is a metal gate. Look through for the ruins of the Gate of Vera Cruz. **(8)** Continue with the City of the Dead on the left. Walk straight ahead down tiny Calle de los Naranjos. Turn first right down another tiny lane to walk along Calle Alberca and to see the Roman bath, La Alberca. **(9)** This is picturesque with water but more interesting when the water level is low and you can see the steps going down and inscribed stones near the bottom. Walk with the baths on the right and ahead is the Church of Vera Cruz. **(10)**

Leave this pretty but ancient area by walking around the left of the church. The Gate of San Andrés is ahead. On the left, pass the Stronghold of the Escobars. **(11)** Walk through the Gate of San Andrés and immediately turn left to walk along the old city wall. **(12)** It has not changed in centuries. Ahead are views of buildings surrounding the Plaza Mayor. To the left, above our heads, is the impressive Alcazarejo de los Altamiranos. **(27)** At a Y junction take the left turning. Within 50m come to the magnificent Palace of Juan Pizarro de Orellana. **(13)** Continue with the palace on our left to turn left at the end of the road. Walk along Canon de la Charcel under the half arch and follow the tiny lane around to the right, through a small tunnel which throws us out, impressively, into the main square dominated by a statue of Pizarro. **(14)**

Pause a moment and take in the whole square, one of the largest

A WALK WITH THE CONQUISTADORES

in Europe. Running all the way around are arched porticos. These were each assigned to a different trading activity in medieval times. There are decorative plaques on the walls naming each area. Look up to the left at the walls of the castle. In the central window sits the statue of Our Lady of Victory, Patroness of Trujillo. The walk has probably already taken an hour and it may be time to stop, take refreshment, visit the tourist office, where there is usually someone who speaks English and buy multi-tickets to enter monuments. Continue our walk from that point.

With our back to the tourist office walk anticlockwise around the square. Starting on the right, the third building along from the right is the Palace of Quintanilla or the House of the Royal Weight. **(15)** The Old Town Hall **(16)** is next in the corner. Coming around to the next side of the square, after the arch, is a bare, old courtyard with government offices. Descend the few steps to walk under the arched portico of the magnificent Palace of the Marquis of the Conquest — the Palace of the Pizarro family. **(17)** Continue around the square while looking around. The best views of what we are passing so closely actually come later by looking back from the other side of the square. Pass Calle de las Tiendas on the right. Continue to the next corner of the square and the side of the Palace of Piedras Albas. **(18)** The tower with the scallop shells, denotes a pilgrimage to Santiago de Compostela. Turn the corner to walk under the arches along the front of the palace to find the information board. Continue to the next corner and the Palace of the Dukes of San Carlos. **(19)** This is now a convent. If you ring the bell before 13.00 and pay €1.00 a nun will allow you to visit the courtyard, chapel and main staircase where you can see the Vargas-Carvajal coat-of-arms painted on the staircase ceiling. You can also buy biscuits. Opposite the palace is the austere-looking Church of San Martín. **(20)** Do not miss going upstairs and on to the balcony for a view of the square. In front of the church is the huge bronze statue of Pizarro. **(21)** This statue was given to the

CITY WALKS 7

The Gate of Santiago, March

A WALK WITH THE CONQUISTADORES

city by the widow of the sculptor, Charles Rumsey, an American. An identical stature stands in Lima, the city Pizarro founded in Peru. Look across for views of the opposite side of the square.

It is time to leave the square. Go up the steps just after the statue of Pizarro with the Church of San Martín behind. Walk along the small road with the Palace of Chaves-Orellana, the House of the Chain, **(22)** on the right. Behind the palace is the Tower of the Pin with the Chavez-Orellana coat-of-arms. **(39)** We pass it later. The road goes up slightly. On the right, pass the Solar de Chaves-Sotomayor **(23)** with its beautiful facade. Continue up the hill, the Cuesta de la Sangre, to the Church of the Precious Blood of Christ. **(24)** The road narrows and continues up. Directly in front we can see an imposing gateway with a huge heraldic device. Behind is an impressive building with a short tower on the left and an irregularly-shaped high tower on the right. This is the Stronghold of Luis Chaves, 'The Old'. **(25)**

After reading the information board, follow the road as it goes around to the right. At the T junction with Calle de los Ballesteros go left towards the Gate of Santiago. **(26)** The return will be back through this gate and right. The Gate of Santiago is extremely old with heraldic devices on both side. Legend has it that the Christian army were led by St. James riding on a horse, in the thick of battle. After the victory, St. James became known in Spain as *Matamoros* (Moor Slayer). On the left of the gate is the tower of Luis Chaves's stronghold and on the right, the other tower that guarded the gate, now incorporated into the Church of Santiago. **(38)** Pass through the gate, past a doorway on the left with wonderful little carvings of faces, and come to a multiple junction. Take the turning first left — we will come back to the Church of Santiago later.

Walk straight ahead on Calle Altamirano. The forbidding-looking fortress high on the left is the other side of the Altamirano **(27)** which we saw from the city walls earlier. Walk ahead to come into Plazuela de los Altamirano. Follow the hill down to the right to come to the Aljibe, the Moorish cistern. **(28)** At a T junction just after the Aljibe, turn left then first right into Calle las Palomas, a pretty 15th century street. On the right is the House of Rol-Zárte y Züiga. **(29)** On the left is the old Palace of Chaves, now a small hotel. **(30)** Higher up on the left is the House of Orellana. **(31)**

At the top of the street, up a few steps, is Plaza de los Moritos and, left, the Church of Santa María la Mayor. **(32)** If you want to visit, go inside now. The altar-piece depicting scenes from Mary's life is beautiful and there are various tombs of past nobles. The best bit is the view from the top of the tower and if you think the last staircase is a bit insubstantial you should have seen it before it was renovated. On leaving the church, turn right back to Plaza de los Moritos. There is a decorated doorway to the church on the right and a covered reservoir and a bronze bust of Francisco Orellana on the left. Orellana was the discoverer and first navigator of the Amazon. Extremadura's extensive canal system, that irrigates so much of the agriculture, is named after him.

Walk straight on to Calle de la Puerta de Coria. Follow the sign for the Universidad Popular de Coria, also known as the Museum. Walk straight ahead, ignoring the turning on the left, to come to the University on the left. **(33)** It is the partly restored Convent of San Francisco, but now houses the Xavier de Salas Foundation which fosters links with Central and South America. Enter during office hours to look at the displays (Spanish only).

Walk along Calle de la Puerta de Coria to reach the Gate of Coria, left. There is a viewing platform to the right of the gate. Continue along Calle el Terrero to the top of Plaza de los Moritos and the back of Santa María la Mayor. Turn left up Calle de Academia. On the left is the beautiful Palace of the Marquis of Lorenzana. **(34)** To the right is the Convent of St. Mary Magdalena of Jerome.

A WALK WITH THE CONQUISTADORES

(35) With the Palace of Lorenzana on the left walk up Calle de los Martires. The next building, also left, is the House of Pizarro. **(36)** Inside is a museum with information in good English. On leaving the museum, turn left to walk straight up the small road to the Castle. **(37)**

On the left are viewing platforms out over the surrounding plain. On the right is the castle and this deserves to be explored thoroughly, inside and outside. The walk along the castle walls gives extensive views in all directions. Take care, however, as the walls do not have rails or much to stop you walking straight off them and the floors, especially the steps, are uneven. The underground cistern and the Chapel which houses Our Lady of Victory are especially noteworthy. Outside it is possible to walk along the right side of the castle to overlook the city below. Surprisingly, because Trujillo is a city, this is an excellent bird-watching site.

Once ready to leave, turn right from the castle entrance, to walk towards the walled garden ahead. The towers of Santa María la Mayor are ahead and slightly left. Turn left to walk down Calle de Mirador de las Monjas. As we walk down the hill, on the left, is an opening on to a patio. This is the *Mirador de las Monjas* (The View of the Nuns) restaurant. I can recommend sitting in the patio, sipping something nice while looking at the castle and the food is excellent.

Continue down the hill to Plaza de Santiago and Calle de la Victoria. On the left is the Church of Santiago. **(38)** Turn left to walk through the Gate of Santiago and walk straight ahead, ignoring the turning right. Walk down the hill. At a Y junction with a restaurant at the centre take the right turning to continue downwards. On the right is the Tower of the Pin, **(39)** seen earlier in the walk from the square. There is an interpretation centre in the tower open during office hours. Further down on the left is a hotel which was the

The Arch of Triumph from outside the city walls, June

A WALK WITH THE CONQUISTADORES

Palace of the Houses of Bejaranos. **(40)**

At the end of the lane we come back to the Church of San Martín and the square. If you stop for refreshments, continue afterwards by walking along the street between the church, on the left, and the Palace of the Dukes of San Carlos, on the right. Take the first right, Calle de San José. Take the first left into Calle San Pedro. At the top, on the left is the little Franciscan Convent of San Pedro. **(41)** Also on the left is a small lane with a series of buttresses from the convent creating half arches. Walk up this lane and reach Plaza de San Judas. It is very quiet — an old part of an old part — but with some lovely buildings. Ignore turnings left and right, and leave the square by Calle de Santa Clara, opposite where we came in. Ahead is the Convent of Santa Clara. **(42)** Turn left to walk around into Calle Santa Beatriz de Silva. On the left is the convent of today, **(43)** because, on the right the old convent is now a Parador. Enter the courtyard to have a look. Turn left on leaving the parador, back into Calle de Santa Clara. Turn left at the T junction with the parador on the left. Walk down the little lane ahead. It bears left around the parador. Turn right into a much wider road going down. In Plazuela de Quiroga there are some lovely old houses. Look back for a view of the unusual bell towers of the convent.

Walk straight down the small road. Ignore the turning left but bear right to see restored houses on the left. We have now walked in a circle because the Convent of San Pedro is before us once more. Turn left to go down Calle de San Pedro. At the T junction, turn left. At the next T junction the main square is right but we are going left. Take the first right to Plazuelo del Altozano and a multiple junction with a main road. Cross the road and take Calle de Sofraga. At the bottom, on the left, is the Palace of the Marquis of Sofraga, notable for its corner balcony with Corinthian columns. **(44)** It is in the little Plaza de San Miguel and lies opposite a Dominican Convent of San Miguel. **(45)** Hostel Blazon, open all the time, is a good place to stop for a drink.

With the convent in front, turn right down Calle de San Miguel. Ignore all turnings until we get to a wide Y junction. Turn right. Within 20m turn left. Walk down a few steps into Plazuelo de Licenciado de Burgos. Walk straight ahead to leave the square through a tiny lane. This comes out at the side of the Church of San Francisco. **(46)** Turn right, then left, to stand in front of the facade of this magnificent church in Plaza de San Francisco. With our backs to the church facade, walk straight ahead down Calle de San Francisco. Keep walking. On the left is the Gabriel y Galán Theatre. Continue ahead. On the left is the Palace of Juan Pizarro de Aragon. **(47)** On the right, our walk ends as we are back at the Town Hall once more.

GLOSSARY

Glossary

acetuna	olive
alcornoque	cork oak
arroyo	stream or ditch
ayuntamiento	town hall
bosque	forest
bravo	fighting bull
cairn	small pile of rocks to indicate direction
calle	street
camino	lane, way
campo	country
cañada	wide sheep moving trail
caza	hunting
cerro	hill
charca	pond
chozo	traditional round hut, often thatched
cordel	line, small sheep moving trail that joined the wider cañada
cortijo	farm estate
dehesa	classic landscape of Extremadura, holm oaks and pastures
embalse	reservoir
encina	holm oak
ermita	hermitage
finca	farm, land or house in the country
fuente	fountain
ganadero	livestock
GR route	Gran Recorrido long distance footpath with white and red waymarking
humilladero	shrine, small chapel near village

GLOSSARY

ida	going, relating to outbound route
jara	gum cistus, flower of Extremadura
llanos	plains
mirador	viewing point
molino	mill
pantano	large pond, reservoir
peligro	danger
peligroso	dangerous
piscina municipal	town swimming pool
presa	dam
PR route	Pequeño Recorrido short distance footpath
puente	bridge
puerto	mountain pass
refugio	refuge, especially in the mountains
rio	river
roble	deciduous oak
ruta	route
senderismo	hiking
sierra	range of mountains
SL-BA routes	routes in Badajoz province
SL-CC routes	routes in Cáceres province
toro	bull
trasumancia	transhumancia, moving sheep from their winter pasture in the south to the north for summer grazing and back
valle	valley
vuelta	return, relating to return route

Identifying flowers around Extremadura

Asphodel
Asphodelus Albus

Dark Mullein
Verbascum Nigrum

Field Gladiolus
Gladiolus Segetum

Gum Cistus
Cistus Ladanifer

Halimium
Halimium Commutatum

Iris
Iris Xiphium

Lupin
Lupinus Angustifolius

Paronychia
Paronychia Capitata

Retama
Retama Sphaerocarpa

Spanish Heath
Ericaceae Australis

Tolpis
Tolpis Barbata

Vipers Bugloss
Echium Vulgare

For many more flowers visit **www.walkingextremadura.com** and click on 'flowers'.